FIRST TIME
EVER

Also by Van Allen Plexico and John Ringer:

Auburn Basketball: From Barkley to Bruce

We Believed: A Lifetime of Auburn Football, Vol. 1: 1975-1998

Decades of Dominance: Auburn Football in the Modern Era

Season of Our Dreams: The 2010 Auburn Tigers

More Auburn Football, from White Rocket Books:

Lorendo, by Ken Ringer

FIRST TIME
EVER

THE UNTOLD STORY OF HOW AUBURN FIRST BROUGHT UNDEFEATED ALABAMA TO JORDAN-HARE STADIUM — AND BEAT THEM

VAN ALLEN PLEXICO
& JOHN RINGER

HOSTS OF THE AU WISHBONE AUBURN PODCAST

WHITE ROCKET BOOKS

FIRST TIME EVER:
THE UNTOLD STORY OF HOW AUBURN FIRST BROUGHT
UNDEFEATED ALABAMA TO JORDAN-HARE STADIUM —
AND BEAT THEM

Copyright 2023 by Van Allen Plexico and John Ringer

Cover design by Van Allen Plexico for White Rocket Books

Game ticket photo contributed by Jim McCrory

Interior illustration by Jarrod Alberich.

A White Rocket Book
www.whiterocketbooks.com

ISBN-13: 978-1-962993-01-2

This book is set in Times and Calibri.

First printing: November 2023

0 9 8 7 6 5 4 3 2 1

Coach Pat Dye talks with Alabama's Bill Curry on the field at Jordan-Hare Stadium prior to the 1989 Iron Bowl—the First Time Ever in Auburn. *Artwork Copyright 2023 by Jarrod Alberich.*

For my own Auburn Family, here in Illinois.
--Van

This book is dedicated to solving a mystery.
At the 1989 First Time Ever game, someone in the student section stole my wife (then girlfriend) Denise's Chic jean jacket.
Hopefully with wide distribution of this book and many fans reading this, the person will come forward and return the jacket or they will be brought forward to justice and the jacket returned to its rightful owner.
--John

– THE AU WISHBONE FAMILY –

Van and John extend their eternal thanks and appreciation to these fine members of the Auburn Family and the AU Wishbone Family (as of November 2023) whose support helps to make our podcasts and other projects (such as this book) a reality. *War Eagle!*

Samuel Salvatore
Phil Amthor
Parker Neill
Carl Von Drunker
Chris and Clinton Stewart
Logan Chilton
In honor of true Auburn Man,
  John Sandy
Anne Pridgen
Bill Weathers
Bradley Blackmon
David Sammons
Eric Morgan
Gary Grant
Matte Flowers
Michael Kirshner
Rich Reimer
Richard Stephens
Steve Trawick
Susan Trawick
Trombone Tiger
William Cardin
William Morgan
Alex Brouns
Ben Bloodworth
Bleeds Orange and Blue
Josh Corbett
Calibrating my fun meter in the
  back booth of Jones BBQ &
  Foot Massage
Chad McDowell
Chris Hilton
Chris Thrash
Dan Thompson
Daniel Odom

Earl Ricks
Bobby P
Harry Zagger
HTown Danny
Critter Sizing
Jacob and Robin Fleming
Kathryn England
Kevin Smith
Lane Middleton
Mickey Bee
George Gaston
OwlGoRhythm and Blues
Paul Miles
Rusty Owens
Shane Bailey
Spanky
Steve Harlan
Theodore Gary
Todd Robinson
Preston Settle
WDERichie Butler
Weagle Weagle
Wes Atkinson
Wilson Beard
Winston Boddie
AuburnBlue
Blake Herrin
Boris the Tiger
Brandon Smith
Carter Glaus
Colby Butler
Cory Smyer
David D
David Simpson
Dyebama

To join their illustrious ranks, go to **www.auwishbone.com** and click on the big orange button that says "Become a Patron!"
Thank you—and *War Patron Eagle!*

– CONTENTS –

NOTES ON TERMINOLOGY

Throughout this book, we often refer to *any* Auburn-Alabama football game by the nickname "Iron Bowl," whether the game was played before Shug Jordan coined that term (reportedly in 1964) or after. This is done purely for the sake of clarity and brevity, and should not be taken as an assertion by the authors that the nickname existed during years that it was not yet in use.

Similarly, the team and the college from the town of Auburn, Alabama is referred to as "Auburn" throughout. Though that institution has been known by a number of different official names over the years, contemporary news reports and game accounts from as far back as their first season uniformly refer to the football team as "Auburn," just as the fans always have. Again, for the sake of clarity and brevity, we maintain that tradition here.

— PROLOGUE —

It happened.

It happened after so many years of being told by the people in power at the University of Alabama, "It won't happen."

And by that, of course, they meant, It will *never* happen.

But it *did*. It happened just as Pat Dye had said it would, when he sat down with Paul "Bear" Bryant for the first time after taking over as Auburn's head coach in 1981. Dye later reported that the first thing Bryant had said to him was, "I guess you're gonna want to play that game in Auburn," and Dye replied, "We're *going* to take it to Auburn." The Bear pointed out that the two schools had an existing contract with the city of Birmingham to play in Legion Field through 1988. Dye responded, "Then we'll play in '89 in Auburn."

The Bear would not live to see that happen.

But it *did* happen.

Campers had filled the spaces in front of Parker Hall as early as Tuesday afternoon, on November 28, 1989. Students walking to class had to wind their way around the orange-and-blue-clad folks sitting in their lawn chairs and cooking on the grill in the middle of campus, in the middle of the day, in the middle of the *week*.

Everyone had game-day excitement, though game-day was still four days away. In truth, many Auburn fans had been feeling that excitement for a lot longer than a week.

13

From the moment the 1988 season ended, there was a buzz around 1989. You could look at the calendar and see why: For the first time in forever, the 1989 Alabama game—the Iron Bowl—didn't have that little parenthesized notation next to it: (*in Birmingham, AL*). Instead, it said one simple word—a word that stirred the blood and shook the very foundations of the college football firmament. It said: (*Auburn*).

It was months away, but it was coming. It was happening. The Alabama Crimson Tide, last holdouts from a group of programs that had always refused to make the journey down to the Plains of east Alabama, had at last given in to the inevitable. Given in? No, they'd been *forced*, their metaphorical arms twisted behind their backs, into agreeing.

They hadn't given in at once, of course. They had to make it difficult.

They'd tried threats. *We will stop playing the series sooner than come to Auburn*, some of them threatened. They had to know how petty that sounded, though. They had to realize that, at some point, such statements go from sounding like manly, principled defiance to childish recalcitrance. To *fear*, even. And the last thing Alabama wanted anyone to think was that they were afraid of *anything*—least of all, of little old Auburn.

Even so, it took a change of leadership at athletic director and head coach for the Tide to finally accept reality. Their previous coach had said, "It won't happen." Their new AD, Steve Sloan—later reviled as a weakling or a traitor by many an Alabama fan—was more willing to accede to Auburn's desire to play the game where they wanted to.

And where Auburn wanted to play it was in the cozy confines of the recently-enlarged Jordan-Hare Stadium.

All week, the crowds on campus grew and grew.

Camper vans and other recreational vehicles covered the lawns of nearly every building on campus. People from all over the state—all over the country—just wanted to be there, and be there for as long as possible, to soak it all up, soak it all in, and be a part of it.

Alabama fans began appearing on campus on Friday, and they were a strange sight, indeed. Oh, certainly there's a long and bizarre tradition of Bama fans, all decked out in their crimson finery, turning up at many sporting events where Auburn is playing (and Alabama isn't). But this was different. This was Alabama fans on the Auburn campus for a football game between the two universities, to be played on the Auburn campus. And that was something Auburn fans had never, ever experienced before. It had the feel of the Visigoths turning up outside the gates of Rome.

The Alabama fans wore red from head to toe. One suspected they believed they needed as much crimson protection as possible from all the sheer "Auburn-ness" radiating out of their surroundings—as if they were entering the Chernobyl reactor site and were worried what all this exposure might do to them.

A few issued half-hearted battle cries, but for the most part they understood that they needed to keep things calm, at least until the lead-up to kickoff the next day. So they roamed around campus and they poked their noses into our academic buildings and they visited the bookstores and generally otherwise stayed out of the way. Somehow, even through their crimson-colored glasses, they understood—they *knew*—that this week, this day, this event was *ours*. Certainly they had hopes and dreams of ruining it for us. But they also knew that could only happen on the football field on Saturday. They were not going to win the pre-game, and ultimately they opted not to try.

At last, after an excruciatingly long Friday night, and week before it, and year before that, Saturday arrived.

No one in Auburn had any desire to hang around the house and just wait some more. We descended on the stadium *en masse* at first light. Crowds had gathered outside Jordan-Hare well before 7 am.

And there we waited, the clock crawling so, so slowly toward noon, and then 1 pm, and the kickoff.

We played cards. We shook the shakers we'd brought with us. We yelled and ran through the standard cheers—but with extra gusto. The very air around us vibrated with energy, with anticipation.

Of course we were excited. At last—at long last—Alabama had capitulated to our will. Not that it wasn't fair; we hadn't asked for (or demanded) anything unreasonable. And yet they'd held out for so long, denying us what common decency dictated we deserved: the right to control our own half of this great series.

It never had to be that way. How much better for them if they'd simply nodded in understanding, on day one, and calmly and peacefully acquiesced to Auburn's desire to play the game in odd-numbered years where Auburn wanted to play it.

But that's not their way. Giving up such a clear advantage has never been their way.

For a time, Tennessee and Georgia Tech also refused to come to Auburn's campus. Eventually they both accepted the inevitable.

Alabama was the last holdout. They had the most excuses, and we heard all of them, over and over. They dug in their heels and refused to come. And they stretched that refusal well past the point of logic—past the point of there being legitimate reasons not to. They dragged the issue out to absurd lengths, until they themselves appeared foolish, stubborn, and just plain wrong. Until it was clear to any neutral observer what they were doing: They'd gained a substantial advantage over their rival in an era when playing the games in Birmingham made sense, and now they wanted to continue doing so even when it no longer made sense—just because they liked it that way, and because it helped them to win.

Thus all of the moral authority on the issue shifted to Auburn, and Alabama's position in the argument became ultimately untenable. Not that they didn't fight it to the very end.

At last, as we shall show here, cooler heads prevailed, and the agreement was made. They couldn't fight it anymore, and they finally accepted reality and stopped trying.

And so it happened. They came. And as that Friday night descended on the Plains, and all the Auburn fans bundled up in their campers and apartments and dorm rooms and tried to sleep, they anticipated what might lie in store the following afternoon.

Victory. Glorious, glorious victory.

To twist Alabama's arm, force them to come down to the Plains, and then *beat them soundly* and send them on their way. That was the desirable goal; the only acceptable outcome.

There was just one problem.

After a decade of mediocre Alabama teams—five of which Auburn had beaten in Birmingham, and two others that had required miracles in order for the Tide to win—this particular Alabama team was coming down to the Plains undefeated and ranked second in the country. Auburn, meanwhile, had lost twice and was ranked 11.

This was not how the scenario was supposed to go, how Auburn fans had expected things to play out.

16

As the sun set on Friday, December 1, 1989, some Auburn fans looked to the next day and—quietly, privately, in their heart of hearts—asked the question, *"What if?"*

"What if... we've dragged Alabama down here to our stadium, kicking and screaming... only to see them win?"

It was a very real possibility.

As David Housel, Auburn historian and then-Sports Information Director, put it:

> *To Auburn people, the unthinkable was about to happen. Their most dreaded, their most horrible fear was about to come to pass. After all of those years, after all of those hopes and dreams, Alabama was coming to Auburn — and it looked as if the Tide was going to win.*
>
> *It would be an event Auburn people would never live down. At what was supposed to be their greatest hour, could it be that they were about to be struck down once again? The ultimate Auburn joke was about to become the ultimate reality.*
>
> *Alabama fans put it more succinctly: "Your ___ on your grass."*

Every Auburn fan that got out of bed that next morning and got ready to head to the stadium knew one thing: We had to do it. We *had* to do it.

Like no other Iron Bowl before, we simply *had* to beat Alabama.

But they weren't going to roll over for us. They were a great team with an outstanding offense, capable of scoring points in bunches.

If we were going to win the "First Time Ever" Iron Bowl in Auburn, we were going to have to *earn* it.

We were going to have to *fight like hell* for it.

Before we dig into all the events of that amazing, astounding, unbelievable day, however, we need to address a larger question:

Why was it such a big deal?

It's a question that doesn't come easily to the minds of fans of either program, because they all know implicitly why it mattered so much. Many Auburn and Alabama fans have lived their entire lives embedded deep in the rivalry, feeling it and seeing it and hearing it around them every single day. They get it.

But, as David Housel once said of December 2, 1989, "Unless you grew up as an Auburn fan you can't possibly understand the significance of the day."

With this book, we will attempt to address that. We will explore every aspect of the "First Time Ever" game, and the great rivalry of which it was but one particularly memorable and important installment. Along the way, we will come to understand the tremendous significance of the overall rivalry and of that one game in 1989—to both sides, and beyond.

We will also lay out the fascinating chain of events, attitudes and actions that began as far back as the 1890s and directly contributed, piece by piece, year by year, decade by decade, to the eventual crisis that erupted between the two camps during the 1980s. A crisis that reached its critical moment when Alabama's leaders said they absolutely would never come to Auburn, and Auburn's leaders told them they absolutely would.

We begin our journey of understanding in the place where it all started: in Lakeview Park in Birmingham, Alabama, on February 22, 1893.

From those humble beginnings arose the greatest rivalry in sports—and perhaps the greatest day in that rivalry's history.

This is its story.

—Van Allen Plexico and John Ringer
Fall 2023

-1-

"IT WAS A GLORIOUS STRUGGLE"

It was the *other* First Time Ever.

From the very beginning, everyone knew it was going to be huge. And the players were under no illusions: They knew they were making history.

There had never been an Iron Bowl before. No one on either side had any past history to go on; to base their emotions or expectations on. There had been no winner the previous year, bragging about a victory for 365 days and rubbing it in the faces of the other side. Nor had there been a loser, vowing, "Wait till next year," and then counting the days until that opportunity came around again.

Auburn and Alabama had never played one another in football before.

Each person coming to this first contest was a blank slate, in terms of the great rivalry being born. No one could yet point to any existing history of the series, whether with pride or with shame. Not the current students, or the alumni, or the faculty of the two colleges.

What about the fans?

The two teams had at this point been competing in the sport itself for less than a year. They'd each played a handful of games the previous fall. The University of Alabama's team hadn't even played against another *college* before this. How many fans could there have been?

And yet, despite all of that, the people of the State of Alabama were excited. Quite a few people, in fact.

The carriages and trains rolled into Birmingham from all across the state. Nearly five hundred fans came from Auburn and Tuscaloosa alone, not to mention all the other interested parties who wanted to witness the event.

One reporter who was present at the scene described it this way:

> *Yesterday by 2 o'clock all Birmingham was on the move. Every private vehicle, stable turn out, and public back was filled with people on the way to Lakeview Park. The (vehicles) were crowded with lovers of the manly sport of foot ball. (sic)*
>
> *Men and women who have heretofore jeered at such exhibitions of brawn and muscle were eager to see the contest. Little children just beginning to toddle about were anxious to see the big boys fight.*
>
> *Every train which arrived at the station brought in foot ball enthusiasts from all parts of the State, and there were over a thousand visitors in the city. All came to see the great game.*

It was February 22, 1893, a cool and blustery day in the Deep South. The crowd had descended on Birmingham to witness the first intercollegiate football game ever played in the State of Alabama, and the first in the series that would one day be named "the Iron Bowl."

While both teams had played during the calendar year 1892, Alabama's three games had been against Birmingham Athletic Club (twice) and Birmingham High School. This first Iron Bowl would be Alabama's first-ever football game against another college football team. Auburn, meanwhile, had played Georgia, Trinity (NC), North Carolina and Georgia Tech in 1892, but had played all four games in Atlanta. This game was, consequently, the first ever played in the state to feature two college football teams playing one another.

No "football season" structure existed yet, in terms of which games should apply to which years. Alabama to this day counts this February 1893 Iron Bowl as the last game of its 1892 season, like a sort of (very late) bowl game. Auburn counts it as the first (very early) game of its 1893 season. Interestingly, using Auburn's definition, Auburn did not play Alabama during Auburn's first season, and Alabama did not play an actual *intercollegiate* football game *at all* until the 1893 season, the year after Auburn started playing. It is therefore easy to see why Alabama prefers their understanding of which season this game belongs to. They don't want to admit that, in terms of intercollegiate competition, Auburn Football predates Alabama Football by an entire year. This would hardly be the last disagreement over football between the two institutions.

But on that cool February day, as the rapidly-multiplying crowd rolled in, all thoughts were focused on the game at hand.

Played on the baseball field area of Lakeview Park, the "grid iron" field was surrounded by ropes that soon held back a standing crowd "a dozen deep."

"The bleachers were filled with as jolly a lot of men as ever sat on hard planks," the *Birmingham News* reported, "and from their faces and their merry talk it was evident that they had come out to make a happy afternoon of it."

Fans arriving in their own vehicles had a special area set aside for watching the game. "The east side of the field had been set apart for those in carriages, and soon from one end to the other it was filled with vehicles of all descriptions, gaily decorated in blue and gold, and in white and red." It's worth noting that while some Auburn fans wore orange and blue, others in this era substituted gold for orange.

Lest one believes that "rushing the field" is a phenomenon going back only as far as, say, the "Kick Six" Iron Bowl of 2013—it was a continuous problem at the very first game, and even *during* the game itself:

> The crush around the ticket window was simply fearful, as the crowd was too big to be handled by one man, and tickets had to be sold on the outside. The vast surging throng kept its temper and the women took being jostled about good naturedly.
>
> As soon as the crowd got on the inside, the men unaccompanied by ladies made a rush for both sides of the grounds, and soon were ranged a dozen deep around the ropes, which were put up around the grid iron.

21

Chief Norton with four officers was there to represent the law and keep the pushing crowd on the outside of the ropes, and although they had the assistance of a number of the members of the athletic club, they were powerless to keep the spectators from rushing under the lines and covering the field, so intense were the onlookers to see every point of the game.

By mid-afternoon, both teams had taken the field. Alabama at the time referred to their team as "Tuskaloosa," and "their uniform was white with red stockings and large red letters U of A, on their sweaters. And then every man, woman and child who wore the red and white rose and shouted themselves hoarse."

Auburn's players—whose average weight was only 152 pounds—entered the field shortly afterward, clad "in white with blue stockings and a large orange A on their blue sweaters. This gave those wearing the blue and orange an opportunity, and they yelled until they almost got 'blue' in the face."

Auburn won the coin toss and "won the ball" (chose to receive the kickoff) and also selected the north goal (end zone). The first Iron Bowl was officially underway.

"It was a Glorious Struggle," enthused the *Birmingham News:*

The game was not only intensely interesting to those who understood the fine plays in football, but fortunately it was a game which, from the start, caught those who were uninitiated into the fine points. The teamwork on both sides was good, and yet there were a number of brilliant individual plays.

A marked feature of the playing was almost a total lack of punting on each side. The game was an offensive one, neither side cared to be on the defensive. This was shown by the few times which the ball was lost by either team on four downs. The reason the Auburn team never punted it was the fact that they found they could make better gains by runs... Both teams had fine runners. Auburn snapped the ball quicker than Tuskaloosa. Goal kicking on both sides was good, but Tuskaloosa's was best.

(Nevertheless) Auburn won by a score of 32 to 22.

Van Allen Plexico

It's humorous to me that the *Birmingham News,* at the very first Iron Bowl, was already spending most of its time praising the play of Alabama, before casually dropping at the end that Auburn actually won the game. Without question a preview of what was to come from them, down through the years.

Having secured the victory, the Auburn players, led by team captain Tom Daniels and along with the head coach, D. M. Balliet, were called up to receive their trophy.

This would be the only Auburn game Balliet ever coached. Immediately after this game, he moved on to become head coach at Purdue. George Roy Harvey took over for the four games of the fall portion of Auburn's 1893 season, the first game of which wouldn't be played until November 6, some eight months later.

Notably absent from the Auburn sidelines that day was George Petrie. In many ways this is unfortunate, as the story of Auburn football begins with Petrie.

The first Alabamian to earn a PhD degree (it was bestowed upon him by Johns Hopkins University), Petrie founded Auburn's History Department, Graduate School, and football program. He coached the team throughout its first season, but had stepped down at the end of 1892, handing the reins over to Balliet. Petrie is also credited with determining that Auburn's colors would be burnt orange and navy blue. Having earned his undergraduate degree from the University of Virginia, he brought that school's colors with him to Auburn when he accepted a faculty job there. He also wrote the famed "Auburn Creed," which ends with the memorable line, "I believe in Auburn and love it."

Following Auburn's win in this first Iron Bowl, a ceremony was held, in which Auburn's Captain Daniels and the rest of the team "gathered around the drag, in which was seated Miss Delma Wilson, who had been elected to present the cup. Miss Sarah Rogan and Miss Mamie Morrow, her maids of honor, were with her."

"Gallant and victorious captain," said Miss Wilson, "in the name of the city of Birmingham, I present you this cup. Drink from it, and remember the victory that you have won this day. May you and your team live to see many more victories."

Captain Daniels replied, "We feel proud of the honor and assure you it is a great pleasure to receive this cup from the city of Birmingham and through your hands."

Everyone cheered, and then "the sun went down, blotting out the day on which the greatest football game was ever played in Alabama."

The two teams would never play at that location again. Lakeview Park is now long-gone, replaced by a golf course and various commercial buildings only a few years after the first Iron Bowl.

A historical marker commemorating the game now sits on a sliver of empty land next to a bank parking lot. The marker reads:

> *Site of the first Alabama-Auburn football game.*
>
> *The first Alabama-Auburn football game was played on this site, formerly known as the Base Ball Park, on February 22, 1893. The Agricultural and Mechanical College's Orange and Blue met the University of Alabama's "Tuskaloosa" squad before a crowd of 5,000 cheering fans. A&M College, now Auburn University, triumphed by a score of 32-22 and still proudly displays the victory cup presented that day by a Birmingham belle. That contest, reported as "the greatest football game ever played in Birmingham," was the beginning of one of the nation's most renowned college football rivalries.*

When Auburn and Alabama met again, the calendar would still read 1893. For Alabama, it was an entirely new season—one that had, in their reckoning, begun on October 13, with the first of two back-to-back losses to the Birmingham Athletic Club. Following those two games, they were shut out, 20-0, by Sewanee, on November 11, in what was only their second intercollegiate game ever. The four-game 1893 season for them ended in Montgomery on November 30, with the second Iron Bowl. Auburn therefore was the opponent in *two-thirds* of all the intercollegiate football games Alabama played during their first two seasons.

That second matchup, played in Montgomery later in 1893, remains the only time the two teams have faced one another twice in the same calendar year. Whether it was the same season, however, remains in dispute to this day.

John Ringer
The fact that we couldn't even agree on that—it just sets the tone for how the rivalry is going to go.

Much bigger disagreements lay in the future. Those disagreements would eventually prove so great as to sever the rivalry entirely—no Iron Bowls at all—for four years, and then forty-one more years after that.

Two of those three incidents were caused directly by Alabama insisting on the game's location. The 1989 Iron Bowl was not the first time the series nearly ended because Alabama refused to play the game where Auburn wanted to play it.

The site where the second game in the series would be played, however, was mutually and happily settled quickly by both schools, because a third party offered them both something that Auburn and Alabama could actually agree on:

Money.

-2-

"THE OUTSIDERS"

Imagine the scene in Montgomery that morning: a train rolls in from the east, orange and blue flags and streamers flapping from its sides. Off of it step a few dozen young men from the Agricultural and Mechanical College of Alabama, referred to by nearly everyone even then by the name of the tiny town in which it was located: Auburn.

A little less than two hours later, another train arrives from the north, carrying the second-ever squad of players from the University of Alabama, at Tuscaloosa. Cries of "War Eagle" surely fill the air, though it's not known precisely what the Alabama fans were yelling, as their team was at that time referred to as the "Cadets" or "Tuskaloosa;" they would not be christened the "Crimson Tide" for a few more years.

The two teams paraded down Commerce Street and Dexter Avenue, cheered on by their partisans both local and newly-arrived for the event. From there they arrived at Riverside Park, to find a gridiron playing field laid out and barricades assembled to keep the fans at bay.

What must have been going through the minds of these young men? Could they have had any inkling of exactly what they were becoming a part of, on that cool, blustery day in the capital city?

They were well aware their first game against their in-state counterparts in red and white had generated a great deal of excitement. Now this second matchup in the same calendar year appeared to be cranking it all up to another level. At some point before kickoff, might one of the players for Auburn or Alabama have closed his eyes and momentarily imagined the rivalry continuing to develop, to grow, to expand, to someday engulf the entire state and the entire nation of college football fans? To give us, over the course of the next century-plus, some of the greatest and most spectacular games in the history of this sport—a sport that was still so very new to these young men about to do battle?

The first game, played in Birmingham, was viewed by most as a resounding success, generating fan interest and bringing throngs of people to town to watch it (and spend money while they were there). The city fathers of Montgomery, seeing the excitement generated by that first battle back in February, paid the two schools $500 (around $17,000 in today's money) to stage a second go-round; a fall edition of the contest, this time to be played in the state's capital city. Only nine months had passed since frantic fans from across the state had descended on Lakeview Park in Birmingham to watch the Tigers battle Alabama. Now, on Wednesday, November 29, 1893, students, professors, alumni and fans of both colleges converged on Riverside Park, to watch two slightly different squads from the two colleges do it all again.

"RAH! RAH!! RAH!!!" shouted the headline of the *Montgomery Advertiser*, on the day of the game. "TO-DAY THE GREAT FOOT-BALL CONTEST COMES OFF," and "Auburn and Tuscaloosa Ready for the Fray—Crowds will be Here from Many Towns—Gossip About the Teams. Now for the battle! Both Auburn and Tuscaloosa are spoiling for the fray."

They will meet in contest at Riverside Park this afternoon and the fight over the pigskin will be a battle royal in every sense.

They will have several thousand people to witness the contest from Montgomery, Selma, Tuscaloosa, Birmingham, Troy,

Eufaula, Auburn, Opelika and other towns. (The cost of a round trip was listed as 4 cents.)

The Tuscaloosa boys have chartered a special train to bring them and their friends over. The train will arrive here (in Montgomery) about 11:30 this morning, decked out in red and white, the colors of the Varsity team. So will the Auburn boys be down in a special train with their friends from miles around. Orange and blue will fly from their train, which will reach here about 10 o'clock this morning. Both trains will be met at the Union station by a delegation of old college boys.

Everything has been arranged at the park for the convenience of the large crowd, and especially have the grounds have been railed off to protect the game from interference on the part of the crowd. The game will (start) at 2:30 o'clock sharp. The umpire and referee will be selected today by agreement between the two teams.

The organizers had learned their lesson from the first meeting, in which onlookers repeatedly pushed through the rope lines and spilled out onto the playing field during the game. Greater precautions would be taken this time.

The *Montgomery Advertiser* had placed a special correspondent on the scene in Auburn, who reported:

The Auburn team has not been practicing as regularly as its wont since the game with Sewanee in Atlanta (a 14-14 tie on November 18). Some of the men have been sick with "the grip" (a term for the flu), and for that reason are not in as good shape as usual. Glenn, Foy, Burym and Dunham have all been on the sick list lately, and their absence from the practice games has somewhat demoralized the team work. But with these exceptions the team is in fairly good shape... They have the determination to conquer to-day and they will come to Montgomery prepared to do their best.

Tuesday was the last practice game of the season, and yesterday the men simply went through their signals and then to bed early for a good night's rest, preparatory to the great battle of to-day.

Auburn's team captain, Rufus Dorsey, was "a veteran half-back" from Atlanta, and was "noted for his long and difficult runs. He plays with vim, and handles his men well."

Dorsey did it all for the Tigers early on. He scored on a 10-yard run, then kicked the extra point to give Auburn a 6-0 lead. (At that time, touchdowns were worth 4 points and the "point after" was worth 2 more.) Alabama answered with a 35-yard touchdown run of their own, but missed the point(s) after. Two more Auburn touchdowns, on runs by J. C. Dunham, gave the Tigers an unorthodox-to-modern-eyes but comfortable 18-4 lead at the half.

Alabama got themselves back in the game in the third quarter with a short run by William Walker, but the Tigers reeled off three touchdowns of their own—by three different players—in quick succession, putting the game out of reach at 34-10. Alabama managed to score once more, but then Auburn's captain, Dorsey, ended the game the way he'd started it, plunging over the goal line to give Auburn the 40-16 victory. Fittingly enough, Dorsey was presented with the game trophy.

Under the headline "AUBURN DEFEATS TUSKALOOSA EASILY," the *Birmingham News* on December 1 noted:

The Tuskaloosa boys were outclassed when they ran up against Auburn here last afternoon. The score was: Auburn 40, Tuskaloosa 16. The game was largely attended, a special train having been run from Tuskaloosa and Birmingham. The Auburn boys were in finer form and had had more practice than their Tuskaloosa friends.

And that's all the *Birmingham News* says about it, after the long article about the first game, earlier that year in Birmingham. Clearly the game didn't matter as much to them, back then, if it wasn't being played in the Magic City.

The Tigers would go on to finish that second season undefeated, with two wins over Alabama and a win over Vanderbilt, as well as a 14-14 draw against mighty (no, really!) Sewanee. A week after the second Iron Bowl, they traveled to Atlanta and tied Georgia Tech in a defensive struggle, with neither team managing to score.

Auburn had played Alabama twice now, in two different cities— neither of which was their home city of Auburn. Nevertheless, Auburn had won both, by an aggregate score of 72-38, and stood 2-0 and undefeated in the rivalry. With one exception, that dominance would continue into the next century.

Meanwhile, Auburn traveling away from home to play Alabama was something the Tigers would have to get used to, as it would become a recurring theme of this series for many years to come.

Van Allen Plexico

It should be a tremendous point of pride for Auburn fans that the Tigers dominated the rivalry early on. If only things could've stayed that way.

Choices were made, however, and paths were chosen by both programs. The way that all played out takes us directly along the path to Legion Field for decades, and then to Auburn on December 2, 1989.

Meanwhile, predictably, the two halves of the rivalry found they couldn't go three games without controversy swirling between them.

The third Iron Bowl was the first to bring with it real contention between the two schools. It also happened to be the first one played on Thanksgiving Day.

Thanksgiving in the late 19th Century was not what it has become. The President of the United States had to issue a statement proclaiming that the holiday was happening at all:

I, Grover Cleveland, president of the United States, do hereby appoint and set apart Thursday, the 29th day of November instant, as a day of thanksgiving and prayer to be kept and observed by all the people of the land.

On that day let our ordinary work and business be suspended and let us meet in our accustomed places of worship and give thanks to Almighty God for our preservation as a nation, for our immunity from disease and pestilence, for the harvests that have

rewarded our husbandry, for a renewal of national prosperity, and for every advance in virtue and intelligence that has marked our growth as a people.
—Grover Cleveland, President of the United States, 1894

It has been argued that Southerners did not fully accept Thanksgiving as a national holiday until it began to involve football. Whether that's true or not, the people of Alabama did set aside their ordinary work and business on that Thanksgiving Day of 1894. Many of them, however, turned their attention to some extraordinary work being done in Montgomery. And that work was indeed a football game, third in the series, between the Auburn Tigers and the University of Alabama. As the Montgomery Advertiser put it,

Fully three thousand people saw the eleven from the University of Alabama triumph over the Auburn team on the gridiron at Riverside Park yesterday afternoon in a hard-fought battle... The great crowd of spectators who saw it pronounced it a game of games, in spite of the fact that the representatives in orange and blue failed to score a touchdown during the contest. Even the Auburn team and its many sympathizers, though they did not relish the defeat, say it was a great game, and commend it for the clean, hard playing that was done on both sides. It was a good-natured crowd, too. About as much so as any that has ever gathered here before in such numbers.

The weather could not have been more favorable. It did seem that the Almighty had recognized the significance of the Day of Thanksgiving and favored His people with a type of weather that made one's soul happy.

On a bright, sunny fall day with a "mellow crispness" in the air—"just cool enough for an overcoat"—the two teams and their fans gathered again in Riverside Park. Trains had been arriving all morning, each bringing more football fans to Montgomery. Most of them wore at least one article of clothing or decoration of red and white or orange and blue.

The Auburn train arrived first, just before 11 a.m. Some fans headed off to their accommodations or to the game site, but others remained in the station, awaiting the Alabama train. Clearly, those fans were aware of a brewing controversy over player eligibility. We know this because, when the Alabama train arrived, a little over an hour later, its passengers were met with this cheer from the Auburn faithful:

Hullabaloo! Konneck! Konneck!
Hullabaloo! Konneck! Konneck!
Wah-hee! Wah-hee!
Look at the men! Look at the men!
Look at the Tuscaloosa hired men!
Preck-a-de-kex! Preck-a-dee-kex!
Wah-hee! Wah-hee!
Siss boom! Hullabaloo!
Auburn!
Je-hah! Je-hah! Je-hah-hah-hah!
Auburn! Auburn! Rah! Rah! Rah!

One should take particular note of line five above. "Tuscaloosa *hired* men."

Taken aback at first, and not particularly prepared to defend the players the Auburn partisans were calling out, the Alabama partisans responded with:

Rackety yack, de yack, de yack!
Rackety yack, de yack, de yack!
Hullabaloo! Hullabaloo!
How do you do? How do you do?
Varsity?
Hiro ke! Hiro ke!
U. A.! U. A.! Varsity!
Rah, who rah!
Rah, who rah!
Let her go, Varsity!
Rah, who rah!

Rah, who ree!
U-ni-V!
Hey up! Hey up! Varsity!
Varsity rah!
Varsity rah!
Varsity tiger!
Siss boom ah-h!

"Then yells and counter yells that no one could make out followed in rapid succession."

Van Allen Plexico
How did they come up with this stuff?? And how did they *remember* it??

John Ringer
They had to have it written down. They *had* to.

Eventually a sizable crowd gathered for the game—including some whose names were familiar to Auburn people then and today. Accounts from that time mention that a large number of ladies accompanied the team to Montgomery, as well as several professors and other Auburn instructors. That number included the very noteworthy professors Petrie, Thach, Glenn, Ross and Noble—each of whom has a building, a street or both on the Auburn campus named for him.

Eventually everyone made their way to the park, the appointed time arrived, and the game kicked off.

Of the actual play on the field that day, the less said, the better.

Suffice it to say, Alabama went on to win the game. They even managed a shutout, with a final score of 18-0.

With the close of the game came a burst of enthusiasm... In the jostling, hurrying crowds ...the noise was deafening. ... So ended a memorable football battle, characterized by clean playing throughout. One remarkable fact stands out—not a player was disabled.

No players were "disabled," no; but Auburn would have preferred, and felt it only just and fair, that some of Alabama's players had not been allowed to participate at all. In fact, the game was played under protest by Auburn.

The *Montgomery Advertiser* points out the following, regarding the days leading up to the third Iron Bowl, in 1894:

> *Considerable talk had been going the rounds about the (Alabama) Varsity boys playing outsiders. Managers Dewberry and Riggs of the (Alabama) Varsity and Auburn elevens respectively met about 11 o'clock and talked the matter over. ... Both agreed to have clean ball by bona fide college boys of the respective teams....*
>
> *Objection was made to Shelly and Abbott playing (for Alabama) and the following protest was handed (to) the sporting editor of this (news)paper about noon:*
>
> *"We, the college football team of the A. and M. College of Alabama (as Auburn was then officially called), do hereby protest against the following men on the University (of Alabama) team in view of the fact that they are not bona fide students, but are grown men who have been out of school and have engaged in regular business for several years—Abbott and Shelley—and under the circumstances we play the game under protest."*
>
> *W. M. Riggs, Manager*
> *Jas V. Brown, Captain*

After discussing the play-by-play of the game itself, the *Montgomery Advertiser* added:

> *It is a noticeable fact that the two men who did the best playing for Tuscaloosa—Abbott and Shelley—are the very men against whom Auburn entered her protest. Abbott made two of Tuscaloosa's touchdowns and Shelley one. Abbott was a substitute end on the University of Pennsylvania team of last year, and Shelley, a son of General Chas. M. Shelley, is an all-around athlete, and is said to be connected with the US Geological Survey.*

Auburn's players pointed out afterward that their team was "a regular college team," with every player having been enrolled for classes at Auburn for at least a year before participating in this game, and with all of them intending to remain there for at least the remainder of the semester. "With the exception of Brown and Riggs, none of the players is twenty years of age. Brown, Riggs and Dunham are (graduate students)."

John Ringer
The trend starts early and often: Alabama cheating by paying to bring in players who should not be playing for them, and tilting the odds in their favor by doing so.

Van Allen Plexico
And this wouldn't be the last time.

John Ringer
We've talked often about the old Lewis Grizzard quote that "losing hurts worse than winning feels good." In this series, it just shows you that the side that's losing is willing to do almost anything to win—to turn things around.

Van Allen Plexico
Unlike (until recently) with Georgia, this is a rivalry that has been marked by bickering, arguments, disagreements and protests literally from Day One. It's not surprising that they quit playing each other, and that they did so more than once.

Alabama had finally won a game in the young series, but they'd brought in "outsiders" to help accomplish it, and indeed those two non-students made all the difference in the outcome. Auburn's official protest went for nought, but the record of it survives, shedding light on this situation.

Thus we see that Auburn learned from very early on exactly what they would be up against in the Iron Bowl: an opponent that would search for any possible advantage, no matter how unsporting or unethical, and exploit it for as long as possible. That could mean using "outsiders." It could also mean insisting—*forcing*, even—the games to be played in a supposedly "neutral site" that actually favored them.

In just its third year, a fissure had appeared between the two sides of the rivalry. That fissure would only grow wider in years to come. On more than one occasion, and for a very long time overall, it would cause the two schools to refuse to play one another *at all*.

-3-

"TUSCALOOSA IS A BIT LACKING"

Maybe you've heard this one before: Auburn was set to play the Iron Bowl in a city they were okay with, but Alabama said it wouldn't happen, and refused to go there.

We're not talking about the 1980s here, but the *1890s*. Specifically, 1895.

Auburn, under new head coach John Heisman, was all set to play the Iron Bowl that year in Montgomery once again. The state's capital city had made another generous offer to both schools to bring the game there, and Auburn had quickly agreed. In the days leading up to it, however, Alabama decided they couldn't and/or wouldn't play there.

The *Montgomery Advertiser* on November 20 describes "disappointment" as "the order of the day," as:

> *Many persons had set their hearts on witnessing a game between the Tuscaloosa and Auburn teams at Montgomery on Saturday, and the Auburn team was counting on it. But it is not to*

39

be. The University (of Alabama) team manager telegraphs that it is impossible. The game, therefore, will take place in Tuscaloosa.

Why was Alabama suddenly unable to travel to Montgomery to play the game?

In the spring of 1895, the administration in Tuscaloosa had passed a rule stating that Alabama's athletic teams could only play in events held on the Alabama campus.

Van Allen Plexico
Suddenly Alabama doesn't want to travel anywhere to play a game. Home games only!

John Ringer
Because they might lose!

Speculation on the motives of the Alabama administrators for passing such a rule tends to focus on two areas. One reason was that they probably thought football as it then existed was too violent of a sport, and sought to end its popularity at the University.

Van Allen Plexico
There actually was a time when the University of Alabama's leaders felt football shouldn't be promoted or even permitted there, and tried to stamp it out. It's like some fantasy dream world. If only they'd stuck to that!

There is something to this, of course, though in 1895 the calls to make football safer for players—or to eliminate the sport entirely—had not become as loud across the nation as they would just a few years later.

It is fair to say that, in the last decade of the Nineteenth Century and the first decade of the Twentieth, football was indeed a violently brutal sport. Players wore very little protective gear at all. The forward pass was illegal, and so most plays consisted of the two teams locking arms and smashing into each other, attempting to move the ball incrementally down the field. Along the way, the cost in gruesome injuries and even deaths spiraled higher and higher.

Some eighteen players *died* during the 1904 season alone, along with the inflicting of hundreds of serious injuries.

In November of 1897, the *New York Times* called for the abolition of two activities it referred to as the "Two Curable Evils." Those activities were lynching and football. Gradually other voices around the country joined in the call to eliminate football entirely.

President Theodore Roosevelt, a lover of all "manly" pursuits involving physical exertion, appreciated the sport, both as entertainment and as a sort of junior-grade battleground for proving one's manliness and worth. In fact, many of the famed "Rough Riders" who fought under him in the Spanish-American War were former football stars, and ten of them listed "football player" as their professional occupation.

As much as he loved the game, however, TR also realized public opinion could quickly bring about its end, if something wasn't done to make it safer for the participants. The fact that Theodore Roosevelt, Jr, was then playing for Harvard's team—and suffered a head injury in practice—probably encouraged that thinking. He decided football needed reforms to "minimize the danger" while preventing it from being eliminated entirely—or, perhaps worse, as he put it, played "on too *ladylike* a basis."

After meeting with leaders of various universities prominent in the football of that era, including Harvard, Yale and Princeton, a number of reforms were put in place. These included legalizing the forward pass to spread out the players on the field, doubling the distance for a first down to ten yards, and creating the "neutral zone" between the two teams, helping to eliminate the mass scrums. By the following decade, the sport had become much less dangerous to the players, and was well on its way to evolving into today's modern game.

Of course, by that time, Alabama had been back playing home and away football games for at least fifteen years. Were they simply ahead of the curve on the need for safety? Perhaps.

The other reason often cited for why Alabama didn't want to play games away from Tuscaloosa amounted simply to the financial costs involved. Fielding a team at all was expensive, especially in those economically lean years across the Deep South. When it came to traveling to away games (usually by train) and putting up a large number of players in some sort of acceptable lodging, the expenses could prove untenable, or at least unacceptable to those administrators.

Van Allen Plexico

The sport was not yet bringing in much revenue, if any. The only source was tickets—gate receipts. There were no TV contracts. Fielding a football team during this era was almost entirely a drain on a school's finances. Auburn was willing to spend the money. Alabama was not.

Regardless of whether Alabama had a legitimate reason or not, for me this is a microcosm of their eternal attitude of "We're the big boys; we're in charge; things will be done the way *we* demand they be done. And if you don't like it, we won't play you." It started here, and continues to this day, in some ways. Certainly it was a big part of their refusal for so long to come to Auburn to play.

John Ringer

Their refusal to play anyone away from home shows that it was always all about *them* and their advantage, and that while they came up with other reasons that they paraded around publicly, it was ultimately about competitive advantage. And they were willing to sacrifice the rivalry to preserve that competitive advantage.

After passing the No-Away-Games rule, Alabama then proceeded to utterly ignore it for the first three games of that four-game season. Alabama played *at* Georgia (in Columbus), *at* Tulane (in New Orleans), and *at* LSU (in Baton Rouge), in the weeks leading up to the season-ending Iron Bowl. With the fourth and final game of the season set to be played against Auburn at a *neutral site* in Montgomery, however, Alabama suddenly felt that a trip a few miles down to the state capital was simply too much. They invoked their months-old, heretofore-ignored rule and insisted the Auburn-Alabama game be moved to *their* campus. Rather than see the game not played at all, Auburn acquiesced to the demand.

Van Allen Plexico

This all seems familiar somehow.

A large number of Auburn students and faculty were away in Atlanta at this time for the "Atlanta Cotton States and International Exposition," a sort of World's Fair event taking place that year in Piedmont Park. The event was intended to attract international trade and business to Georgia and the other states of the "New South," but is mostly remembered today for a famous speech given there by Booker T. Washington.

Auburn fans started looking past the game with Alabama—a game that looked like it might not happen at all—to the *other* big rivalry game, scheduled for November 28. Yes, *Georgia* was on the Tigers' minds.

"Next week Auburn will nearly empty itself into Atlanta," one reporter noted, not just to see the Exhibition but also because "the great football game between (Auburn's) team and that of the University of Georgia will be played in Atlanta on Thanksgiving Day." (That game, played on November 30 in Piedmont Park, was won by Auburn by a score of 16-6, giving Auburn a 2-1 lead in the series.)

But then reports surfaced that the Alabama game might yet take place. There was talk of it being moved to the "Tuskaloosa" campus the following Saturday, "notwithstanding all contrary reports." Clearly, this issue was still being debated until nearly the day of the game. Ultimately, Auburn did, as it happened, give in and agree to make the trip to the Tide's campus. The Tigers arrived in Birmingham on Friday morning at 11:35, before setting out for Tuscaloosa later that day.

"It is probable," one observer noted, "an excursion train will be run from Birmingham on Saturday in ample time for (fans to make it to) the game," which would return after a party that night. The Alabama team was described as "a little worse for wear from their recent trip to New Orleans and Baton Rouge," where they'd lost to both LSU and Tulane.

Despite having to travel at the last moment to the campus of their opponents—making this the first Iron Bowl played on either school's *home* campus—Auburn prevailed. The headline afterward read, "AUBURN HAD THINGS THEIR OWN WAY AT TUSCALOOSA," and described the game as "distinctly a one-sided affair."

43

It was apparent to spectators as soon as the two teams came on the field that Auburn greatly outclassed the University in the matter of size, and when the playing began it was a battle of fresh recruits (Alabama) against veterans (Auburn). The University boys put up a plucky game, but it was of no avail against the heavyweights of Auburn's seasoned veterans, who drove through the University line for touchdown after touchdown.

After the game, Alabama did in fact host "a brilliant hop" (dance party) in their "red Mess Hall in honor of their victorious rivals," as one report put it, with the hall sporting as much orange and blue decoration as red and white.

This would be the last Iron Bowl played until five years later. Presumably, Auburn was willing to travel to Tuscaloosa to play Alabama *once*, but wouldn't agree to making it an annual thing. Consequently, the series ended and Auburn moved the Georgia game into the big Thanksgiving rivalry spot on the schedule.

John Ringer

Here we see their willingness to cancel the Iron Bowl unless they get exactly what they want, the way they want it.

Van Allen Plexico

Yeah—honestly, their excuses aside, this is all not much different from how they talked in the 1980s (as we shall see later).

John Ringer

I think people focus on that long break prior to 1948, but here's another one, years earlier; a five-year break in the rivalry. There's a reason other old rivalries, like Auburn-Georgia or North Carolina-Virginia, have been played so many more times than the Iron Bowl has. Those teams didn't engage in this silliness.

Mysteries linger after this 1895 game. What happened to Alabama's team between the 1894 and 1895 seasons, to cause them to be so outclassed by Auburn's players? Were they still bringing in "hired men," and if not, why not?

Why did Alabama, in what appears to have been a sudden and unexpected move, invoke a rule they'd clearly ignored during the first three-fourths of the season, forcing Auburn to travel to Tuscaloosa or let the series end?

In any case, the following year, Alabama *did* enforce the rule. They played only three games in 1896, all of them at home in "the Quad." They defeated their old nemesis, the mighty Birmingham Athletic Club, as well as Mississippi A&M (the future Mississippi State), but lost to Sewanee, 10-6. They didn't play Auburn at all.

Meanwhile, on November 26, 1896, Auburn played Georgia in Brisbine Park (also spelled "Brisbane") in Atlanta on Thanksgiving Day. The Tigers fell to the Bulldogs, 6-12, completing an undefeated season for Georgia and evening that series at two wins each. One reporter mentioned that the game between the Tigers and Bulldogs "next Thanksgiving (1897) will be decidedly interesting and it is to be hoped that Montgomery will be able to secure it." Clearly by this time Georgia had replaced Alabama as Auburn's Thanksgiving opponent, with Montgomery wishing to be the host when Auburn's turn came to be the home team in that series.

Van Allen Plexico

I have to interrupt our narrative here for a really fascinating side story involving Georgia that I uncovered during our research.

The Bulldogs went undefeated in that 1896 season and won their first two games in 1897 as well. But on October 30, they faced the University of Virginia in the same Brisbine Park where they'd played Auburn the year before. Apparently that location was sort of Georgia's Legion Field, where they'd play some of their out-of-state opponents in the "big city."

Georgia lost that game to Virginia, 17-4. More importantly, however, during the game a Georgia player, Von Gammon, struck his head on the ground and was then piled on by a mass of his teammates and their opponents. When the players were separated, Gammon was unresponsive, taken to Grady Hospital, and declared dead.

A huge uproar ensued. The Bulldogs canceled the rest of their season after only three games, and the Georgia state legislature actually passed a bill *outlawing* football in the state of Georgia!

Before Governor William Yates Atkinson could sign the bill, however, Gammon's mother wrote an impassioned letter to the legislators, arguing that Gammon loved football more than anything else, and would never have wanted to be the cause of the sport's demise. In response, the governor vetoed the bill. Gammon and his mother are hailed as martyrs in the cause of preserving UGA football to this day.

And, beyond that—just think how close we came to both the University of Georgia and the University of Alabama ending their football programs! It's interesting to contemplate what would have become of Auburn's football program without either of its biggest rivals even participating in the sport, for at least some number of years.

Now, back to Alabama:

In 1897, with other actual college teams apparently refusing to agree to play Alabama exclusively on their home field, the Tide only played one football game, defeating the Tuscaloosa Athletic Club, 6-0. The following year, Alabama did not even bother to field a team.

We say again: In 1898, the University of Alabama *did not even bother to field a football team*, because they would only play opponents who agreed to their demands to play in Tuscaloosa. And nobody did. Consequently, they didn't play at all.

John Ringer

It's surprising—and I didn't realize this until we researched this book—that Alabama had multiple seasons where they didn't play actual college football opponents, or else they didn't play any games at all. While other teams, like Auburn and Georgia, were playing real schedules against real teams, Alabama took their ball and stayed home.

Van Allen Plexico

Think about this: Alabama didn't play an actual *college* team until the Auburn game in February 1893—a game

Auburn officially considers part of the *1893* season. And then, in 1898, Alabama didn't play football *at all*. So, while Auburn and Alabama both trace their football programs back to 1892, such that both have played football for the same amount of time, Alabama has actually played the sport *one fewer year* than Auburn has—and arguably *two fewer years* than Auburn!

With regard to their "self-imposed travel ban," it's not quite as shocking to think that Alabama would not play on Auburn's campus until 1989, when you realize they once went multiple seasons refusing to play on anyone else's campus—and they actually shut their program down rather than play a single away game.

John Ringer

A pattern of behavior emerges much earlier than any would have predicted: The University of Alabama, its supporters and administration, wanted to only play in situations that were an advantage and benefit to them. They were not interested in sportsmanship or competition but in what benefited them directly.

As hard as it is to imagine, in 1898 Alabama voluntarily and unilaterally abandoned the sport of football.

Their students and fans, however, did not.

By 1899, the pressure upon the University's administration over lack of football grew so great, they at last rescinded the rule and agreed to allow their teams to play away from home. Thus they were able to assemble a football team once again.

Alabama had developed a tradition of playing against local high schools and "athletic clubs" in addition to other actual colleges, to the point that ten of their first twenty-four football opponents included such fearsome rivals as the Birmingham Athletic Club, the Tuscaloosa Athletic Club and Birmingham *High School*. They faced no fewer than *three* of these in 1899, though they did also travel to Ole Miss for their one game against another university. It was too late to schedule Auburn for that season, however, so another year went by with no Iron Bowl.

Van Allen Plexico

It's probably a good thing for Alabama that they didn't resume the series with Auburn in 1899. That was John Heisman's fifth and final Auburn squad, and he later called it his best.

"I don't think I have ever seen so fast a team as that (1899 team) was," Heisman recalled, saying they were "the first to show what could be done with speedy play, and it wasn't long before all other teams (were copying it)."

That Auburn team shut out every opponent they faced, with the exception of mighty Sewanee's Iron Men at the end of the season—to whom they fell, 11-10. It's worth noting that the undefeated 1899 Sewanee squad beat five teams in an unfathomable *six-day* span of glory, including Texas, Texas A&M, Tulane, LSU and Ole Miss. Auburn was the only opponent to score a point on them—and only lost by one!

The Iron Bowl returned in 1900, again played in Montgomery as Auburn preferred. The Tigers responded to the resumption of the series by opening up a can on their cross-state rivals. Auburn crushed Alabama, 53-5.

A big crowd witnessed this renewal of the rivalry. "Grandstand and bleachers were comfortably filled, while on every side of the big quadrangle the side lines were packed to the ropes with a mass of people," reported the *Montgomery Advertiser*. They then said this of the two teams:

> *Auburn presented nearly a team of veterans. That college has been playing football for years and years and it has come to pass that Auburn ranks among the kingpins of the South in that line. On the other hand this is practically the first year that Tuscaloosa has had a regular team since 1893.*
>
> *Of the Auburn team nothing need be said. The people of Montgomery have seen them before, and it is sufficient to say that yesterday the brilliancy and dash of the team was kept up to the Auburn standard. Montgomerians know what that means.*

The teamwork of Auburn, too, was something beautiful. The men worked together like clockwork. This matter of teamwork is something that Tuscaloosa is a bit lacking in.

Alabama couldn't contain Auburn's backs. Left halfback Yarborough scored three touchdowns for the Tigers, including a run of 75 yards, while Noll scored twice, with one run going for 55 yards.

Auburn finished the season undefeated at 4-0. Alabama was the only team to score a point against them all year. The Tigers' aggregate score for the season was 148-5. Twelve days after crushing Alabama, Auburn traveled to Brisbane (or "Brisbine") Park in Atlanta and shut out the University of Georgia, 44-0. (Clemson, Texas and Tulane finished ahead of them in the Southern conference standings, based on number of games played. Those teams played five or more games and also finished undefeated.)

Auburn would go on to shut Alabama out the following two seasons, giving this three-game series since the resumption an aggregate score of 93-5 in Auburn's favor.

The 1901 victory by Auburn, 17-0, took place on the Quad in Tuscaloosa, and was Alabama's only loss that season. In two games played on Alabama's home field to that point, Auburn had held their rivals scoreless. That 1901 game would be the last Iron Bowl played in Tuscaloosa for almost a century; when they returned in 2000, Auburn again shut out Alabama. The Crimson Tide did not score on Auburn in their own home stadium until the *fourth* game there, in 2002—but they still lost. (Auburn Coach Tommy Tubervillle noted after that game, "At least they finally scored on us!") Alabama's first win against Auburn in Tuscaloosa would not come until the *seventh* Iron Bowl played there, in 2008.

For the first time since the very first Iron Bowl, the series returned to Birmingham in 1902.

The game was set to begin at 3 pm, but Alabama's team was inexplicably late arriving at West End Park. Game officials delayed the kickoff until 3:30, by which time the Varsity boys from Tuscaloosa at last showed up and play could begin.

After numerous reports in previous years of fans pushing out onto the field of play during the game, the Birmingham organizers spared few efforts at restricting the field of play for this game:

A fence of wire netting has been erected around the entire gridiron proper so that no one can enter the field except players and officials. This fence is held securely in place by posts driven deep into the ground every eight feet. To further prevent any trouble a barbed wire fence has been run around the outside of the screen so as to prevent spectators from leaning against it.

John Ringer
The idea of players playing inside a fence and the out-of-bounds is a fence... the players being inside and the fans on the outside, like a WWE cage match... it's disturbing and amusing.

Van Allen Plexico
Not to mention—*barbed wire* on the outside!
Is this the answer the SEC has been searching for, to stop fans from storming the fields?? Ha.

Auburn defeated Alabama yet again. The headlines of the day read:

VARSITY COLORS DRAGGED IN THE DUST BY
WEARERS OF THE ORANGE AND BLUE

AUBURN OUTCLASSES HER HEAVIER OPPONENTS

"Tuscaloosa outweighs Auburn several pounds to the man," stated the *Birmingham Post-Herald*, "but the orange and blue admirers say Auburn's swiftness will offset this handicap in flesh and bone." Clearly this turned out to be the case, just as John Heisman had said of his earlier Auburn teams. Speed had replaced size as the determining factor in southern football.
The report added:

Men from Tuscaloosa fail to make any impression on the Tiger line and lose by score of 23-0. From the moment the first toe struck the pigskin it was evident that Tuscaloosa had no chance.

The overall record at that point stood at six wins for Auburn to one for Alabama. Auburn remained as dominant in the series with its renewal as it had been before Alabama had stopped playing it. That would soon change, however, as the rivalry quickly became one of winning streaks by both teams, back and forth—something that continues to this day.

Alabama would mark their second-ever victory over the Tigers the following year—1903, in Montgomery—by a score of 18-6. Auburn wrestled the crown back in Birmingham the next season, winning 29-5.

Beginning with that 1904 game, the Iron Bowl would only be played in Birmingham… until eighty-five years later, on December 2, 1989.

Shockingly, that 1904 victory also would turn out to be the Tigers' last Iron Bowl win for forty-five years. Of course, Alabama would only secure three more wins in the series themselves during all that time. The rest of the time, it simply *wasn't played*.

What could possibly have caused the series to end again, so soon after it had resumed?

-4-

"THE BREACH"

Without question, by 1907, the students, faculty, and alumni of
Auburn and Alabama had embraced this new sports rivalry with
massive enthusiasm, and without any traces of hesitancy or
qualification. So too had many other people across the state. After
only a handful of years, the rivalry that would one day be named "the
Iron Bowl" had become a cultural touchstone; a statewide event; an
institution unto itself. How remarkable, then, that only fourteen years
after it had begun, the series would be allowed to *end*—to simply die
out. How shocking that the two schools could find themselves in
such disagreement that they would choose to stop playing one
another, depriving their own student-athletes—not to mention their
large-and-growing football fan bases—of even the opportunity to
compete against one another.

What possibly could have caused this breach? What could have
been seen by the leaders of both colleges as so serious, and so
irreconcilable, as to bar the two from engaging in competition
against one another in football for decades?

The truth is muddled. Many have commented on the topic in the
time since the breach occurred. They have claimed different factors

were involved. Some have made accusations, while others have refuted them. The weight of years has distorted it all further.

There are a few things we know.

The two sides had disagreed from the very beginning over at least one issue: which season their first contest counted toward. That alone would not have been enough to kill the series. But it was a start. It indicated that each institution believed only its view was correct, and would not compromise with the other.

By the third Iron Bowl, however, a far more serious disagreement occurred: Auburn accused Alabama of using ineligible, non-student-athletes in the game. Essentially, Auburn said that Alabama hired what amounted to professional football players for the Iron Bowl, while Auburn used only their own, fully-enrolled student-athletes.

That controversy caused official protests to be filed, though the games were still played. It settled down a bit—though it would arise again soon—after the series took a break from 1896-1899. But then a newer controversy emerged.

Alabama won the 1905 game in Montgomery and the 1906 game in Birmingham, both with shutouts. After years of Auburn dominance, the "Varsity" from Tuscaloosa had found a way to tilt the series in their favor.

Some of the Auburn folks of that era had a word for what Alabama was doing. They felt that word just might be "cheating."

Auburn objected to Alabama, under new head coach J.W.H. "Doc" Pollard, running what they considered an illegal offense. Alabama had sprung it on Auburn at the start of the 1905 game, to some success. It was called the "military shift." *Sports Illustrated* describes it as, "every player except the center lining up on the line of scrimmage and joining hands, but then turning right or left to form an unbalanced line." They would do this before the ball was snapped, overpowering the defense at the point of attack. Pollard was said to have brought this style of play to Alabama from Dartmouth, his undergraduate school. It had not been used in Southern football before, and the rules were unclear on it. Auburn felt it should be disallowed. Alabama didn't see it that way, and the game referee agreed.

A year later, in the 1906 Iron Bowl, Pollard used another, similar strategy that colored around the edges of legality: the "Varsity Two-Step." After that game, the exasperated Auburn officials proposed a solution to the problem going forward: In future games, use a referee from the north, who was more familiar with that style of play, understood such tactics better, and would be better prepared to decide on it—in other words, more likely to penalize Alabama for doing it.

Alabama, of course, rejected the idea of a northern referee. They insisted that only a southern referee was acceptable—a southern referee who either wouldn't be aware that kind of play was illegal, or who at least could be counted on to overlook such shenanigans.

Another issue pointed to by fans, years afterward, was supposed violence between supporters at the Auburn-Alabama games—particularly at the 1907 game, the last before the breach. Some argued the two teams should not be allowed to play one another any longer, simply because their fans at the games could not be trusted to interact peacefully.

Auburn's then-coach, Mike Donahue, pushed back against some of these accounts later in his life. "The game was always very cleanly played during the time I was coaching at Auburn, beginning with the 1904 game," he said. "I have heard that riots and the conduct of the players were responsible for the severance of relations. I want to tell you that this is not true."

At this same time, the "Alabama using ineligible players" issue reappeared. In this case it was a guard, T.S. Sims, who scored the first touchdown against Auburn in the 1905 Iron Bowl, and was selected to the All-Southern team for that season. In 1906, Auburn protested that Sims was an illegal player. The protest was heard by officials of the Southern Intercollegiate Athletic Association, but they ruled in favor of Sims and Alabama.

The disputes between the two programs were mounting. Ultimately, it wouldn't prove to be any one thing that divided them and kept them from playing for so long. The Iron Bowl died a death of a thousand cuts; little things, here and there, that mounted up.

In addition to the refereeing issue, the final cuts were disputes over the number of players participating, the amounts of the per diem payments to them, and scheduling.

The two schools argued and debated one another for months over these issues. Auburn proposed four possible dates for the game. By the time Alabama got around to responding, two of the dates had already gone by. Alabama had a game scheduled on one of the other dates, against the Haskell Indian Institute. Auburn suggested they cancel it and play the Iron Bowl on that date instead. Alabama refused.

Van Allen Plexico

Good thing, too—the Tide went on to roll to a massive 9-8 victory over the mighty Haskell Indian Institute!

Alabama then proposed the game be played after Thanksgiving, but Auburn had a rule in place that it would not play any games after that holiday. The Auburn Board of Trustees rejected changing the rule. With that, it was too late to schedule a game for that season. Thus 1908 came and went with no Iron Bowl.

Coach Donahue stated:

> *Failure to agree on details, where the teams would stay, the expenses and how many players each squad would be permitted to have and the officials caused the breaking of the relations.*
>
> *I was in Tuscaloosa, with Tom Bragg, director of athletics, and met with Hill Ferguson and (Alabama) Coach Doc Pollard at the old McLester Hotel. The meeting took place after the ball game between Auburn and Alabama in the late spring of 1907. There was no agreement on officials and details of the game. Reaching an impasse, the game was called off for 1908.*

Phillip Marshall of the *Montgomery Advertiser* summarized the causes of the breach thusly:

> *The widespread rumor for years has been that separation was caused by a fight. It wasn't. Auburn wanted expenses of $3.50 per day for twenty players. Alabama countered with a proposal for $3 per player. Auburn coach Mike Donahue wanted a northern official for the game. Alabama wanted a southerner. So it was that the series that by a century later would be considered one of the great rivalries in American sports went dormant over 50 cents per player for a total of $10 per team and where the official—there was only one on the field in those days—came from.*

In 1944, Alabama's athletic director, B. L. Noojin, noted:

It probably had its beginnings in Auburn's objection to the shift plays — "varsity two step" — which Dr. J.W.H Pollard ... used in his football formations and which Auburn contended were always "offside." These plays, ahead of their day, were but a forerunner of the many varied shifts employed today and were allowed by some officials and penalized by others. My recollection is that inability to agree on officials — scarce in those days — was the crux of the "break-up."

Some referees saw what Alabama was doing on offense as illegal, and some thought it was perfectly fine. From that came the "inability to agree on officials."

In terms of how the players themselves comported themselves, Coach Donahue added, "The game was always very cleanly played during the time I was coaching at Auburn, beginning with the 1904 game."

Before the series came to a sudden and screeching halt, however, the two teams put on an exhibition for the ages, with the 1907 edition of the Iron Bowl, played at the Fair Grounds in Birmingham.

Nobody could have guessed, in the days leading up to that game, that they were about to see the last clash between Auburn and Alabama in the lifetimes of a great many of them.

Fans across the state were as excited as ever. A *Birmingham News* headline three days before the game read, "INTENSE INTEREST AMONG ENTHUSIASTS," and explained that the "experts" favored Auburn this time around, "if the 'dope' has been figured out right."

Auburn to win appears to be the accepted result of the battle and if Alabama does happen to back Auburn off the boards there will be many a "fooled man" in this town Saturday.

Auburn never was afraid of Alabama... With the strength of the team and the knowledge of football the Auburn players (this year) will not fear Alabama at all and will go in for blood.

A score of about twelve to nothing is expected but Alabama may spring a surprise as a result of much practice and succeed in scoring once.

All arrangements for the game have been made and the fair grounds are in fine shape.

The game did not go the way those with "the dope" had expected. While Alabama did only succeed in scoring once, they held Auburn to that same total.

On Sunday, the same newspaper summarized it thusly:

Birmingham Turned Out Saturday to Witness the Best Football Contest Seen Here in Years.

Both Elevens Had Many Friends On Hand.

Before the largest crowd that ever saw a football game in Alabama the rival state institutions played each other to a standstill at the Fair Grounds Saturday afternoon. Final score, University of Alabama, six, Alabama Polytechnic Institute, six.

The result is hailed as a victory by Tuscaloosa, against whom the odds of three to one were freely made, and even money was put up that the Crimson and White would not score. Auburn is greatly disappointed, their expectation being that Alabama would be defeated by at least three touchdowns.

As one report noted, "Alabama did not play straight football to any extent throughout the game," relying instead on a plethora of trick plays. This time, however, Auburn was prepared. The 1907 game turned into a defensive slugfest, with neither team able to generate much offense.

Auburn scored first. Just at the end of the first half the Orange and Blue was shoved over the line for a touchdown, and the (extra point) was easy. A great crowd, headed by Auburn's college band of twenty pieces, yelled themselves hoarse.

In the second half, after twenty minutes of play, Alabama, using the famous military formation, and the dance trick to perfection, drove the ball down the field from the forty yard line to a score. The goal followed with ease and the other half of the crowded grandstand went wild with delight.

After the game, though Auburn was upset about Alabama's continuing use of what it considered illegal formations, it was Alabama's turn to complain. Their coach, Doc Pollard, filed a protest alleging that the referee had given Auburn an extra down on their lone scoring drive.

Auburn had moved the ball to Alabama's one-yard-line, only to be flagged for "offsides" (likely illegal motion by the offense). The Tigers were penalized five yards, but scored on the following play, which was effectively fourth down. Alabama argued that the previous play was the effective "fourth down" and that Auburn should have turned the ball over to Alabama at that point. The referee, however, followed the rules and did not count the penalty as a loss of down, therefore allowing Auburn to replay the down from five yards farther back, and score. In dismissing Alabama's protest after the game, the referee stated he was confident the downs had been correctly counted.

Auburn had one last opportunity to win, but they fumbled on the final play of the game. The referee blew the whistle to signal the game's end just as Alabama recovered the ball.

The scenes at the finish were the most inspiring seen in this city at any football game. The players of both teams were carried off in the arms of their fellow students and "You did great old boy" was about all that could be heard. Every supporter of both teams was satisfied.

The fans went home. The organizers took down the ropes and the posts and the barbed wire. The Alabama players went back to Tuscaloosa. The Auburn players headed back down to Lee County. Alabama still had games remaining against LSU and Tennessee. Auburn had to face the University of Georgia twelve days later, in Macon. Both teams had other things to worry about on the immediate horizon. They couldn't be distracted thinking about the future of their series with one another. But—why should they? It was a huge event. It had become an occasion the whole state came to a stop for, every year. Crowds descended upon whichever city happened to be hosting it that year. Yes, certainly, there were issues being disputed between the two schools. But those would be worked out in the days ahead, wouldn't they? Nothing could stop this great rivalry from continuing to grow and to capture the imagination of players, students, faculty, alumni and fans all over the state and the Southeast.

It had become too big to fail.

And then... *it failed*.

Just like that, the series ended.

The two teams, the two universities, simply stopped playing each other.

As unthinkable as it now seems, Auburn and Alabama did not face one another in football for the next *forty-one years*.

Through a World War, a Great Depression, and another World War, they did not play one another.

As the sport grew in popularity and impact, across the state and across the South and across the country, they did not play one another.

For forty-one years there were no Iron Bowls.

None.

During those long years, both teams made occasional, perhaps half-hearted efforts to revive the series. None of them yielded anything tangible.

John Ringer

Imagine: Both Auburn and Alabama playing football, but just not ever against each other. Both were members of the Southeastern Conference (SEC), which was formed in 1933. But even as conference members they could not be made to play each other—which says something about the power of the SEC in the early days, that it could not require the two teams to play! Much as Texas and Texas A&M have refused to play annually since the Aggies left the Big 12 for the SEC, the Auburn-Alabama series ending was a case of pretending the two sides did not care, when they both cared a little too deeply.

During the early and middle portions of the Twentieth Century, and especially during these four decades of not playing Auburn in football, the University of Alabama made numerous tentative efforts to actually *take control* of Auburn—of the entire university—if not absorb it outright. There were moments it seemed Auburn might cease to exist entirely, except as a branch campus of the University of Alabama. Another UAB or UAH, but down in Lee County—and with Tuscaloosa able to shut down its sports programs whenever it felt like it.

Van Allen Plexico

Ask UAB football fans how they have enjoyed that particular arrangement!

Two things in particular allowed Auburn to stay separate and independent of Alabama, much to the chagrin of those in Tuscaloosa.

During the 1930s and 1940s, Auburn became the regional center for a number of President Franklin Roosevelt's New Deal agencies, including the Agricultural Adjustment Administration (AAA), the Soil Conservation Service, and the Resettlement Administration. This brought federal funding to Auburn in a big way. It didn't hurt that both Auburn's president, Luther Duncan, and Governor Bibb Graves were outspoken supporters of FDR and the New Deal.

By the end of World War II, Alabama again engaged in efforts to make Auburn "the dangling tail of a Tuscaloosa kite," as one state official described it. They intimated in a report to the state legislature that giving Auburn money and power was "illogical." Auburn's Duncan described this Alabama report as "this evil monster" and compared it to "the doctrine of Hitler."

Auburn's independence was saved this time by Harry Truman and the G.I. Bill, which provided federal funding for former servicemen to attend college. With more money now flowing from Washington, DC, to the Plains, Auburn's survival was ensured.

Van Allen Plexico

I like the fact that I'm not the only person who has at some point compared the University of Alabama to Hitler. Ha.

William Falkner said that the main economic activity powering the South before World War II was agriculture. After World War II, it was the federal government. That includes military bases, defense contracts, and eventually the space

61

program in Huntsville, Houston, and Florida, among other things.

Certainly if Alabama had tried to absorb Auburn again in the 1980s, again they would have been deflected by more massive federal funds flowing toward the Plains—this time in the form of money for the Strategic Defense Initiative (SDI, or "Star Wars," the missile defense system research), which poured into the aerospace engineering program, among others, and pumped Auburn up during the Reagan years in particular.

Auburn had survived as an institution of higher learning, separate from the control of its great rival, despite the best efforts of Tuscaloosa to swallow it up.

During those long years that the two schools didn't play each other, however, Alabama's football fortunes slowly rose, while Auburn's slowly fell. By the time they got back to playing one another, Auburn was no longer the dominant football power of the two. Some people point to this as the most absolutely critical period in shaping how the rivalry exists to this day. Alabama decided they were the top dogs in terms of football in the state, and they would dictate to everyone else how, when and especially *where* the games would be played. Having coaches like Bryant and Saban come along and generate great success only added to that public perception. Auburn found itself in a hole it has never entirely managed to dig itself out of.

Van Allen Plexico

I think that's one reason the 1989 Iron Bowl coming to Auburn was so very important—as we shall show. It didn't entirely reverse that public perception, nor did Auburn's success during that entire decade. But it helped. It was one very big step in the right direction, and everyone—on both sides of the rivalry—knew it.

Meanwhile, forty years passed after 1907 with no Iron Bowls.

Today, such a thing is almost unthinkable. At the time, however, neither school and neither fan base seemed to mind all that much.

A few token efforts were made to reconcile the two universities and restart the football series. Nothing came of any of it.

Eventually, however, the pressure on both schools grew to the point that even the state government couldn't ignore it any longer.

Something had to give. Someone in authority had to step up and step in and make it happen.

Prior to the 1948 season, someone did.

- 5 -

"YOU CAN FEEL IT
IN YOUR BONES"

Some thought it would never happen.

At last, after forty-one years, it *did* happen.

After more than four decades of no Iron Bowls—of Auburn and Alabama never playing one another in football—the two sides finally came together again on a field in Birmingham on December 4, 1948.

And it happened because a higher power chose to intervene.

No, not *that* higher power—though fans on both sides have always claimed He supported their side of the rivalry. No, the Iron Bowl resumed in 1948, at least in part, because the Alabama state legislature was fed up. It did not threaten to immediately cut off funding for the two schools, as has oft been claimed. Instead, it voted in favor of multiple *non-binding* resolutions *urging* the two schools to resume the series—all of which were ignored.

The lingering, long-term threat behind those resolutions, however, was the idea that the state government *did* control the purse strings of both schools, so money was indeed involved. That largesse, it was to be understood by all parties involved, might be made to dry up. Very quickly then, in 1948, the impasse at last gave way and the two teams placed one another on the schedule again—only forty-one years after the last time.

Van Allen Plexico

It's amazing—and I'm being totally sarcastic here—how quickly four decades of outstanding issues and division got resolved when the bottom lines for both universities were threatened!

John Ringer

This is a pattern we've seen in other states, with other rivalries. The universities themselves can't settle matters, so state legislatures get involved and pass legislation requiring the schools to play one another. It's happened before, and here it clearly had to happen again.

Eventually they would have had to play one another, being members of the SEC. But it's good the legislature got involved when it did, back when the conference couldn't make it happen by itself. There may be too much legislation in general, but this is an example of one of the rare useful pieces of legislation.

In the buildup to that 1948 game, folks all across the state were buzzing. As the *Birmingham News* colorfully described it:

You can feel it in your bones.
You can hear it with your own ears.
You can see it with your own eyes.
All Alabama is talking and singing of Saturday's first tussle in 41 years between the state's two top institutions of higher learning.
But most of Alabama will listen to the game over the wireless.
Tickets to the Tide-Tiger scraperoo are as tight as a pair of mail-order shoes. The beautiful ducats are harder to find than a Dixiecrat on the federal payroll.

And when that game was over, Auburn had suffered the biggest defeat it has ever suffered, before or after, in the series.

Before getting into that, however—and the glorious redemption earned just one short year after it—let's turn our attention to that long break that led up to it.

Following the failure to schedule an Iron Bowl in 1908, both schools continued along, for the most part, as if nothing had changed. Auburn focused on the rivalry with Georgia— "the Oldest Football Rivalry in the Deep South" —which predated the Iron Bowl rivalry by nearly a year. Alabama came to adopt Tennessee— on "the Third Saturday in October" —as their main rival.

Auburn enjoyed tremendous success during the first two decades after the end of the series with Alabama. Under Mike Donahue, the Tigers went 91-26-4 from 1907-1922. During that span they won the Southern Intercollegiate Athletic Association championship three times—in 1913, 1914 and 1919. The 1913 team finished 8-0 and outscored their opponents by an astounding 223-13.

Van Allen Plexico

The 1913 and 1914 teams both can make strong claims to being national champions. There were no "official" rankings in those days, so—as Alabama, among others, has famously proven—schools can just "claim" to have been champions of whatever years they like, and it's left to the court of public opinion to decide how valid such claims might be.

Playing only two of their eight games at home, the Tigers of 1913 shut out their first six opponents, then allowed one score each to Vanderbilt and Georgia, on the way to an 8-0 finish. The Billingsley Report, a ranking service recognized as legitimate by the NCAA, retroactively named this Auburn team the national champions of 1913. It's an absolute mystery to me why Auburn doesn't officially claim that title. In the context of its time, it is as legitimate as 2010 and probably even more legit than 1957, honestly.

John Ringer

Auburn should claim 1913 for sure.

The fact that we don't (other than a recent and very brief mention on the Athletic Department's web site) just shows that either we don't care about these things, or we pretend we don't care.

Other schools made the move to retroactively claim titles like this before the Internet made it more noticeable to do that.

Van Allen Plexico

That's a good point. Alabama first claimed their batch of extremely dubious titles by simply adding them to the list they printed in their media guides one year in the 1980s. Back when there was no easy way to start a giant controversy over it.

John Ringer

National title or not, the 1913 team was one of the greatest teams in Auburn history.

In 1914, Auburn scored 193 points while not allowing the opposition to score on them a single time. Unfortunately, there *is* one scenario in which holding an opponent to zero points doesn't necessarily mean you won the game, and Auburn discovered that fact the hard way. They tied Georgia 0-0 in Atlanta, to finish with 8 wins, no losses, and one draw.

The 1919 team won Donahue his final conference championship by going 8-1-0. The only loss was to Vanderbilt, 7-6, in a game played in Nashville.

The 1922 season was Coach Donahue's last on the Plains. He finished up having coached Auburn to the same number of wins as Pat Dye. His overall record for the Tigers was 99-35-5.

Van Allen Plexico

The case can be made for a 1914 national title as well, on the twin strengths that they didn't lose a game all season and they shut out every team they played. I mean, think about that for a second: In the entire season, no one scored on that Auburn team.

The 0-0 tie with Georgia, unfortunately, drops them one spot below an undefeated and untied Tennessee team that season, within the conference.

And I have to say, Vanderbilt wasn't bad during some of those seasons back then. It's disappointing that they beat Auburn in 1919 to ruin a perfect season, but there's no real shame in it. They won a lot of early games over the teams that today dominate the SEC.

Oddly enough, the fact that everyone knew a renewed Iron Bowl would be a big deal was the justification given by Auburn for not renewing it in 1923. When Alabama made a few hesitant overtures to that effect, Auburn president Dr. Spright Dowell turned them down, saying that if the two schools played each other, it would render "other games, contests and events subservient to the one supreme event of the year." Too big to fail? Now the mere thought of the Iron Bowl ever taking place again was too big to consider!

Alabama football enjoyed its first true golden years beginning in the mid-1920s, including their famous trips to the Rose Bowl. It's easy to see how both programs were likely content with their success and not dying to shake things up again.

Nevertheless, occasional efforts were made by individuals from both sides, here and there, to renew the series—notably in 1911, 1919, 1932, and 1944—but to no avail.

Van Allen Plexico
Honestly, in retrospect, the various efforts to start the series back up seem rather half-hearted.

One account expands a bit on the animosity Auburn felt towards Doc Pollard of Alabama, and how that might have figured into the breach in the series. It perhaps sheds a little light on why things played out the way they did.

The story goes that, in early 1908, Auburn's Coach Donahue and President Thach traveled up to Tuscaloosa on what amounted to Alabama's A-Day spring game. They were scheduled to have a meeting with Alabama's Coach Pollard and President Abercrombie to discuss the details of the contract to continue the football series.

One must recall that Auburn people were already upset with Pollard for what they considered "illegal shifts" by Alabama's offense in previous Iron Bowls, none of which were penalized by the referee.

Before these people all got together for their meeting, the two schools played a baseball doubleheader. It turns out the baseball team was also managed by Pollard. In an era of very low scores, Alabama won the two games by a combined score of 19-0.

As you might imagine, and as the story goes, Coach Donahue and President Thach were not in the best of moods when the contract meeting finally commenced, later that day. Worse, they felt they were dealing with a cheater. They also felt that Auburn didn't need to play Alabama, so there would be no real negative fallout if the series simply didn't continue. The meeting broke down into an impasse and never progressed further. The series ended.

Auburn Coach Mike Donahue later stated, "I tried to bring the schools together several times after relations were broken in the spring of 1908." But nothing came of it.

It didn't help that, early on, the leaders at Alabama weren't particularly keen on the idea. They cited violence taking place at other rivalry games around the country, including Texas, Georgia, Tennessee and others, when their Committee on Physical Education and Athletics issued a report that stated, "We hazard nothing in saying that the game would not make a single constructive contribution to education in the state."

John Ringer

I love that last quote there. That should be the motto of the Iron Bowl.

The report went on to add, "The fundamental question is: Do the people of Alabama need a tranquil, sane kind of athletics in their two major institutions, or an irrational rabid kind?" Clearly Alabama felt that any contest with Auburn would inevitably become the latter; better, then, in their view, not to play at all.

John Ringer

Whoever did this study clearly knew what they were talking about! (Says an irrational, rabid Auburn fan.)

Eventually, people all over the state got behind the push to have the two universities resume the series. As Alex Scarborough of ESPN notes:

In 1930, there was a movement to make the Iron Bowl a postseason game, with proceeds going to charity. The Robert E. Lee Memorial Foundation wanted in. So did the American Legion. The Native Sons of Birmingham, fearing the impact of the stock market crash a year earlier, asked that the estimated $75,000 gate go toward the unemployed.

"We challenge you in the name of humanity to accept this invitation," the Native Sons wrote. "There can be no POSSIBLE REASON sufficient to warrant your refusal. Your acceptance will earn for the University of Alabama a place in the heart of every Alabamian. Your refusal COULD AND SHOULD mean an IRREPARABLE LOSS to you and the University—that of good will and future support of the citizens of Alabama, and more especially the citizens of Birmingham."

(University of Alabama president George) Denny gave his answer in ink atop the letter. It would not be practical, he wrote, to "comply with your request."

Van Allen Plexico

During the later part of the forty-year hiatus, more often than not, Auburn was the side pushing harder for a renewal of the series, while Alabama was the side refusing to play. I'm sure the Alabama leaders in those years saw themselves as just somehow "above" playing Auburn, and refusing to stoop down to Auburn's level. Slowly, however, I think they realized that it was starting to look like they didn't want to play Auburn for *other* reasons. Like, perhaps, they were *afraid* to. Afraid they might *lose*.

At one point, Gessner McCorvey, a member of Alabama's board of trustees, wrote to Alabama president Raymond Paty, telling him about how he was being besieged by Alabama fans demanding the Tide play Auburn again.

"Some of them," McCorvey added, "have even gone so far as to say we are acting like a bunch of babies and were afraid we might get beat. Auburn, of course, will encourage this thought."

Van Allen Plexico
I am 100% here to encourage that thought!

Sooner or later, it seemed every organization in the state, no matter how small or unrelated to sports and education, wanted to get on the record as calling for the return of the Iron Bowl.
Scarborough continues:

> Why the Ensley Real Estate Board felt compelled to pass a resolution in favor of resuming the series, no one knows. But there it was, mixed in with Alabama president George Denny's papers (in the University of Alabama Special Collections Library).

Eventually, Alabama's leaders grew resentful of the fact that they were looking like the side afraid to play. They felt that the Tigers didn't really want to resume the series either, but that Auburn's leaders were speaking out publicly as if they *did*, purely to make Alabama look bad.
Alabama commissioned and issued a report supporting and justifying their position of not playing Auburn. Upon its publication, Alabama's faculty chair of athletics, A.B. Moore, wrote to trustee McCorvey:

> It took courage, if I do say so, to do what we did. (Publish the report saying the two teams should not resume the series).
>
> (Auburn president Luther) Duncan does not want to see the two institutions play football, but believing that WE would not agree to play, he put us behind the eight ball. We understood the situation and could easily have moved out in the clear, but to have done this... would have been a cowardly and faithless act.
>
> In this sad hour (of World War II) when our boys are dying on the seven seas and on battlefields all over the globe ... the press of the state has been seriously discussing the question of whether or not Auburn and the University should play football. ... Does not all this represent a fearful overemphasis of football in the public mind of Alabama?

Van Allen Plexico

My takeaway from that letter is that, even while we as a country were collectively battling the Nazis and the Japanese, the good people of the state of Alabama had their eyes on what *really* mattered: playing the Iron Bowl! Ha.

In the years just prior to 1944, Auburn once again reached out to Alabama to judge their interest in a renewal. Alabama's board of trustees turned them down flat. They felt it could lead to "an overemphasis on football in Alabama (imagine that!) and an unhealthy increase in rumor and rancor between the two schools."

Van Allen Plexico

It might also lead to Paul Finebaum!

The Tuscaloosa trustees also warned that a resumption of the series might "make it impossible for either school to hire coaches of high character and proven ability," because the pressure to always beat the cross-state rival might lead to a continuous and ongoing condition of what we today would call "the hot seat" for both coaches. Who would want such a job? Who would take it, if offered? Better surely to avoid such a situation by simply not playing the one game guaranteed to bring that kind of pressure with it.

During the years Auburn had the stronger program, it was Alabama trying harder to restore the series. But then a shift took place at both programs.

Van Allen Plexico

Alabama started emphasizing football in the 1920s, just as Auburn was de-emphasizing it. We lost Coach Donahue around the time they hired Wallace Wade. The whole balance of power flipped from Auburn to Tuscaloosa. We mostly languished while they went to the Rose Bowl. It didn't have to go that way, but decisions were made and emphasis was placed where it was placed by the leadership at both schools.

The story goes that Alabama's President Abercrombie kicked one of the star players off the Tide team, provoking Coach Pollard to resign. Alabama alumni and fans directed their ire not at Pollard or the player, of course, but at

Abercrombie, for kicking the player off the team. He was forced out and replaced by—and you'll recognize this name—Dr. George Denny. (He would go on to serve as president at UA, on and off, from 1912 all the way to 1942, and they later named the tower with the chimes after him.)

Denny was the one who pushed for football to be of greater importance at Alabama, because he knew it would make money. (If he'd only known just *how much* money it would someday make!) Denny in turn brought in Wallace Wade, who enjoyed great success with the Tide during his years there.

Clearly there could be no reconciliation between Auburn and Alabama as long as that particular leadership was in charge in Tuscaloosa. And Denny was still president there during World War II!

As a friend put it, if not for all of this happening, the Auburn-Alabama rivalry would look today a lot like Clemson-South Carolina.

The thought of that—of what could have been—is enough to make even a strong Auburn man cry.

Because of this, great Auburn players like Billy Hitchcock, who starred on the Plains from 1935-1937, never got the opportunity to play against Alabama.

We thought about it. We were friends with them. In summer baseball, we played in the amateur league with Alabama players. We didn't know why we weren't playing. We all wanted to play. It took a long time, but they finally got around to it.
—Billy Hitchcock

They got around to it after multiple attempts by the Alabama legislature to twist the arms of both schools—attempts that amounted to very little.

As World War II was drawing to a close, the state legislature passed multiple resolutions that simply called for a resumption of the series. Lacking any kind of force to back them up, however, Auburn and Alabama were free to ignore or reject these overtures.

Van Allen Plexico

Nearly every account of the series resumption I've ever read or heard has indicated the state legislature basically drew a line in the sand and told both schools to play each other or lose state funding. But here we find accounts stating that the metaphorical "funding" gun was never pointed directly at either university. It does, however, sound like that metaphorical gun was waved around in the air a lot, and suddenly the leaders of the two schools just happened to find religion and worked things out. Religion in this state, of course, being football.

One other important note: As mentioned earlier, there were efforts by Alabama, over the entire 20th Century, to simply *absorb* Auburn into the University of Alabama system, making it into—in effect—another UAB or UAH. And we all know how much Alabama likes scheduling its satellite campuses in sports. (Spoiler: It doesn't! At all!)

So the thinking by some is that Alabama always assumed they'd be gobbling up Auburn (or, rather, Alabama Polytechnic Institute) "any day now," and therefore there was *no need* to schedule them for football. But when Auburn's enrollment suddenly took off during those years, it became obvious to everyone that Auburn would remain its own university, completely separate from Tuscaloosa. At that point, getting the two schools back together on the football field might have become a tiny bit easier.

After the legislature finally stepped in, Auburn's President Draughon wrote to Alabama's McCorvey that, while no one liked feeling "bludgeoned into the game through such legislation, we need to recognize the possibility that we may make an ever-greater mistake in persisting in our refusal."

In March of 1947, Auburn's Board of Trustees approved a resolution to resume athletic competition between Auburn and Alabama.

Carl Voyles, Auburn's athletic director, told a committee of the state legislature that Auburn wasn't the problem here. The Tigers were, in fact, holding open a date for a possible resumption of the series "on the last Saturday in November and the first in December" of 1948.

By that time, Alabama fully appreciated the corner they'd been painted into. They commissioned yet another report on the situation, which laid out their predicament in dire terms:

> *If athletic relations should not be resumed the University (of Alabama) would have to bear the brunt of public displeasure and criticism. The public ill-will engendered toward the University, we fear, will be highly injurious to it. In such a situation, we feel that we cannot afford to hold out for our convictions, though they are deep and well sustained.*
> *—University of Alabama report on the resumption of the Auburn-Alabama series, 1947-48*

In other words, Auburn had won the public relations battle. The Tigers looked like the team that wanted to play the game again. Alabama looked like the one that was dodging its cross-state rival. If the two sides didn't start playing again, everyone in the state would blame Alabama.

Van Allen Plexico

War Chicken? Oh no—more like Cringing Tide!

Well played, Auburn. Well played.

By this point, Alabama knew they had no choice but to give in and play Auburn. All that remained was for the leaders of the two universities to "happen to run into each other" somewhere and start the process moving forward.

As Auburn's former Athletic Director, David Housel, tells the story, Auburn president Ralph B. Draughon ran into Alabama president John M. Gallalee at a meeting in Birmingham at some point prior to 1948. There, Dr. Gallalee reportedly said to Draughon, "There's no reason in the world why Alabama and Auburn can't play one another." Draughon supposedly agreed. Anyone unaware of all the machinations going on behind the scenes would have certainly wondered, "Then why haven't you played for the last four decades? What happened to all those objections?"

Putting all that bad blood aside, the two presidents agreed to meet later to discuss the situation. They rendezvoused in April at the Ann Jordan Farm near Kellyton on Highway 280 near Alexander City, whereupon they hammered out the details to resume the series with games in early December of that year and the next.

Van Allen Plexico
Hey, Kellyton! That's just a few miles south of where I was born. I drove past there on Highway 280 a million times when I was a student, going back and forth between Sylacauga and Auburn. It's exciting to think that history was made such a short distance away.

John Ringer
Should we erect a historical marker in Kellyton on the site of the negotiations?

Van Allen Plexico
Something like the train car where Germany surrendered to the Allies after World War I!

Auburn's president, Ralph B. Draughon, sent a letter marked "personal and confidential" to Alabama's president, John M. Gallalee, dated April 24, 1948. In it, Draughn thanks Gallalee for "your hospitality on Thursday, April 22." He then lists twelve things "from memory" that were "tentatively agreed upon" in their mutual efforts toward the "resumption of athletic relations" between the two schools. Of particular note, they agree "it is unfortunate that this question has become a political matter," meaning that the state legislature has gotten involved.

They fear that "pressures for resumption (of athletic relations) from sources outside the institutions may be expected to increase to the point of interfering with the normal educational programs of the two institutions." In other words, they're trying to run colleges but it's increasingly getting to be all about sports. Maybe if they play each other again, folks will settle down and let them get back to teaching!

They agree to start scheduling one another in sports starting in the fall of 1948, including a football game on December 4. The location of that game would be decided "by our respective Athletic Staffs."

This new arrangement would be for no more than three years, "in order that we may test the practicality of the action and its effects upon the two institutions." In other words, let's try this a few times and see what happens.

Item nine is of particular interest. It reads: "...It is the considered judgment of the responsible officials of the two institutions that we should look forward to the playing of football *on a home and home basis*, therefore, that joint effort should be planned whereby the Legislature may appropriate funds *for the enlargement of the stadiums of Auburn and the University (of Alabama)*. However, such appropriations should be in addition to appropriations for the maintenance and operation of the two institutions. (Emphasis added.)

Van Allen Plexico

Okay, this part is huge.

Both Auburn and Alabama are saying the Iron Bowl should be played *on the campuses of the two schools*—not at some neutral site every year.

They are also saying the two campus stadiums need to be *bigger* in order to accommodate this.

So, to translate: Attention, state legislature! You've gotten involved in this situation, and you're demanding we play one another. So give us some *money* to enlarge our facilities so that we *can*. And make sure it's not money we were already due to receive, being redirected from other programs. No, we want *new money* for this, separate from what's already coming our way.

I think we've finally found something Alabama and Auburn completely agree on: "The state legislature should give us *more money!*"

John Ringer

But instead, playing the game in Birmingham became an expectation, and people on both sides just forgot the original plan was to use this as leverage on the state government to fund expansion of both home stadiums.

Van Allen Plexico

And once you start playing it in that one location, it becomes easy to keep on, and harder to move it anywhere else.

Forty years later, that would become a huge roadblock to Auburn when we wanted to bring the game home: Everyone was simply used to it being played in Birmingham, as if that was where it was always supposed to be played.

The letter more or less concludes with one more important point: "Pending the building of adequate facilities on the two campuses, no commitments be made to any civic or athletic group whereby the game will be played continuously on any given field. On the other hand, the site of the football game each year to be left in the hands of the responsible athletic officials of the two institutions, acting jointly and in mutual agreement."

Van Allen Plexico

This part seems extremely important as well. I take it to mean that, until the stadiums in Auburn and Tuscaloosa have been improved and are up to par, neither school is able to make a deal, on its own, that the game will be played in any specific non-campus location, under the control of any outside organization. Instead, the two schools would have to *agree* on the temporary, off-campus location where it should be played.

Now, if they both did agree early on to play in Birmingham "pending the building of adequate facilities" in Auburn and Tuscaloosa, that's fine. But it also says the two sides have to *agree* on such a location. I take that to mean "going forward," as in, on a continuing basis. Which in turn means that if Auburn decides it doesn't want to play at a particular non-campus location anymore, then a "mutual agreement" to play there no longer exists, and by the language of this letter, the game *will not be played there.*

Presumably that was the purpose of those multi-year contracts like the one mentioned by Bryant to Dye. The two universities, over the years, had been occasionally re-upping the *mutual agreement* to play at Legion Field, with the most recent one running through 1988 (not counting the mysterious amendment Alabama discovered later).

That seems pretty iron-clad to me. After 1988, Coach Dye was withdrawing Auburn's approval to have the Tigers play in Legion Field. Lacking "mutual agreement," we didn't have to play there anymore.

What happens if the two cannot agree on a non-campus location, however, is not addressed.

John Ringer

This was a trend of the time. Georgia-Florida, Texas-Oklahoma, and others. Local committees and chambers of commerce got involved, promoting the games and encouraging the teams to play there. That's probably what Auburn and Alabama were attempting to avoid here, with this language in the agreement, but it happened anyway.

Two days later, Dr. Gallalee wrote back with a one-sentence letter: "Dear Dr. Draughon: There is attached an outline of our understanding of the results of a recent meeting."

The document attached listed eight bullet points, agreeing in principle with Draughon's letter.

Of note, Gallalee says the two universities will "make agreement for two years for games at a non-campus site to be selected," those two years being 1948 and 1949. He continues, "Football games after 1949 to be played on a campus-campus basis with request to legislature to appropriate equal amounts to each school for stadium seats.

Van Allen Plexico

So the Iron Bowl was intended to be played on the Auburn and Alabama campuses starting in 1950! And, at the time, Alabama was okay with that.

In this statement from Gallalee, Alabama pretty much agreed with President Draughon's memo, other than narrowing the agreement down to just two years initially.

What I really love about these documents is that they both agree that if the state legislature is so determined that Auburn and Alabama play each other that it's willing to make a big political issue out of it, then that same legislature can danged sure fork over some extra cash to both schools to build bigger stadiums for that game!

David Housel

When the game was first renewed back in 1948, the intention all along was to play the game in Birmingham until they could build a stadium big enough in Auburn and big enough in Tuscaloosa to host the game on both campuses. But as the Birmingham stadium began to grow, and frankly Alabama's stadium did *not* begin to grow—it's passed Auburn now, but if you go back, Auburn enlarged the stadium in 1960, 1970, (1980), 1987, Auburn's stadium grew at a faster rate than Alabama's.

The original intention was to go home-and-home. It just (over time) became a Birmingham thing. Nobody did anything, it just kind of "osmosed" into a Birmingham thing. And Birmingham at that time had the political power to pretty much run the state.

Auburn's rule against playing games after Thanksgiving had ended years earlier—the 1932 and 1933 Auburn teams played South Carolina in early December—and so those dates were available.

Left undecided in all the back-and-forth between the two presidents was the answer to the question: Exactly *where* would the newly-resumed Iron Bowl be played?

For decades, whether out of preference or necessity, Auburn hosted many of its home games in other cities. At different times, Birmingham, Montgomery, and Columbus, Georgia all served as homes away from home for the Tigers. Because of that, Auburn playing Alabama in Birmingham, when Auburn was the home team, did not seem like much of a stretch at all, back in the Forties, and for a long time afterward. In 1949 Auburn's stadium was expanded to 21,500 seats and renamed "Cliff Hare Stadium," but it still lacked the capacity to accommodate the number of fans expected for such a game. The town of Auburn, likewise, possessed nothing like the lodging or restroom facilities to accommodate an Iron Bowl crowd. Auburn continued to play Tennessee and Georgia Tech in Legion

Field until well into the 1970s. Playing the Alabama game on the Plains simply wasn't a realistic possibility in that era.

Alabama in those days, however—and for many years afterward—also preferred to play their bigger games away from Tuscaloosa. Legion Field, with a capacity at that time of 47,000, was larger than their on-campus stadium, which held only 31,000 fans.

Thus in 1948 it made perfect sense for both teams to play the game in Birmingham, and to divide the stadium (at least on paper) down the middle, half Auburn fans and half Alabama fans.

John Ringer

One thing that really hits me is Georgia being the only school that came to play games in Auburn without a fight or major complaint.

After years of playing every year in Columbus, Georgia, the series moved to home-and-home beginning in 1959, in Athens, and then 1960, in Cliff Hare Stadium in Auburn.

It honestly changes how I feel about them and about the rivalry. Now I dislike Alabama and Georgia Tech more and dislike Georgia a little less.

It also makes me really want to preserve that rivalry in the face of current scheduling complications as the SEC expands.

Van Allen Plexico

The problem, as I see it, is that both programs needed to play in Birmingham at the start of the resumption of the series, for various reasons. It was just the most practical solution for both of them. As time went by, however, circumstances changed. Alabama enjoyed playing the game there, did so out of preference, and wanted to continue doing so indefinitely. Auburn played there only out of necessity, and as that "necessity" situation changed, Auburn increasingly wished to get out of Birmingham.

Why did the situation change for Auburn? Several things happened over time. The city of Auburn grew, and continues to grow. Infrastructure there became more developed—more and bigger roads and highways, more hotels, restaurants, parking areas, rest rooms, and so on. And above all, Jordan-

Hare Stadium expanded its capacity from 21,500 in 1949 to 85,214 in 1989.

Alabama was used to how things were, though, and liked it. They liked playing every year in Birmingham, yes—but they also simply liked giving the orders and getting their way. Bossing Auburn around. All the other things gradually became excuses. They were not interested in changing anything.

I tried explaining this to my young daughter recently. Saying it all out loud, it became very obvious how unreasonable Alabama's position on where Auburn played its home game had become over the years. She just shook her head and asked, "If it's our year, why couldn't they just let us play it where we wanted?" I replied, "That's the response any normal person, looking in from outside the rivalry—or back into history—would have. But we're not talking about normal people here—we're talking about Alabama! (Pause while we both laughed at my joke.) Alabama had become fully invested in this setup, they'd enjoyed its benefits for decades, and they were going to find any excuses and invoke any threats they could, to keep things from changing."

One other factor is this: I think a lot of Alabama people simply couldn't or wouldn't believe that Auburn had grown so much, and that Jordan-Hare Stadium had grown so much and was, by the late 1980s, the largest and by far the nicest stadium in the state. I can remember hearing the astonishment from quite a few Alabama fans when they came to Auburn and saw our stadium for the first time, be it in 1989 or over the next few years.

On December 4, 1948, Alabama student body president Gillis Cammack met with his counterpart at Auburn, Willie Johns, in Woodrow Wilson Park in Birmingham. There they metaphorically *and* literally "buried the hatchet"—they dug a hole and put a real hatchet in it—symbolizing the reconciliation between the two universities and their return to athletic competition against one another.

Said Cammack in 2010, "The idea was we bury the hatchet and we'd forget about all the bad things between the schools. I threw the hatchet in. Just dropped it in a hole is all. I don't imagine it stayed there long. Someone probably dug it up before we left."

Van Allen Plexico
In terms of "forgetting the bad things between the schools," it certainly has always *felt* like someone dug that hatchet up immediately!

The ceremony was overseen by Birmingham public safety commissioner Theophilus Eugene "Bull" Connor. Yes, the same Bull Connor who set attack dogs and fire hoses on peaceful civil rights demonstrators a few years later.

Said Cammack of Connor, "He warned us there would not be any hard feelings. If anybody got out of line, it was going to be jail right then. He really laid it down to us."

Van Allen Plexico
One can only imagine what Bull Connor might have done to a bunch of college students from Auburn and Alabama if he'd had a mind to intervene with them. Good heavens.

The hatchet—and forty-one years of animosity—now successfully buried, or at least temporarily covered over, the game was on!

With the two teams playing again for the first time in decades, and football having gotten (relatively) more sophisticated since 1907, a whole new way of staging the game had to be worked out.

Gone were the ropes and the barbed wire. Tickets were split evenly between the two schools. Students entered Legion Field hours before kickoff, yelling "War Eagle" and "Roll Tide," and keeping up the cheers the whole time, until they lost their voices. As game time approached, the two bands marched onto the field and formed the "UA" and the "AU," played the alma maters and fight songs, and then combined to perform the National Anthem.

Van Allen Plexico
This arrangement would continue through the 1987 game— the last time the stadium was divided evenly between the two fan bases. I was fortunate to be in attendance at that one, and

got to see the alleged "50-50 split" for myself. Maybe it was "even" on paper, but in real life, inside that old stadium, it wasn't remotely divided evenly. The fact that the stadium was always an Alabama venue with a Tide home crowd was one of the main arguments by Auburn that the series needed to move to Jordan-Hare in Auburn's years.

On the Thursday before the renewal game, Walling Keith of the *Birmingham News* wrote an article under the headline, "Will The Tide Wash The Plains Or The Plains Stem The Tide?" He described the scene in the days leading up to the big game:

> *The flower of Alabama lung power is at loose today—in polite, restrained sort of way—going over the scales in training for Saturday's grandstand spectacle supreme for all Alabama lovers of pig flesh.*
>
> *Strange jargon emits from the lips of portly old boys who will "lay you five to one" what something or other dark and dire will come to the scoreboards at Legion Field (on the) day after tomorrow.*
>
> *Already there are cries of "War Eagle!"*
>
> *Two dawns and a couple of dusks away from the historical Alabama-Auburn clutch here in Birmingham you can hear the "Yeah, 'Bama!" throating in the otherwise calm December breezes.*
>
> *Spies in Montgomery, Mobile, Jasper, Gadsden and over the hills, valleys and mudflats of Alabama report that there is a joyous and pigskin happy spirit of deepest unrest in a generation.*
>
> *An old-fashioned football parade, the kind that used to send electric sparks shooting up the spine and cause even staid deans of old Scandinavian literature to yell "War Eagle" will be staged at 10:30 Saturday.*
>
> *Bama's 1,300-man pep "squad," a small army of student pepper-uppers will stage some new and fancy stunts.*

Unfortunately for Auburn, the Alabama team they faced on Saturday completely overwhelmed them.

Auburn's most dangerous player, "Triple Threat" Travis Tidwell, suffered an ankle injury in the second quarter and was taken to the hospital for x-rays. He did not return to the game. Without him, Auburn couldn't generate any real offense, and Alabama began to wear the Tigers' defense down.

Alabama led 21-0 at halftime, and only piled on more points in the second half, scoring six more touchdowns after the break.

The *Birmingham News* said:

"Big Shoe" Ed Salem, a strapping 190-pound fullback from Ramsay High, cut loose with fire, thunder and lightning in spearheading Alabama to a 55 to 0 victory over Auburn Saturday. Never has a sophomore back done so much damage in Legion Field, as 46,000 watched the first football game between Alabama and Auburn in 41 years.

John Ringer
We just couldn't stop Big Shoe.

Van Allen Plexico
At least now we know what—or who—caused all the damage to Legion Field!

This remains the most lopsided win by either team in the history of the Iron Bowl. Auburn did still lead the overall series, however, at 7-5-1. But the trend lines did not appear to be going in the Tigers' favor. Fans from the Plains looked ahead to the 1949 game with perhaps equal measures of hope and worry. They had to be asking themselves, "Can we pull back ahead of Alabama in football again, or has dominance in the state permanently swung to the western side?"

Fortunately, it took only one game to restore competitive balance to the series.

Fast forward one year. The date is December 3, 1949. Alabama hasn't lost since October 1, a run of seven straight games. The week before, they'd trounced Florida in Gainesville by a score of 35-13. Auburn, meanwhile, enters the game with a record of 1 win, four losses and three ties. In addition to the clear differences between these two editions of the Tide and Tigers, most folks in attendance at

Legion Field that day surely remember how the previous Iron Bowl played out, and don't give Auburn much of a chance at all.

But, to quote Lee Corso: "Not so fast, my friend."

Auburn's bend-but-don't break defense gave up 354 yards of total offense, but held Alabama's prolific scoring machine under control in the first quarter. Then, in the second quarter, things got interesting:

> *Johnny Wallis (of Auburn), the former Ensley carrier, intercepted an Eddie Salem pass in the first 45 seconds of the second period. He raced like mad down the sidelines for 18 yards and the first touchdown Auburn had scored (against) Alabama since 1907. Tucker converted (the extra point).*

With that pick-six, it looked as if the Tigers would take a shut-out lead to halftime, but the Tide (yes, by this point they were called the Crimson Tide) equalized mere seconds before the end of the first half, as quarterback Salem scampered for a 13-yard touchdown.

After a scoreless third quarter, a healthy Travis Tidwell (who stood 5 foot 10 inches and weighed 185 pounds) finally managed to lead the Tigers down the field, battling against the tough Alabama defense. Auburn went up 14-7 when George Davis carried the ball into Legion Field's checkerboard end zone from ten yards away. Alabama was running out of time, but they managed another last-minute drive, punctuated by Tom Calvin bulldozing in from three yards out. It looked like the Tide would escape with a tie, but quarterback Salem, doubling as the kicker, missed the extra point. Auburn escaped with what has been called by some the greatest upset in the history of the Iron Bowl.

Legendary sportswriter Zipp Newman of the *Birmingham News* wrote of it:

> *There has never been a sweeter Auburn victory in all the 58 years of football on the Plains than the Tigers 14—13 win over Alabama.*
>
> *No Auburn team ever came from as far behind in one year as the 1949 Tigers. They lost to Alabama, 55-0, just 364 days ago. It was to avenge the dregs of hemlock that this Auburn team*

entered its 14th game since 1893 with Alabama—and in atoning for the loss a year ago, won on the toe of Billy Tucker.

Forty-four thousand fans jammed into the stadium to watch the state's two big football powers do battle.

Van Allen Plexico

The Alabama quarterback threw a pick six for the first Auburn score, and missed the extra point that would have tied the game at the end.

John Ringer

He cost them the biggest upset in the series history. Alabama was a three-touchdown favorite.

Van Allen Plexico

We need to put up a statue of him, right next to the one for Jamie Howard, the 1994 LSU quarterback.

It's good to know that Alabama losing to Auburn by melting down in the kicking game didn't start in the 2000s, or even in 1972, but is a long and proud tradition going way back!

I have to mention one thing here: The Alabama back who scored at the end was Tom Calvin. When I saw that name, it immediately rang a bell, but I had to look him up to be sure. He went on to play for the Pittsburgh Steelers for a few years, then took a job coaching high school football back home in Alabama. The school was Sylacauga High, my alma mater, where he led the Aggies to four state championships. When I was a kid, we all knew him as "Coach Calvin." He coached my brother, who was the backup quarterback there, and he was my PE teacher one year when I was in elementary school. I still remember him teaching us the proper form for running—hold your hands like "Os" and not as fists, so they're more aerodynamic—and for catching a football—you look it into your arms! (The face he would make while "looking the ball into his arms" in slow motion was just priceless.) He also taught us that if you're running down the field and you see an opponent ahead, you run right at him and try to run him over! I don't think Coach Calvin would've approved of all this "running out of bounds" and "sliding" stuff that players do now.

He was a great guy, despite his choice of colleges. Ha. He lived just down the road from where I grew up. Later he moved back home to north Alabama, and didn't pass away until he was well into his 90s, in 2020. He is still remembered and honored as a Sylacauga sports legend.

After the huge upset win by Auburn in 1949, the Iron Bowl turned into a game of streaks.

Alabama would go on to win the next four, and to do so decisively, by a combined score of 90-14. Then Auburn turned the tables and won five in a row, from 1954-58, by an even bigger combined score of 142-15, under the leadership of new head coach Ralph "Shug" Jordan.

Jordan was incredibly important to Auburn. The program had, for the most part, languished in the years just before and after World War II. He came in and shook things up immediately.

David Housel

Auburn Football was a wasteland, a desert, when Coach Jordan came back as head coach in 1951. An Auburn Man, he gave Auburn people the greatest thing that could ever be given: *hope*. And he delivered. Whatever Auburn Football is today, whatever it may become in years to come will be due in no small measure to Coach Jordan and his many contributions to his alma mater.

Phillip Marshall wrote in the *Montgomery Advertiser*:

Shug Jordan and Jeff Beard, the fathers of modern Auburn football, had together taken a program that was 0-10 in 1950 and won a national championship in 1957. From the start, they dreamed of one day playing all of Auburn's home games on campus. But (that simply wasn't possible during those years because) Bear Bryant built a monster program at Alabama (while) Auburn hit on hard times, losing nine out of 10 to

Alabama between 1959 and 1968 and nine straight from 1973 through 1981.

During Shug's twenty-five-year reign on the Plains, he led the Tigers to nineteen winning seasons, twelve bowl games and thirteen appearances in the final Associated Press poll, including seven Top 10 finishes. He coached twenty-five All-Americans and eight Academic All-Americans. In 1958, lineman Zeke Smith won the Outland Award and in 1971 quarterback Pat Sullivan became Auburn's first Heisman Trophy winner. He was AP SEC Coach of the Year in 1957 and 1972, and remains among the winningest coaches in SEC history.

Van Allen Plexico
Coach Jordan was wounded fighting Nazis on the Normandy beaches. I mean, what else do you need to say? He certainly wasn't going to be afraid of Alabama or the Bear.

Alabama, with their new head coach, Paul "Bear" Bryant, won the next four in a row, from 1959-62. Auburn hit back in 1963, with Jimmy Sidle's team pulling out a 10-8 victory over 6th-ranked Alabama. They would go on to the Orange Bowl for the only time in program history.

Van Allen Plexico
From 1950 to 1963, the losing team in the Iron Bowl never scored more than 8 points, and was shut out nine times in fourteen games. And it wasn't just one of the teams dominating—it was divided pretty evenly between them.

After Auburn's 1963 win, Alabama got hot again and reeled off five straight, from 1964-68. Each of those Crimson Tide teams was ranked in the Top 20, and four of them were in the Top 10.

It was during this time that Shug Jordan gave the series its iconic name—the Iron Bowl—derived from Birmingham's old iron and steel industry. That city was, after all, long known as the "Pittsburgh of the South."

The 1964 Auburn team came to Birmingham for the game with a 6-3 record. A reporter asked Coach Jordan about the prospect that

90

Auburn might miss out on going to a bowl game. Jordan reportedly replied, "We've got our bowl game. We have it every year. It's the Iron Bowl in Birmingham."

Obviously, the name stuck.

Van Allen Plexico

At the 1993 Georgia game in Athens, Auburn was undefeated, but we were on probation and couldn't play in the postseason. As Auburn was winning late, an irate Georgia fan who clearly thought he was pretty clever yelled at me and my friends, "Yeah, but what bowl game are you going to?" I yelled back, "The Iron Bowl!" So, thanks, Shug, for that ammunition. (Georgia had only won four games to that point in the season. My friend next to me called back to the guy, "What bowl game are *you* going to?")

Pat Sullivan and Terry Beasley brought the Iron Bowl trophy back to Auburn in 1969 and 1970 with two high-scoring wins. The twelfth-ranked Tigers in 1969 hung 49 points on Alabama, while the 1970 squad outscored them, 33-28.

Alabama got some revenge on Sullivan in 1971, beating him in his senior and Heisman Trophy-winning season, 31-7, when both teams entered the game ranked in the Top 5 (Alabama at 3 and Auburn at 5).

The next year looked to most fans to be more of the same. Alabama was at the mountaintop during those years of dominance by Bryant. They would come into the 1972 Iron Bowl ranked number 2 in the country. Auburn, meanwhile, was playing without their Heisman-winning quarterback for the first time in three years. Surely the Tigers had no chance at all.

For most of the 1972 game, the expected storyline held true.

But then Alabama had to punt. And as Greg Gantt dropped back, let go of the football and swung his leg, a very strange sequence of events began to play out in Legion Field; events nobody there, or watching on television, would or could ever forget.

-6-

"UNCONTROLLED PANDEMONIUM"

On December 2, 1972—seventeen years to the day before an undefeated and second-ranked Alabama team would come to Auburn for the first time ever—Auburn engineered one of the most shocking upsets in college football history, over another undefeated and second-ranked Alabama team.

The 1972 Iron Bowl, of course, went down in history as the "Punt, Bama, Punt" game. In it, the Auburn team known as "the Amazins" pulled one of the most memorable upsets in the history of the series.

That "Amazin" team arrived in Birmingham ranked a surprising ninth in the country, having suffered only one loss all year. They'd achieved that record despite the absence of Heisman Trophy winner Pat Sullivan, who was by that time playing in the NFL. They didn't possess anything like the prolific offense of previous seasons, but they were opportunistic on that side of the ball, and they combined a stingy defense with strong special teams to make up the difference.

Even so, Alabama was considered to be the stronger team by far. Indeed, as the game progressed, Auburn's defense kept it relatively close, but the offense couldn't dent the Tide's defense. Well into the fourth quarter, Alabama was shutting out Auburn, 16-0. It could've been worse, but the Tide's kicker had missed an extra point earlier in the game. Few watching would have thought a missed extra point mattered much at that stage, but how big it would loom later in the game.

With time winding down, Auburn finally put together a drive that moved the ball deep into Alabama territory. Alabama managed to hold them out of the end zone, however, and bring up fourth down. Instead of going for it, Coach Jordan chose to send out kicker Gardner Jett for a field goal. It has been said that fans of both teams booed; Auburn people booed because they felt the Tigers, down 16 late, might as well go for the touchdown, and Alabama fans booed because it cost them the shutout and ruined the point spread.

After Jett's successful field goal, Alabama got the ball back, but an increasingly desperate Auburn quickly stopped them and forced them to punt. The Tigers rushed punter Greg Gantt with everything they had, overwhelming the blocking from all sides, and Bill Newton slapped the ball down, whereupon it bounced up perfectly into the arms of the onrushing David Langner, who easily carried it into the end zone.

Just like that, over the space of only a few seconds of game time, the score had been transformed from a 16-0 Alabama shutout to the Tide clinging to a slender, 6-point lead.

Even so, time was now rapidly ticking away, and Auburn's offense had shown little ability to score on its own. The Tigers would need a miracle, an absolute *miracle*, to score any more points in this game.

Fortunately, they *got* that miracle.

Once again holding Alabama's offense in check, the Tigers forced the Tide to punt. Again Auburn brought the house, and again Bill Newton found his way through the blockers and to the foot of Greg Gantt.

People watching on television assumed they were seeing an instant replay. Indeed, it played out exactly the same way as the previous blocked punt. After Newton knocked the ball down, it again bounced up into the arms of David Langner, who again carried it untouched into the end zone.

Gardner Jett knocked through what radio play-by-play man Gary Sanders described as "that all-important extra point," and now two stunned fan bases found themselves staring at a Legion Field scoreboard that read Auburn 17, Alabama 16.

The Tigers had to survive one more scary moment. They themselves were forced to punt near the very end of the game, and Alabama's onrushing defenders came very close to returning the favor and blocking the Auburn punt. But the kick got away a split-second before the lead Alabama player could get a hand on it.

David Langner wasn't done with the heroics. Alabama could still win the game with just a field goal. The Tide attempted to get down the field quickly, but Langner intercepted a pass to ice the game.

The *Montgomery Advertiser* described the scene that followed:

Uncontrolled pandemonium struck like lightning at Legion Field Saturday when an astonishingly sudden turnaround gave the Auburn Tigers 17 points in the fourth quarter and a sweeter-than-sweet, one-point victory over Alabama in the annual Iron Bowl Classic.

The Auburn thrills were entirely as late as they were astonishing. The Plainsmen didn't have much to cheer about until Gardner Jett's 42-yard field goal got Auburn's first points with only 9:15 remaining in the game. After that, ecstatic moments for the Plainsmen were in rapid succession, Langner's touchdowns coming, respectfully, with 5:30 and 1:34 on the stadium clock.

"Never in all my coaching experience have I ever had a defense make a greater effort than this (team) did out there today."
—Shug Jordan, after the game

"The best-coached team won today."
—Paul "Bear" Bryant, after the game

"The boys say we are No. 1 and I have to agree with them."
—Shug Jordan, after the game

Clyde Prather, former Auburn Public Safety Director

(My wife and I were) at the 1972 game. There were two Alabama couples sitting behind us, and they were so obnoxious. You wanted to get up and just blast (one of the guys). But we took it and took it and took it. And finally, we blocked that first punt, and one of the couples got up and left. And the other one started carrying on. And I turned around and said, "When we block the next one, I hope you'll stay to see it." Never dreaming something like that could happen. But it happened! By the time we blocked it, by the time the ball hit the ground, that couple was headed down the steps.

That was an unbelievable game. Nobody could believe it.

Van Allen Plexico

Auburn sent out little 45-RPM records containing the audio highlights of this game, and I remember my dad having one and playing it on our record player. I don't remember watching that game live, but the radio play-by-play is as familiar to me as the Kick Six or any other famous Auburn game broadcast because of that little record. I recorded it with a tape recorder and played it all the time.

The story goes that Bear Bryant told reporters later that he wouldn't retire from coaching until he blocked an Auburn punt. Supposedly, Shug Jordan heard this and replied, "In that case, I'll let him block one in the next game."

John Ringer

David Langner is and always will be an Auburn legend.

He came to my dad's pregame tailgate cookouts a good bit. Players were much smaller back then. If you walked by him on the street, you'd never guess he was a football player that made two of the biggest plays in Auburn history.

After the 1972 Auburn win, the record in Iron Bowls stood at 19-17-1 in favor of Alabama. To this day, it has not been that close again, as Alabama was about to reel off the longest winning streak in the history of the series.

In addition to padding Alabama's lead in the series, the Crimson Tide's run from 1973-1981 should've demonstrated conclusively for everyone how valuable playing in Legion Field was for Alabama. In the words of ABC's Keith Jackson, "Coach Bryant knew he had a little advantage playing the game in Birmingham, and he didn't want to give it up."

Mike McClendon

Alabama liked playing in Birmingham, and that preceded Bryant. Bryant preferred playing in Birmingham to playing in Denny Stadium. Legion Field was larger, it was an hour's drive from Tuscaloosa and he had a huge fan base in Birmingham. In the 1960s Denny stadium was a real dump. Since Alabama played half their home games in Birmingham, and all their major games there, it wasn't worth them spending money to do any serious renovations in Tuscaloosa. Plus the city of Birmingham was more than willing to accommodate whatever Bryant wanted. In a lot of respects, it was a better arrangement for them (to play in Birmingham than to play at home). They got all the benefits of home games and none of the costs associated with facilities. Legion Field was really their home stadium. So, every game at Legion Field was a home game for them.

Of course, during those years, Auburn played some of their home games in Legion Field as well.

Mike McClendon

In the 1960s Auburn would schedule three games or so each year in Birmingham. It helped with recruiting, and it made sense from a political viewpoint. Other than that, it was never a good deal for Auburn. The road from Birmingham to Auburn was mostly a two-lane winding road that went through a lot of small towns. It was a three-hour drive on a good day, and longer sometimes. Those games in Legion Field were never true "Home Games" for Auburn.

Van Allen Plexico

I am here to testify about that road from Birmingham to Auburn, otherwise known as US Highway 280. From 1986 to 1990, I drove the Sylacauga to Auburn portion of it many,

many times. During my freshman year I drove it pretty much every weekend, home and back, both ways!

And let's be clear—the problem with the road wasn't from Birmingham to Sylacauga. That part was just fine. It was a nice, four-lane highway, going back to the 1960s. A bit later they extended the four-lane down to Alexander City, just over halfway from Birmingham. But that still left all the distance from basically north of Lake Martin all the way to Columbus, Georgia, as two-lane roads that ran through the middle of towns like Dadeville, Camp Hill and Waverly, complete with their intersections and traffic lights, causing terrible bottlenecks. And let's don't forget all the logging trucks you'd inevitably get stuck behind! It would take me, on average, ninety minutes to get from Sylacauga to Auburn back then. Today it's a lot faster, because they've finally made the entire route a four-lane modern highway. But it took them forever, and the State of Alabama was never in a particular hurry to do it. In fact, I used to hear the story that Alabama graduates ran the highway department, and were deliberately keeping the road to Auburn as primitive as possible, as their contribution to the success of the Crimson Tide. Knowing everything else I know about the rivalry in the state, that seems perfectly plausible to me.

On top of that, most of the road south of Alexander City— and, honestly, in places north of it, like Childersburg and Harpersville—were notorious speed traps. The local police and the state troopers understood that most drivers were going nuts, stuck behind logging trucks and other slow-moving vehicles for miles and miles. So they would lurk out of sight, just over the hills, in the spots where you could most easily pass someone, and they'd pounce on you as soon as you topped a rise, going the slightest bit over the suddenly-dropping speed limit. I accumulated a nice collection of tickets along that stretch, during the late Eighties.

(And—no joke—I only got out of a ticket one time, when the officer's pen ran out of ink while he was writing me up! I guess he never thought to ask a college student if he had a pen in the car with him, thank goodness!)

John Ringer
I have much more experience on I-85, coming to and from Atlanta. As a federal Interstate, it was much better maintained. A much easier, better drive. Because Alabama people didn't have control of it!

It was always much easier to get to Auburn from Atlanta than from the northern part of Alabama. That had to have had an impact on the student body, on recruiting, everything.

One hallmark through the history of the Iron Bowl has been Alabama's stubbornness. They insisted on counting the very first Iron Bowl, played in February, as happening in the previous season. They insisted on playing all their games, home and away, on their own campus. They insisted on using plays and formations that were considered illegal in most of college football. They insisted on only employing referees for the Iron Bowl that agreed with their interpretations of the rules. And they insisted on playing the game every year in Birmingham, where they knew they had an advantage.

Of course, that would all come to an end seventeen years later, in 1989. And the parallels between the 1972 and 1989 Iron Bowls are remarkable. Brace yourself, because this gets *crazy*:

Alabama entered the 1972 Iron Bowl with a 10-0 record. They entered the 1989 Iron Bowl with a 10-0 record.

Alabama was ranked 2nd in the country prior to the 1972 Iron Bowl and 2nd in the country prior to the 1989 Iron Bowl.

Auburn entered the 1972 Iron Bowl with 8 wins. They entered the 1989 Iron Bowl with 8 wins.

Auburn's major out-of-conference opponent in 1972 was Florida State. Auburn's major out-of-conference opponent in 1989 was Florida State.

In Auburn's game just before the 1972 Iron Bowl, they played Georgia. The same is true of 1989.

Coming into the 1972 Georgia game, Auburn was ranked 11th in the country. Coming into the 1989 Georgia game, Auburn was ranked 11th in the country.

In 1972, Auburn beat Georgia by 17 points. In 1989, Auburn beat Georgia by 17 points.

In 1972, an undefeated Alabama lost to Auburn, then went on to lose their bowl game. In 1989, an undefeated Alabama lost to Auburn, then went on to lose their bowl game.

The Auburn head coaches in both games remained in that job for three more seasons, then retired just after that year's Iron Bowl. Both cited health issues as part of the reason for retirement. Both lost at least 5 games in their final season. Both also tied a team from the old Southwestern Conference. Both have their names on at least part of the stadium. Both were replaced by offensive-minded head coaches who lasted five full seasons before being fired. (Doug Barfield was fired at the conclusion of year five; Terry Bowden made it a few games into his sixth season in 1998 before his controversial exit.)

In both 1972 and 1989, Alabama finished with a record of 10-2.

In both 1972 and 1989, Alabama won at least a share of the SEC Championship despite the loss to Auburn.

In 1972, Alabama was awarded the SEC title outright, despite losing to Auburn head-to-head, having the same number of conference losses, the same number of wins overall, and a lower national ranking than Auburn. What made the difference was that Auburn kept playing Georgia Tech even after the Yellowjackets left the SEC, causing the Tigers to play one fewer conference game than Alabama, and thus finishing with one fewer SEC win.

Van Allen Plexico

It blows my mind that SEC teams played different numbers of conference games back then, on a regular basis. And that Bryant was gaming the system to make sure Alabama had what amounted to a permanent "tie breaker."

If Auburn had played Ole Miss or Vanderbilt in 1972, instead of non-SEC Chattanooga, they likely would've won their first SEC Championship since 1957 that year, instead of having to wait another twenty-six years.

But I guess it's really on Auburn for not realizing that could happen, and doing something about it.

John Ringer

This really shows that, back then, the SEC was a shell of what it would become later. It didn't have the power to enforce standardized schedules on its teams. It shows that Alabama continued to take advantage of the situation and game the system to advance their own interests.

The nine-game win streak by Bear Bryant's Alabama team from 1973-1981 is the longest in the series. As of the 2022 Iron Bowl, Alabama hasn't won more than three in a row since then.

More than anything else, it was probably this nine-game win streak by Alabama—in Legion Field in Birmingham—that made Auburn people realize they needed to move their half of the series to Auburn. They were not *afraid* of playing Alabama in Birmingham, they just came to realize they were giving the Crimson Tide a massive advantage in the rivalry. Why do that? After all, Alabama had a top-ranked team most of the decade of the Seventies. They didn't *need* any additional help.

By the time Pat Dye was hired, prior to the 1981 season, most Auburn people had made up their minds that it was time to bring the big game *home*.

- 7 -

"GO HIRE
WHO YOU WANT"

Ralph "Shug" Jordan retired after the 1975 Iron Bowl—a shutout, 28-0 win by fourth-ranked Alabama.

The Tigers kept it close, trailing only 7-0 in the third quarter, before Alabama pulled away late.

> *"Sure, I'd like to have another time at bat, but it just can't happen. I'm sitting here right now wishing I could come back another year.*
>
> *"I am not saying goodbye to anyone because I'm still going to be around. However, I told the team just a few minutes ago that they are now Doug Barfield's team and I wished them all the best for the future and thanked them for 25 great years.*
>
> *"I'm sorry we couldn't end up a little better, but we didn't and that's that."*
>
> *—Ralph "Shug" Jordan, after the 1975 Iron Bowl*

"First of all, I'd like to say something of a sad note that Coach Jordan's last game was one of the best we ever played. I wish they had played someone else and he had gone out a winner. He's a fine gentleman and a credit to the game."
—Paul "Bear" Bryant, after the 1975 Iron Bowl

Jordan's replacement was his former offensive coordinator, Doug Barfield. Barfield did not fare well in the job, nor in the Iron Bowl. After four straight losses to the Crimson Tide, from 1976-1979, Barfield came into the 1980 Iron Bowl with very little chance of hanging onto his job. The Tigers were winless in the SEC at 0-5, and 5-5 overall, with their only wins over TCU, Duke, Richmond, Georgia Tech and Southern Miss. They'd been pounded, 42-0, at home by Tennessee. If the Grim Reaper wasn't standing next to Barfield on the sidelines, he was definitely watching from the press box.

The Tigers pulled within three points of Alabama late in the second quarter after a Charles Thomas to Byron Franklin long touchdown pass, along with a Greg Peoples 2-point conversion run, made it 21-18. The score remained that way until less than six minutes remained in the game, whereupon the Tide scored twice very quickly and won, 34-18.

After the game, Bryant told reporters he felt bad for Auburn, because Coach Barfield had suffered some "bad luck" that season.

Van Allen Plexico

All I'll say is, when an Alabama coach starts propping up an Auburn coach, you know the Alabama coach probably wants the Auburn coach to stay employed there and not be fired. And there's usually a reason for that.

Barfield was struggling just to make Auburn competitive in its winnable games. There was certainly no danger of him ever trying to rock the boat with Bryant. The thought of Auburn having the leverage during these years to force Alabama to move the Iron Bowl out of Birmingham is laughable. No, Alabama was very happy with Doug Barfield being the Auburn coach, and they had no desire to see him terminated.

(The same was true with regard to Georgia. They loved them some Barfield, too. The late, great humorist Lewis

Grizzard, a Bulldogs fan extraordinaire, wrote an entire chapter of one of his books about how wrong it was of Auburn to fire Barfield after year five. I always enjoyed Grizzard's comedy stylings, and I appreciated that he loved college football so much. But let's be honest here: He wouldn't have put up with Georgia winning four or five games a year. He didn't like it when they hired Ray Goff! Sadly, he didn't live long enough to write a column about whether it was right of UGA to fire Goff after the 1995 season, much as Auburn had done with Barfield.)

While Barfield never attempted to move the location of the Iron Bowl and, to the best of what the records show, never even broached the topic, Bear Bryant privately was thinking about it. And that's because he was sure Auburn's new coach, Pat Dye, would be thinking about it. It was therefore one of the first topics Bryant broached with Dye after Dye was hired at Auburn.

Van Allen Plexico

I think it took Pat Dye's personality and willpower to push the issue to the forefront and make it happen. The Bear knew Pat Dye very well, and knew from Day One that Dye would try to assert an amount of control over the series similar to what Alabama had been enjoying.

Doug Barfield, by all accounts, is a very good guy. But Pat Dye was a bulldog. Pun intended. And that's what it would take.

Dye was not the first choice to be Auburn's new head coach, however.

Before Auburn's leaders turned to Dye, they had another coach in mind to take over from Barfield. As early as the Tennessee game of 1980, the Powers That Be on the Plains had made up their mind what they wanted to do: They wanted to hire Vince Dooley away from the University of Georgia.

John Ringer

Dooley *should* have been the first choice. It was a no-brainer. He was an Auburn alum, as was his wife. And he was an excellent, up-and-coming coach.

Under the headline, "Dooley going to Auburn?" Phillip Marshall, writing in the *Montgomery Advertiser* on the day after the 1980 Iron Bowl, states, "Vince Dooley is apparently on the verge of becoming Auburn's next head football coach.

"The *Advertiser* has learned that members of a committee searching for a new head coach flew to Atlanta last Wednesday to meet with Dooley."

"They talked with Coach Dooley and he was very receptive to what they had to say," a source told Marshall. "It looks like he's going to be the man."

"I won't say positively that I wouldn't consider it," Dooley told reporters after the Bulldogs defeated Georgia Tech that same day.

Doug Barfield's status as head coach was due to be evaluated by the Board of Trustees on December 8, nine days after the Iron Bowl.

Dooley was, of course, a former Auburn quarterback. The timing seemed perfect to bring him home. It had worked for Alabama years earlier, in securing Paul "Bear" Bryant as their new coach, when, upon receiving the offer from Alabama, Bryant had packed up and left Kentucky with the words, "Mama called."

Auburn reportedly offered Dooley $1.8 million per year to come back to the Plains.

Ultimately, however, Dooley chose to remain in Athens.

Former Auburn trustee and head of Colonial Broadcasting, Bobby Lowder, said of the process:

We met (Dooley) in Birmingham. I was going to pay him $50,000 and the school was going to pay, I think, $100,000. I still have the agreement he signed with me for what I would pay him. He gets on a plane and flies to Tampa. By the time he gets back to Athens, he's changed his mind because they were going to make him athletic director the next year.

(Alabama Governor and former Auburn player) Fob (James) said, "I'm through. Go hire who you want."

At a press conference in Athens on December 2, 1980—nine years to the day before the First Time Ever game—Dooley explained to the press how he came to his decision:

I have reached a decision that was most difficult in coming and that decision is to remain at the University of Georgia. There were emotional ties to my alma mater involved and I hope everyone can understand that.

(Tuesday night) was the first chance I had to discuss it with (wife Barbara). My wife had heard so many things by Monday night she was distressed. It bothered me, too. I've never had trouble sleeping, not even the night before a big game. But I had no sleep at all the past two nights.

The overriding factor was I had too much invested here. I couldn't leave. This has been my home for 17 years. I couldn't, in the final analysis, put it all away and start over at age 48 with something I started here at age 31.

I'm confident the Auburn program will be a good one, but I'm a Bulldog and proud to be one.

Unspoken here was the fact that Dooley was preparing to coach Georgia, with freshman sensation running back Herschel Walker, in the Sugar Bowl against Notre Dame, for the 1980 national championship.

Van Allen Plexico

Imagine how hard would it have been for Dooley to leave Athens before that bowl game. And imagine abandoning one of the greatest backs of all time after just one season with him, knowing his potential.

It's hardly surprising to me that Dooley chose to stay where he was. I'd have been far more shocked if he'd left. And I think ultimately it worked out for the best for both schools.

John Ringer

The timing was just bad. Sometimes things don't work out. He was the right candidate and Auburn made a good pitch for him, but he had a great team and player, and a chance to win the national title. And the core of that team was coming back, so they had more chances to have great success. So it's understandable that he stayed in Athens. I don't blame him for that.

Alabama's governor and former running back, Fob James, along with the Auburn Board of Trustees, were apparently so confident that Dooley would accept the offer that they had no one else immediately in mind to interview. Said Hanly Funderburk, the Auburn president:

I appreciate his (Dooley's) prompt decision and his candor and I wish him continued success at the University of Georgia. We will begin a thorough search process immediately to obtain the best available coach for Auburn.

Having been turned down by their first option, Auburn officials began an entirely new search which quickly focused on one individual: Florida State's Bobby Bowden.

Van Allen Plexico

It makes sense that we would go after Bowden. Not only was he leading FSU to unprecedented heights right around that time, he was from Birmingham and had coached at Howard (Samford) University there, and so was familiar with the program. And he was being recognized already as a coach on the rise.

It turns out Bowden also turned down Alabama, LSU, and even the Atlanta Falcons over the years, to remain at FSU.

John Ringer

He was from Alabama and I think he would've been an excellent hire. He had a tremendous run of success in the late Eighties and Nineties at Florida State. Auburn had more resources than FSU did. It would've been very interesting to see what he would have accomplished at Auburn.

Of course, that doesn't mean I didn't hate him later! In particular, that one night at the Sugar Bowl after the 1988 season.

Florida State had finished that season with a record of 10-2, including a shutout win at LSU, a four-point victory at number 3 Nebraska, a two-touchdown win over number 4 Pitt, and a win over 19th-ranked Florida. Both of their losses took place in the same stadium: the Orange Bowl, first against Miami in September and then against number 4 Oklahoma on January 1—by one point. The year before, they'd gone undefeated until losing to the same team in the same bowl game.

Van Allen Plexico

I didn't realize that, from 1979-1980, Florida State had a record of 21-3.

All three of their losses happened in the Orange Bowl stadium. One was a regular-season game at the University of Miami; the other two came in the actual Orange Bowl post-season game on January 1.

Their Miami curse began a lot earlier than people think!

And get this: Both bowl losses—two-thirds of all their losses over those two seasons—were to Oklahoma.

On the Tuesday before the 1980 Iron Bowl, however, Bowden decided to stay in Tallahassee.

Van Allen Plexico

Honestly, knowing that Bobby Bowden turned us down just makes our wins over his FSU teams from 1983-1990 all the sweeter. Especially that 59-27 beat-down in 1985.

Having missed out on both Dooley and Bowden, two other coaches came onto the Auburn radar, and the people in charge were divided over which of them they should hire. One was the Pittsburgh Panthers head coach, Jackie Sherrill.

By all accounts, Sherrill was ready to accept the job if it was offered. "Send a plane up here and get me and I'll sign," he told Auburn.

John Ringer

I for one am thankful this did not work out!

He was a fine coach, but he had a reputation for infractions with the NCAA, and I don't think he was nearly as good a coach as Pat Dye turned out to be.

Van Allen Plexico
I agree. He had his moments of big success, but he also had some really odd moments over the years.

For various reasons, Lowder and others were not sold on Sherrill. They were more interested in one of Bear Bryant's former assistants, who had also once been an All-American guard at Georgia and was now head coach of Wyoming. His name was Patrick Fain Dye.

Dye was flown to Auburn to meet with the board, and by all accounts he convinced them he was the man. The vote was not unanimous, but it went Dye's way. He would earn $50,000 per year from the university as his regular salary, and another $50,000 from Lowder's media company.

Some have speculated that Dye was already watching this situation closely because he thought he might have a shot at the job at his alma mater, Georgia, if Dooley left for Auburn. As it turned out, that wasn't the job that came open. Both Ivan Maisel (ESPN) and Creg Stephenson (AL dot com) have written of how two hugely important conversations between Pat Dye and Bear Bryant played out, with regard to this situation, and we amalgamate them here:

Given an ultimatum by his employers at Wyoming—are you going to be here next season or not?—Dye simply resigned. Such was his confidence and his determination to get the Auburn job that he simply walked away from that job security with the Cowboys. He remained unemployed for ten days while waiting to hear from Auburn.

Meanwhile, over in Tuscaloosa, Bear Bryant was not happy to see Dye in the running to be the next Auburn coach. He tried to talk Dye out of even considering the Auburn job. When Dye called his old boss to discuss the matter, the Bear told him, "You aren't going to take that job."

"I am if they offer it," Dye replied.

Bryant had a different vision for Dye. "You're going to get this (job)," he said. While Bryant was in no hurry to retire, at age 67 he knew the end was coming. Dye was his choice to take over in Tuscaloosa.

Dye was not swayed by such a prospect. "If I come to Alabama, I'd be running a maintenance program," he told the Bear. "I'd be trying to maintain what you've already done. I can go to Auburn and build a program."

The Bear couldn't talk him out of it. Dye was determined to take the Auburn job.

Auburn made the offer, and officially hired him on January 4, 1981.

At his introductory press conference, Dye stated:

> *Auburn is what I consider one of the top jobs in the South. It's a school that has tremendous football tradition, and it is a school that I remember playing against and watching my older brothers playing against back in the Fifties and having coached against the University of Auburn at times when they were certainly a feared football power in the South. And I'm confident that, with the support of the Auburn people, the alumni, the former players, the student body, the faculty, the administration, that we will be able to bring this great football tradition back to what it once was. And we're looking forward to this challenge with great anticipation, a lot of enthusiasm, and realizing fully that it is going to take a lot of hard work and probably a lot of patience on your part and our part. But we will get the job done in the end.*

Randy Campbell, who would rise up the depth chart to become Dye's starting quarterback as a junior and senior in 1982 and 1983, said this of the new coach:

> *He came across a little different probably than we expected, because he...told us they had won when he was playing, they had won when he was coaching, and we were going to win here. And it was just like a matter of fact.*

In his autobiography, *In the Arena*, Dye says:

When I first got to Auburn, I wasn't thinking about the size of the stadium, or where we played Alabama. I was trying to build a football team, trying to survive.

Coach Dye had told Bear Bryant he would "build a program" on the Plains, and that is what he set out to do. He would go on to be the most successful of Bryant's former assistants, winning 153 games overall, including 99 at Auburn. As the head coach of the Tigers for the next twelve seasons, he would win six Iron Bowls and four SEC Championships—the first since Shug's national championship season of 1957. He would also bring the Iron Bowl game itself to Auburn, for the First Time Ever. And he did so while immeasurably boosting the pride and self-confidence of the Auburn Family.

When Pat Dye took up the reins as head coach of the Auburn Tigers, he walked into an environment different from how it had been only a short time earlier, in terms of goals and expectations. And what wasn't already different, he quickly made different himself.

Van Allen Plexico

When Pat Dye became our coach at the end of 1980, he wasted little time in making a few things clear. One was, Auburn could be and *should* be a top team in the SEC and in the country, and he intended to get us back to that level. Another thing was that we should control our own destiny with regard to things we could actually control, and he felt very strongly that we had every right to control where we played our home games.

It might have made sense years earlier to call it a "neutral site" game in Birmingham, back when both Auburn and Alabama were playing a number of their home games there. By the 1980s, though, the Iron Bowl was the only game Auburn still played in Birmingham. Alabama, on the other hand, continued to use Legion Field for some of its bigger home games, reserving Bryant-Denny Stadium in Tuscaloosa for their lesser opponents. That meant Legion Field was rapidly becoming a home game for Alabama every single year, and certainly a home environment, regardless of how the tickets were divided up or which team got to wear the home jerseys. Add to that the fact that Alabama *wanted* to play there, while Auburn didn't—and was basically being *forced* to, against our wishes—and it's easy to see how Auburn people would be ready to say goodbye to Birmingham by the 1980s.

Coach Dye understood that growing sentiment immediately, and he bent his efforts toward making it a reality.

A short time later, now as the Auburn head coach, Pat Dye sat down with Paul Bryant for another conversation. Before Dye could even bring up the topic of where future games in their series would be played, Bryant broached the subject.

"When I saw Coach Bryant when I first got to Auburn, the first thing he said to me, very first thing, he said, 'Well, I guess you're going to want to take that game to Auburn,'" Dye told Creg Stephenson of AL dot com in 2019. "I said, 'We're *going* to take it to Auburn.'"

Bryant wasn't impressed. He told his former assistant that such a thing would never happen while Bryant was coaching.

"You ain't gon' coach forever," Dye replied.

If Bryant was surprised by this sort of pushback—something he'd never received from gentlemanly Shug Jordan or struggling Doug Barfield—he didn't show it. The fact that he'd brought up the subject at all showed that he knew Pat Dye very well, and knew exactly what he could expect from him.

"Well, we've got a contract through (19)88," Bryant retorted.

Dye shrugged. "Well, we'll play '89 in Auburn."

That pronouncement, so quickly tossed out in a back-and-forth with his former boss and a coaching legend, would become a line in the sand for Dye and for Auburn; a non-negotiable point; a deal-breaker, as they say. Alabama would later try various stratagems to secure the 1989 game for Legion Field. Even though the Tide knew by then that their days of unilaterally dictating terms in the series were ending, they also knew that forcing Dye to back off the 1989 demand would represent at least one small victory for Alabama.

Pat Dye would have none of it. Playing the game in Auburn in 1989 became a point of honor for him and for Auburn.

Van Allen Plexico

I've always loved this story, but two things jump out at me about it.

First, it's fascinating that it was Bear Bryant who first brought up the idea of moving the game to Auburn. Clearly Coach Dye was thinking about it, but Bryant asked him about it before he could even mention it himself. If you asked a hundred Auburn fans which football coach first brought up the idea of moving the game to Jordan-Hare, I doubt a single one of them would reply, "Bear Bryant!"

The other thing it makes me wonder is if Coach Dye was the first Auburn coach to seriously talk about moving the game. Did Shug Jordan ever talk about it? Did Doug Barfield ever entertain the notion? We're so used to thinking of this as something that Pat Dye managed, entirely through his own will power and determination, we don't necessarily stop and think, "Was he the first to even consider doing it?"

So I went back to the man who would know best about such things—David Housel:

David Housel

Coach Jordan mentioned wanting to bring (the Iron Bowl) to Auburn, then laughed and said, "but there will have to be a few prominent funerals first..."

Presumably he meant Coach Bryant, but he never specifically said that.

(It was) never a serious topic before Coach Dye.

Third-generation Auburn fan Jim McCrory was fifteen years old in 1976 when Coach Jordan came to visit his granddad, former player Red Northcutt, in Dothan, and Jim brought this exact topic up with the coach: When will Auburn make Alabama come to Auburn to play football?

Jim McCrory

Coach Jordan looked at me, smiled and replied, "Son, there will be a prominent funeral in Tuscaloosa, and then we will make it happen". That wasn't the answer I wanted, and frankly it made me dislike the Bear and Alabama even more. Imagine

114

a coach and a university that had so much power in the state, that they could force another successful conference school to play where they told them to play every year. It was wrong and I hated them even more for it.

In February of 1983 I was a student at Auburn, and I got a knock on my door. A friend in my apartment complex came to ask me if I had heard the news. I replied, "What News"? He told me that Bear Bryant had passed away. My mind immediately went back to what Coach Jordan had told me that day. My first words were, "Do you know what this means?" My friend looked puzzled and said, "What?" I said, "It means those SOBs are going to have to come to Auburn to play us."

I was genuinely sad Coach Bryant had passed away, but I also knew what it meant for the Auburn and Alabama game.

And in fact, Alabama wasn't even the first SEC school to take the "We will never play in your stadium" position with another school. The Tide may have perfected it and dragged it out the longest, but they learned it from another dynastic program that carried a certain level of arrogance with it—and one they knew very well: Georgia Tech.

David Housel
The Times, They Do Change…

I see where Georgia Tech is playing Ole Miss in Oxford, Mississippi on Saturday (in September 2023).

There was a time when that would never have happened.

Return with us to the early sixties, about 1962-1963:

Georgia Tech was still in its glory, but nearing the end of its glory days. For many years, Georgia Tech was the crown jewel of SEC football, the biggest stadium, the biggest fan base, the most money, in the biggest city in the South. Tech fans still call those days the "Golden Era."

Georgia Tech was so strong, others so weak, that the Yellow Jackets were able to force Clemson and Auburn to play at Grant Field every year. Auburn and Clemson made more money by taking a guarantee payment from Georgia Tech than by playing a home game on their home fields.

115

Then things began to change. Alabama hired a new coach, a man named Bryant, and Tech no longer ruled on the field. The SEC began moving toward league arranged schedules rather than having schools make their own schedules. Rotating conference schedules that would have each school play all other conference members on a rotating home and home basis or at mutually agreed upon neutral site was becoming the order of the day.

Georgia Tech head coach and athletic director Bobby Dodd, one of the greatest and most innovative coaches in the history of college football, was having none of it. "Georgie Tech," as he enunciated it would never play, would never go to Oxford, MS or Starkville to play. Never. A touch of arrogance and condescension? Definitely.

And now, here we are, days away from Georgia Tech playing a game in Oxford against Ole Miss. Times do change.

Scheduling was one the main reasons Tech left the SEC in 1964. The reason given for their leaving was academics, but there were other reasons, too. Diminishing success on the field, diminishing influence in the conference office and in conference affairs were factors, too.

Tech went it alone as an independent until 1978, when it joined the ACC. It is no secret that Georgia Tech's prestige and success have never equaled what it was in their days in the SEC. Maybe they like it that way. I don't know.

But I know this: Southern football is better, more exciting when Georgia Tech is good. Southern football is better and more exciting now that Tennessee is good again, and Southern football will be better and more exciting when Auburn is good again.

As much as I used to envy them, I, for one, would like to see Georgia Tech become good again.

All of this comes to mind thinking how it's going to be, watching the once-vaunted Georgia Tech Yellow Jackets take the field in Vaught-Hemingway Stadium Saturday in Oxford, a place they once swore they would never play.

Thing do change…

Never say "never."

Van Allen Plexico

We sometimes forget today that Georgia Tech used to have the reputation—and the attitude—that David describes. For a long time, they could back it up. And their clashes with Alabama during that era are legendary, as are the events surrounding the games. For example, there's the story that Bear Bryant took to wearing a football helmet on the sidelines of Grant Field, because the Tech fans in the stands would throw liquor bottles at him. According to one telling, Bear dodged a bottle, then reached down, picked it up and looked at it. A reporter asked him about it, and Bear replied with words to the effect of, *I'm not surprised they threw their liquor bottles at me, I'm just surprised Tech fans drink such cheap liquor!*

It is interesting to note, though, that Alabama apparently did absorb some of that arrogance from Tech, and then applied it to Auburn.

While no Auburn coach before Pat Dye seriously considered pushing to move the game to Jordan-Hare permanently, it's obvious that Bear Bryant was concerned about that very thing when Dye took the Auburn job. Would the Bear have ever agreed to it?

"Coach Bryant was smart. He knew the value of playing in Birmingham."
—*Pat Dye, 2019*

Mike McClendon

Bryant liked it the way it was set up in Birmingham.

When Auburn and Alabama restarted the series in the 1940s, the state legislature made the two state schools come to terms. Those terms included that it would be played at a "neutral" site, Birmingham, with a 50/50 split on tickets. Neither of those things was ever true. Birmingham is and always has been a heavily Alabama football city. It is probably better today than it has been in the past, but it has never been close to an even split. That gave Alabama an advantage in fan support.

And that fan support edge translated into the makeup of the crowd for the game each year.

Mike McClendon

Alabama always had a huge advantage in tickets. When they expanded Legion Field in the 1960s, part of the arrangement was that the city would withhold a certain number of tickets to be sold to the public on a first-come, first-served basis. In reality the majority of those tickets always ended up in the hands of Alabama fans. They would put those tickets on sale to the public in August every year. I remember standing in line to get them, and they rarely got past the first few people in line. Then, of course, the Alabama folks would snap up any tickets that went on the open market. The result was that it was always a lot closer to a 2/3rd split in favor of Alabama than a 50/50 split.

Basically, everyone at Alabama loved the way it worked out and pretty much everyone at Auburn hated it. There just wasn't much the Auburn people could do about it. Bryant ran football in this state, and whatever he wanted was the way it was.

Birmingham had a legitimate shot at an NFL team in the late 1960s, until Bryant came out against it. He did not want the NFL competing against Alabama football.

Somewhere in the 1970s Bryant was asked about moving the game onto the two campuses, and he promised the Alabama fans that they would never have to make the trip to Auburn. In his lifetime, he was right. I think Shug wanted to move out of Birmingham, but he realized it was futile.

As Shug had said, "A few prominent funerals first," indeed.
And one of them would not be long in coming.

- 8 -

"SIXTY MINUTES"

Before Auburn could worry about moving the home game to Jordan-Hare, other issues took priority. At the top of the list, as understood by all concerned, was finding a way to end the then-eight-game losing streak to Alabama. In fact, one of the questions the interviewers at Auburn hit Pat Dye with was, "How long will it take you to beat Alabama?" His reply has become legendary: "Sixty minutes."

His first opportunity to coach those sixty minutes came later, of course. First there were ten other opponents to deal with; six hundred minutes before the sixty.

Going into the season, Dye conducted what he described as some of the toughest off-season workouts of his career. He intended to find out who was physically and mentally tough enough to help lift the program to a higher level. He also meant to run off any players who couldn't or wouldn't give their all for the team.

In an interview for the "Decade of the Eighties" video the school produced years later, defensive tackle Edmund Nelson summed up what the transition to the Dye regime was like:

It started in the winter, and he'd work us—he'd just dog work us. It was short enough; we had nine weeks for winter workouts instead of the usual eleven, and he basically ran just about everybody off. It was survival of the fittest. And I remember, in fact, I always wanted to get a t-shirt that said, "I survived winter and spring with Coach Dye."

Randy Campbell, who would serve as the starting quarterback the following two seasons, described it this way:

Our practices before had been real organized but it wasn't a real physical practice. They (the new coaching staff) came in and really got after us. There were bodies flying here and there, and of course everybody knows about the coaches jumping on fumbles and things like that. It was almost at the point of the coaches saying, "If y'all don't pick it up, we'll go put the pads on and we'll come out here ourselves and whip your butts." But we all learned how to work and we learned about being accountable and being responsible and I guess that was a start of learning how to win.

Van Allen Plexico

These were also the infamous "wolf sign" practice sessions, where players described the aftermath of practices as looking like "wolf sign" was everywhere—blood and hair and broken limbs. Maybe it wasn't quite to the level of Bryant's infamous 1954 "Junction Boys" practices in Texas, but it apparently wasn't far from that, either.

Auburn in its first season under the Dye regime, in 1981, was a hungry and scrappy team. They didn't have a lot of offense, but the defense was strong, and they held every team they played to 28 points or less. Facing mighty Nebraska in Lincoln, they limited the Cornhuskers to just 17 points. On September 26, in Knoxville, facing a Tennessee team that had pounded them at home the year before—and effectively gotten their coach fired—they came within three points of handing the Vols a massive upset, in a 10-7 slugfest.

The scene in the locker room after that Tennessee game is legendary. They'd lost by a field goal, on the road, against a strong rival that had hung 42 on them in their own house the year before. And yet the players were emotional; utterly disappointed. In only a matter of months, the players' standards and expectations had risen dramatically. Coach Dye rallied them in the Neyland Stadium locker room afterward:

> *There's gonna be a lot of days where you lay your guts on the line and you come away empty-handed. Ain't a damn thing you can do about it but go back and lay 'em on the line again. And again. And again.*
>
> *Every coach, manager, glad to be associated with you. You keep fighting like you did today, you keep playing like that, we'll build a foundation we can live a long, long time on at Auburn.*

After falling 13-24 at fourth-ranked Georgia, Auburn's record stood at 5-5. They had the following Saturday off, as did Alabama, before the two teams faced one another in Legion Field.

This first clash between Bryant and Dye would have been big enough anyway, but fate had determined that another element was in play that day: The Bear was going for his 315th win, which would move him past Amos Alonzo Stagg and into sole possession of first place in lifetime wins in major college football.

Van Allen Plexico

Alabama had gone undefeated, or nearly so, the last two or three years. When, near the beginning of the 1981 season, reporters and fans started buzzing about how Bryant likely would be playing for his then-record-setting 315th win at some point that year, I immediately worried that it would come against Auburn. You could see the Tide fans were going to make a huge deal out of him achieving that record. I couldn't have cared less if he achieved it, but I certainly didn't want it to happen against *us*. You knew the Alabama fans would absolutely relish it and would rub it in our faces forever. On top of that—the last thing I wanted was for Alabama to have *extra* incentive to beat us.

So I got out the SEC schedule and counted how many wins he needed to make it to 315. I was relieved to see he would likely accomplish the record against Mississippi State on Halloween, two games before the Iron Bowl. Whew!

But then Alabama did something shocking and unexpected: They *lost to Georgia Tech* in week 2! And when they were ranked second in the country! (And even more shocking—this was a Georgia Tech team Auburn would later beat in Atlanta by four touchdowns!)

Back to the schedule I went. The timeline had shifted. Now the Bear would likely be going for his 315th win on the road, against Penn State, in the game before the Iron Bowl. Good, fine. As long as it wasn't against us. Let them achieve that huge, emotional win up in Happy Valley, and then come back down to Birmingham, all full of themselves, and we could ambush them! To quote Admiral Ackbar, "It's a trap!" Perfect!

And then *something else* shocking and unexpected happened: On October 10, Alabama tied Southern Miss, 13-13, in Legion Field.

Oh no.

A sense of dread fell upon me. The timeline shifted again. The two-game padding between us and Bear's 315 game was gone. I couldn't believe it, and yet I absolutely could believe it.

It was one of those things that, in hindsight, seemed inevitable: Bear Bryant would be going for his 315th win, the all-time record, *against Auburn.*

Instead of our game being a "trap game" after breaking the record—we were now the team he'd have to beat to break the record! The players would be jacked up and determined. The fans would be insane beforehand and insufferable after.

Ugggh.

Pat Dye and the Tigers were not about to lie down for Bryant and the Tide, though.

Auburn arguably outplayed Alabama in the first half, but squandered it by way of penalties, a couple of missed scoring chances and turnovers.

A motivated but mistake-prone Auburn against a perhaps too-hyped Alabama resulted in the game being tied 7-7 at the half.

122

In the third quarter, the Tigers tacked on ten more points to Alabama's seven, and by the time the fourth quarter started, Auburn was ahead, 17-14.

But then Alabama's depth wore the Tigers down. Two late rushing touchdowns put the Tide up, 28-17, and Auburn couldn't respond.

Auburn fullback George Peoples led the game with 155 yards rushing on 26 carries, but it wasn't enough.

Bear had his 315th win, and it happened against Auburn.

Van Allen Plexico

So predictable. *Of course* they won it. *Of course* it came against Auburn. They got everything they could have wanted out of that game. And meanwhile they were giving us the stiff-arm with regard to letting us play our home game where we wanted.

Nevertheless, Auburn had come to play that day, and had come very close to upsetting the Tide on their coach's big day. Everyone could see the improvement from the Barfield era—particularly on defense. One couldn't help but think that Auburn was on its way back.

I hope we didn't disappoint anybody. I'd like to congratulate Coach Bryant and the Alabama football team on their accomplishment here today.

It was evident that it (the 315 win record) was going to come and I'm sure they'll have a lot of fun because it was over Auburn. But we'll have to live with that. That's part of losing.

—Pat Dye, after the 1981 Iron Bowl

Dye met with Bryant briefly on the field before the game, and their mutual affection and respect were obvious. So, too, was Dye's determination and defiance. He honored his legendary mentor, but he was never going to bow down to the man.

"I told him we were going to get after them. He smiled and said, 'You can't scare me.'"
—*Pat Dye*

After the game, Dye had nothing but respect for Bryant.

"I didn't get to spend much time with Coach Bryant after the game, but he knows how I feel about him and I know how he feels about me. We just went to war for a couple of hours today. He is the greatest coach in history."
—*Pat Dye*

Their quick post-game exchange was described thusly:
Dye: "I'll tell you what, Coach, we beat your tail in the stats. I just wish I could add them up to 29 points."
Bryant: "You might be interested to know Governor (President Jimmy) Carter just called."
Dye: "Did the President (Reagan) call?"
Bryant: "Well sure he did."
Bryant might have thought Dye, as a Georgia native, would be more interested in hearing about his receiving a congratulatory call from Carter than from Reagan.
Dye also was quick to point out the strides the Tigers had made over the course of just one year.

"There's no question we've made a lot of progress with our program. Nobody likes to lose, but our players have accepted our way and I think they believe in our way. I'd rather have that than have a couple more wins and face problems down the road."
—*Pat Dye*

Bryant acknowledged the tough time the Tigers gave his team that day:

"In the third quarter, I didn't know what to think. I didn't know what we were going to have to do to win after we lost almost 80 yards on fumbled punts. To turn it around and come back the

way we did is one of the greatest victories I've ever been associated with.

"We have better personnel than Auburn, but they were very well-prepared. Pat Dye has done a great, great job. I told (assistant athletic director) Charley Thornton to vote for him for Coach of the Year.

"Those players fought their hearts out."
—Bear Bryant

At least some of the Alabama players agreed with their coach's assessment:

"We were lucky to come out victorious. We knew they were tough and we expected that type of game. We expect great things from them (Auburn) in the future."
—an unnamed Alabama linebacker

And the fact that the coaching wins record was on the line did indeed provide extra motivation for the Tide players—at least, according to one:

"Every time we lined up in the third and fourth quarter, we would say in the huddle, 'We can't give up. This is for 315 and the record.'"
—Alabama defensive back Benny Perrin

The 1981 season had come to an end, and Auburn was 5-6, the same record they'd finished with the year before, under Doug Barfield.

But this 1981 team was very different from that team.

The wins had been exhilarating, as LSU, Florida and Georgia Tech all fell to the Tigers. The win over Tech, a team that had beaten Alabama earlier that season, was by 24 points—at Grant Field!

The losses had been close—heartbreakingly close, as with the road games at Tennessee and at Nebraska. They'd fallen to a top ten-ranked Mississippi State by only four.

They'd faced fourth-ranked Georgia in Athens and then fourth-ranked Alabama in Birmingham and they'd held both powerful teams to 28 points or fewer.

Why does all this matter, with regard to the First Time Ever game? Because it was all about establishing the credibility of the program. Auburn had to prove itself to be a legitimate contender, able to stand toe-to-toe with Alabama, before it could be taken seriously in terms of moving the game.

The 1981 season had shown Auburn *could* be great. Everyone could see that 1982 was most likely going to be an even better year. And that was before anyone really knew about the young freshman running back from McAdory High School that would be joining the program. He'd grown up in Birmingham as an Alabama fan, but Pat Dye convinced him he'd find a true home—and lots more playing time—on the Plains.

Van Allen Plexico

The story of Bo Jackson's recruitment to Auburn by Pat Dye has been told many times, and in many places, including in our *We Believed* book.

Suffice to say, Alabama really blew it with his recruitment. They told him if he came to Alabama, he might get on the field by his junior season. That Alabama arrogance didn't serve them so well for once.

"You could tell he was different," said quarterback Randy Campbell, looking back years later. "He was bigger and stronger than anybody we had who wasn't a lineman. He was faster than anybody, period."

Was there jealousy on the part of the other players, that a true freshman was getting so much attention and playing time?

"No," said Campbell, adding, "The thing is, he was so much better than everybody. Nobody went back to their rooms saying 'I can't believe they put that freshman ahead of me.' It was like if I was playing quarterback and all of a sudden John Elway transferred to Auburn. It was that obvious."

126

Van Allen Plexico

Pat Dye told Bo that his presence on the team gave us a real chance against any team we played. Consequently, he got on the field immediately, alongside Lionel "Little Train" James, in the Wishbone backfield.

Bo is such a huge piece of the puzzle we're assembling here. It was all about establishing Auburn Football's legitimacy and credibility, so that we'd have leverage over Alabama going forward—particularly with regard to moving the Iron Bowl to Auburn. As long as we were getting pushed around by Alabama on a yearly basis, we had no leverage over them at all. If they couldn't be made to take us seriously as a football program, they would never give us the time of day when it came to where future editions of the series would be played.

Pat Dye and Bo Jackson both gave Auburn instant credibility. Dye was the coach *Alabama* had wanted; the coach the Bear had hand-picked to be his successor. Bo Jackson was a phenomenon; a player Alabama would have killed to get, once they realized what they'd missed out on with him. Auburn was suddenly a team with a great coach and great players. It was a team that overpowered its opponents the way Bryant's Alabama teams always had. It was a team that won games. That was something Alabama could understand, and what they could—slowly and grudgingly—come to respect. Perhaps they still couldn't treat Auburn as an *equal*, because that's just not in the Crimson Tide DNA. But they'd have no choice but to show a good deal more respect. Much more than they had in decades.

Pat Dye had converted Auburn's offense to the triple-option Wishbone attack upon his arrival, just as Bryant had done at Alabama to great success a few years earlier. Both Lionel James and Bo Jackson would find great success running from that formation.

In his freshman season, Jackson rushed for 829 yards on 127 carries, averaging 6.5 yards per carry, with 9 touchdowns. James added 779 yards on 113 carries, topping Bo with 6.9 yards per carry, along with 7 touchdowns.

After uncertainty at quarterback throughout his first year on the Plains, Dye settled on his man early in 1982 and stuck with him. He reached down to fourth string and named junior Randy Campbell the starter under center. Campbell wasn't flashy or a great passer or super-athletic; it was easy to see why he had been so far down on the depth chart up to this point. But the Wishbone demands a quarterback who can quickly read the defense and make good decisions on the fly. He does have to be able to throw the ball occasionally, and execute a quarterback keeper now and then (that being one of the three options in the triple option). Mainly, though, he has to quickly decide whether to give the ball to the fullback, pitch it to one of the halfbacks, or keep it and dive forward. Campbell excelled at the field general aspects of the position, and the team would only lose four games during his two seasons as the starter.

Along with an improving defense and kicking game, the rejuvenated offense put the Tigers in contention for a win every week in 1982. They stumbled only three times in twelve tries, falling to Nebraska, Florida, and a powerful Georgia team on its way to play for the national championship. As with Tennessee the year before, the Tigers took the heavily-favored Bulldogs to the limit and to the final seconds.

Going into the 1982 Iron Bowl, Auburn fans could just feel something was different. They remembered how close they'd come to knocking off the Tide the year before, when all the advantages seemed to run Alabama's way. This time, it just felt like the tide was about to turn.

John Ringer

It felt like we had hope again. We'd been on the mat through the late 1970s, but suddenly it felt like we had a real chance to beat Alabama. And not just in a fluke sort of way, as sometimes happens in this series, but because we were becoming a fundamentally better team.

Van Allen Plexico

I was a freshman in high school in 1982. Some of my friends were big Alabama fans. The week before the Iron Bowl, I told them that this would be the year their streak ended. I almost guaranteed it. I could just *feel* it. I remember one of them laughing, and saying, "Auburn's getting better, and maybe *next* year will be the year, but you won't do it *this* year." I was so confident he was wrong.

Honestly, at least for me, the outcome of the 1982 Iron Bowl was almost as emotional as that of the 1989 game. I was too young to have watched and appreciated the 1972 game. The next year I started first grade. I'd never *seen* Auburn beat Alabama. It had never happened while I'd been in school, with all those Alabama fan classmates. For so long, it seemed *impossible*. To hear my friends talk, it might as well have never happened in all of history. That nine-game streak might as well have been *ninety* years, or *nine hundred*.

So when Auburn won the First Time Ever game in Jordan-Hare, yes, it was absolutely huge—but I'd seen Auburn beat Alabama before. When Auburn won in 1982, I'd *never* seen that before. I'd never experienced it in my life. That's the one thing that game has over the 1989 game for me. The 1989 Iron Bowl was the First Time Ever in Auburn, but the 1982 game was the first time ever—*at all*—for me.

In the days leading up to that 1982 Iron Bowl, it was clear that two unusual topics were on the minds of the fans and the press: Could Auburn actually win this time, and break the long streak? And what would Coach Bryant do if that happened?

Keith Jackson broached both topics with one question to Bryant, prior to that game: "Coach, let me ask you a hard question. If Auburn beats you, are you going to retire?"

Bryant shook his head and replied:

"I'm not going to retire, period. If Auburn beats us tomorrow, I've already invited the University to look into the situation. It's not gonna make me very popular with the people I work with, the players or anyone else, because I'm supposed to win... We have enough players to win. We have enough players to have a great team next year... But in answer to your question... I've invited the president to look into it, and he'll look into it. But I want to do what's best for the University of Alabama."

129

John Ringer

Anytime they lost to Auburn, Alabama people felt like somebody needed to "look into the situation." Launch an internal investigation. Because clearly something wrong had happened.

Van Allen Plexico

I'd love to know what became of the University "looking into" the situation. Bryant did announce his retirement shortly after this game, so maybe that was it.

Bear had a lot of mileage on him. It's amazing to me that he was only 69 when he retired and then passed away. He seemed more like 89.

And he didn't retire just because "he lost one Iron Bowl in ten years," as my Alabama friends all described it afterward. Alabama retired him, and they did so because they'd gotten spoiled by how good they were in the late Seventies. They expected to stay there, but they could see they were in decline, even as Auburn under Pat Dye was clearly on the rise. The 1982 Iron Bowl marked the moment that the trajectories of the two programs crossed paths. After this game, Auburn was 8-3 while Alabama was just 7-4. That wasn't acceptable in Tuscaloosa—even if the coach who earned that record was Bear Bryant himself. Something had to be done. Something had to change. Alabama knew they had a 69-year-old coach— who, frankly, looked and seemed a lot older than that. That's not who you turn to when you need big changes. The Alabama powers-that-be knew the Bear was in no shape to start the process of building them back up again, to compete with the younger and more dynamic Dye. They wanted what *we* had. They couldn't get Dye, but they were darned sure ready to get *somebody* new.

The 1982 Iron Bowl was an exciting game from start to finish.

Auburn led at the half, 14-13, but Alabama scored 9 points in the third quarter while shutting Auburn out, to go up 22-14 as the fourth quarter began. Al Del Greco kicked a field goal to pull the Tigers within 5, and then Auburn mounted one last epic drive to take the lead. That drive was capped off by Bo Jackson leaping "over the top"

130

and into the end zone on fourth-and-one. Auburn managed to hold on from there, ending the nine-year win streak by Alabama and causing Tigers fans to tear down the Legion Field goalposts.

The *Birmingham News* the next day ran the headline, "AUBURN ENDS A NINE-YEAR WAIT," over a photo of an emotional Pat Dye hugging his old boss, Bryant, on the field after the game. Beneath the photo, a smaller headline read, "PAT DYE AND A TEAR FOR THE BEAR."

In Auburn's locker room after the game, chaos reigned. Coach Dye, the assistant coaches and staff, and the players were joined by the university president and representatives from the Tangerine Bowl, there to invite the 8-3 Tigers to their first bowl game since 1974. After his post-game speech, Dye added this:

"What I'd like for you to do, is I'd like for you, the ones that want to... I'm gonna go back out there, and thank our people."

The players then left the locker room and went back on the field, where they celebrated with the delirious Auburn fans. Seemingly the only ones who had left were the ones last seen carrying the goal posts down Graymont Avenue.

"We were mighty fortunate to win... Alabama played a really outstanding football game... The thing that won for us of course was the thing that has won for us at other times this year: not turning the football over, not making the mistakes that will beat you. I thought our kicking game was outstanding. Lewis Colbert did a great job of punting the football under a lot of pressure... and I think in the fourth quarter, after Bo made the long run and we got the field goal, was the first time our players really realized they could win the football game. Up until that point it had been all Alabama."
—Pat Dye, on the Auburn Football Review, the day after the 1982 Iron Bowl

"And to give a program that's been such a class program and a bunch of class people and dedicated fans that have followed us,

to give them back something after all these years, is the best feeling you can have."
—Mark Dorminey, Auburn defensive back

"My football career is complete now. I can live easy for the rest of my life."
—Bob Harris, Auburn

"You have to tell me how it feels to beat Alabama."
"I don't have to tell you how it feels. You know."
—Phil Snow and David Housel, locker room after the 1982 Iron Bowl

"We've waited for it a long time... We don't intend for it to be ten years again. We're gonna meet them head on."
—Dr. Hanly Funderburk, Auburn President, locker room after the 1982 Iron Bowl

"Head on."

Even Auburn's president understood the enormity of what had just happened on that artificial turf in Birmingham. The two programs might not have drawn level—not immediately. Not after just one Iron Bowl win. But the momentum was all with Auburn. That much was plain to everyone to see and to feel.

Meanwhile, the story was quite different in the other locker room, and in the days to come just afterward.

A heavy smoker and drinker for most of his life, Paul Bryant's health was already in decline throughout the previous decade. He experienced a cardiac episode in 1977, spent time in rehab, and suffered a stroke in 1980, followed by another cardiac episode in 1981.

Following the Iron Bowl, Bryant coached Alabama one last time, in a win over Illinois in the Liberty Bowl. After that game, a reporter asked him what he planned to do in his retirement. His answer: "Probably croak in a week."

He actually made it *four* weeks before suffering a massive heart attack while at the hospital. He passed away on January 26, 1983.

Van Allen Plexico

When legendary Ole Miss coach John Vaught passed away in 2006, some raised the question: Why did Bear Bryant's Alabama teams so rarely schedule Ole Miss under Vaught?

Alabama played Ole Miss in the Sugar Bowl after the 1963 season, marking only the second time in thirty years the two teams—both Southeastern Conference members! —had played each other.

Why didn't Alabama schedule one of the conference's better teams more often, back then?

One might just as well ask why Alabama played Georgia so infrequently.

Or why they thought of Vanderbilt as a major rival.

Or why Bryant lined up extra conference games for his squads, beyond what the other SEC teams scheduled, so their conference win totals would have some padding.

Or why they liked to play the Iron Bowl in Birmingham.

Each of these things represented an advantage Alabama held over their opponents, and over the rest of the conference. As long as Bear Bryant ruled Alabama and the SEC, none of those things would or could change.

But now Bryant was gone. And change was coming, and it was coming rapidly.

- 9 -

"A BONE FOR FOREVER"

With Bear Bryant out of the picture and Auburn on the rise as a football power in the state and in the SEC, Pat Dye and other Auburn officials began—quietly, at first—to talk about moving the Iron Bowl to the Plains.

Legion Field continued to be (allegedly) divided fifty-fifty between the two fan bases every year, with the "home team" designation really only indicating which team wore dark jerseys and which wore white. But for Auburn fans, the stadium and the city itself were rapidly becoming enemy territory, regardless of which team was "home."

"You've got Coach Bryant's statue out front—and it ought to be out front. ... But it gets kind of rough when the overwhelming majority of concessions sellers, both in the stands and in the booths, had on Alabama (clothing). The ushers had on Alabama stuff. I remember going up there one time and parking in the officials' lot, and the guy said, 'Hey, Auburn boy, park over there if you can figure out how to get there.'

135

"Morris Savage, one of our trustees, who played on the 1957 national championship team, said it best. He said, 'Legion Field was as neutral a location as Normandy was on D-Day in 1944.'

"I think Auburn developed a complex about going to Birmingham. I don't necessarily think that spilled over into the team, but Auburn's fans sure had a complex about going. We played Oregon State up there in 1973, and we played Louisville up there in 1974, and a lot of Auburn season-ticket holders just said they weren't going."

—David Housel, Auburn Athletic Director Emeritus

"Auburn had done more than win the Iron Bowl (in 1982). It had made a statement that things were changing, that it would not bow before Alabama or anyone else. That included insisting that it could play its home games, including the Iron Bowl, wherever it chose."

—Phillip Marshall

"It really got serious after we won the 1982 game. We had moved the Georgia Tech game and the Tennessee game and the Georgia game. Everybody was home and home. We wanted to move Alabama, too."

—Bobby Lowder, former chair, Auburn Board of Trustees

"It is worth noting that, of all of Auburn's major 'neutral site' rivals, only Georgia—time-honored, honorable ancient foe Georgia—came without a fight, proof once again of the deep respect the two schools have had for each other since the very earliest days of college football in the Deep South. Georgia alone marched to Auburn with colors held high. All of the others said, 'No...' Alabama said 'Never.'"

—David Housel

Van Allen Plexico

David Housel here is describing what he calls our "neutral site" rivals, meaning the teams that, for years, we would play at a neutral site instead of ever playing in Auburn. Florida, however, is not included in that batch of teams, because they came to Auburn as soon as it was possible to do so. The first game ever played in our stadium was against the Gators in 1939, and ended in a 7-7 tie. Our players even re-enacted the Auburn touchdown pass and catch during the 1989 Florida game. The Gators deserve acknowledgement for this.

The Tide aside, Tennessee had been the last holdout; the last opponent to refuse to play in Auburn. They played in Jordan-Hare in 1974, but then the game was moved back to Legion Field in 1976 and 1978. It returned to the Plains for good in 1980. By the time Pat Dye took over as coach the following year, Alabama was the only team Auburn still played in Birmingham.

Van Allen Plexico

Tennessee came to Auburn for the first time in 1974, for the third game of the season. They were ranked 14th in the country, but an unranked Auburn squad shut them out, 21-0. It's not surprising they wanted to go back to playing us at Legion Field after that.

Of course, some Auburn people had been agitating to move the Iron Bowl to Jordan-Hare for years. Van and John spoke extensively for this book with Mark Murphy, the longtime head of *Inside the Auburn Tigers* and Auburn Undercover.

Mark began his career in sports media at the age of four, as a "gofer" for Buddy Rutledge in the Auburn radio booth at what was then Cliff Hare Stadium. His father was the engineer for the radio broadcasts. In the years since graduating from Auburn, where he served as Sports Editor for the *Plainsman* newspaper, Mark has covered the Tigers' athletics programs extensively.

Mark Murphy

In 1974-75, as the *Plainsman* Sports Editor, I wrote a column saying that Auburn needed to quit playing football games in Birmingham. Basically, I said the university president, board of trustees and other people needed to quit bowing down to money, the interests in Birmingham, and tell

Alabama that college football belongs on the Auburn campus. And it was highly critical.

I remember having professors stopping me walking across campus and saying, "Yeah, you needed to say that." I remember students at the *Plainsman* then saying, "You think you're gonna get a visit from the dean?" And Jack Sims—the head of the journalism department at that time—it got him in trouble. I'm pretty sure he thought I might get in a little hot water, too. But Dean Foy, who I actually knew, said, "Look, I can't say this officially, but you're exactly right."

It was important for Auburn to do that. Because, financially, it was a big deal to sell season ticket packages. And Alabama folks knew that. The Alabama administrators wanted to do whatever they could to keep Auburn from getting that type of money into the football program and become more of a threat to Alabama, which was really in one of its heydays back then in the 1970s.

So I think a lot of Auburn people had been working for years to do that. But they just didn't have the backbone or insight to stand up to Alabama. Coach Dye had worked on the Alabama staff, and he understood the importance for Auburn getting that game moved. It took him a while, but he had some real good allies on the Board of Trustees who helped him with it and ended up making a compromise, (which was that we had) to play one more game in their sandbox.

Van Allen Plexico
The "throw them a bone" game in 1991.

Mark Murphy
Exactly right.

It was really important financially for Auburn to move the Alabama game to Jordan-Hare, and it was the last one that Auburn moved (after Georgia, Georgia Tech and Tennessee).

John Ringer
I hadn't thought about the money side of it like that—that by having the Alabama game you increase season tickets and

you allow Auburn to have more financial resources to build more down the road.

Mark Murphy

And that's why the situation isn't great right now (in 2022, with both the Alabama and Georgia games being played away), because we used to have it where Georgia played here one year and Alabama the next. Those are the two biggest draws for season tickets. And they didn't have a great year, I don't think, this year (2022), selling season tickets, because neither one of those games was played here.

John Ringer

So there can actually be some ups and downs.

Mark Murphy

Oh, yeah, there are definitely ups and downs. But more than just the ticket sales, there's the ticket *priority*. That's where the big money is, you know, for being that GAF (Greater Auburn Fund) and getting your ticket priorities. That's where they really make the big money to operate the athletic department, plus what television pays right now (Disney and CBS) that's providing a lot of money.

That's why you're seeing so much building going on across the entire SEC. It's like (new athletic director) John Cohen mentioned; it's a term I've used a lot: There's like an arms race in the SEC with facilities. You see what Auburn has done recently. And it's not just Auburn. Look at Mississippi State last Saturday night, how their stadium is so nice compared to what it used to be. They're redoing their basketball arena. Their baseball park is fabulous. And they've done other athletic projects over there. So everybody's doing it.

Van Allen Plexico

What can you tell us from the Alabama side of it? People now figure, "Well, Alabama just didn't want to give up an advantage." And then we kind of got them over a barrel. Was there more going on behind the scenes on their side of it?

Mark Murphy

I think they were working with some of the city officials in Birmingham, because it was a big economic deal for Birmingham to have that game every year. And also, Alabama played most of their really big games at Legion Field. And so, finally, it's interesting that Alabama saw what was going on at Auburn. Auburn was making improvements to the stadium and bringing recruits in and seeing how nice the campus and stadium were, (and they said) "Heck, we're going to do the same thing ourselves." And they ended up (eventually) pulling out of Birmingham, too.

John Ringer

Was there a point when we were expanding, refurbishing Jordan-Hare that we thought, "We're doing this thing, and this is going to be the tipping point, and we'll be able to get Alabama here?"

Mark Murphy

I think without a doubt. That was the longtime goal, to get the game to Jordan-Hare Stadium. And it started long before Coach Dye (arrived). It was just sort of a slow process. But I think Coach (Shug) Jordan was very into doing it, too. He talked about the importance of upgrading the stadium and being able to bring in teams from outside the region for home-and-home type games. I think he actually had a home-and-home game agreed to with Penn State many, many years ago. But they ended up backing out of it. And I remember him at a Board of Trustees meeting talking about the importance of improving the stadium, just for the overall revenue enhancement and status of the football program.

Coach Jeff Beard was the athletic director for many, many years, back in the days when they were really tight financially in the budget, and Auburn didn't have a whole lot of money. A lot of colleges didn't have a whole lot of money, back before the big TV deals and before they were charging a lot of money to go to games. Coach Beard was sitting there next to me at the 1989 Auburn-Alabama game. He was retired. He was living up north of Auburn, out in the country. I talked to him before and during the (1989 Iron Bowl). He was so excited. And I remember right at the start of the game, the look on his face, when the team came out. The crowd went crazy. And they had those orange and blue shakers—they were paper shakers—and it was like a sea of orange and blue. He was just looking at the whole thing in amazement. And then, in the fourth quarter, when Auburn kicked the field goal to go up by 10, tears came in his eyes. He was so excited. I'll never forget the look on his face, just how happy he was. Because he knew—he *knew*—things had changed forever, with Auburn getting that game. That was the final thing the football program needed to do to secure its financial well-being.

How did Coach Beard come to be at that game? He hadn't attended an Auburn football game since retiring from Auburn after the 1971 season. David Housel wasn't going to allow him to miss this one, though. He sent an assistant to go and pick him up and drive him straight to the stadium. Years later, Housel explained:

"I made sure (Coach Beard) had a seat in the press box. That man had a smile on his face the whole day. I went up to him before the game and said 'What do you think?' He said 'We're going to win.' We were behind at halftime, and he said 'we're going to win.' That man had confidence.

"(The 1989 Iron Bowl) meant a great deal to me personally. I also thought about what it must have meant to him. (He and Coach Jordan) had that dream of Auburn having good enough facilities to have its home games on campus. In my formative years, I bought into that because I bought into Coach Jordan and Coach Beard. My feelings for the game went much further back than just my experience with it. There is no way to put into words what it meant."

Van Allen Plexico
Was the number of seats always the main thing? As long as Alabama could say, "We have a bigger facility in Birmingham," they didn't want to play here? I know there

were other factors that were talked about by some, like "not enough hotel rooms and restrooms in the area," and so on.

Mark Murphy
Those were definitely excuses used.

The Auburn folks understood in the Athletic Department that it never was a 50-50 ticket split in Birmingham. There were Legion Field stadium bondholders—there were thousands of them—who helped finance the expansion of Legion Field (which gave them access to buying tickets). And those folks were Alabama fans, which made sense because Alabama played home games there regularly. And so it never was an equal split of the fans at those games.

And that's another reason to move it: Enhancing the whole Auburn football program, playing all the home games on campus.

Auburn finished the 1983 season with just one loss, narrowly missing the national championship as a result of a convoluted set of bowl outcomes.

One-loss Miami, ranked 5th and playing in their home stadium, defeated Nebraska in the Orange Bowl. Meanwhile, one-loss Auburn, ranked 3rd, defeated Michigan in the Sugar Bowl, while Georgia beat Texas (the only team to beat Auburn all year) in the Cotton Bowl. With numbers 1 and 2 both losing, Auburn fans went to bed that night sure their winning Tigers would move up into first place in the final poll. Instead, voters kept Auburn 3rd, dropped Nebraska to 2nd, and jumped the Hurricanes from 5th all the way up to 1st.

Van Allen Plexico
We can talk endlessly about the way that season ended, but that's not really our point here. Yes, Auburn deserved the national title, and the computer rankings named us number one. If only the powers that be on the Plains would acknowledge that. Pat Dye always said he'd claim 1983 if we could win another one on top of it. I don't see why that's necessary—but we did win another (and arguably more than that!) since then. So let's claim it.

As disappointing as it was to be denied a championship—especially when it was decided by popularity contest rather than on the field—the mere fact that Auburn was there at the end, in full contention for the national title, spoke volumes about how far and how quickly the program had risen. Alabama, meanwhile, finished the year at 8-4. The shoe truly was on the other foot now. Auburn was the dominant program in the state, if only for the moment. Leverage was growing. Soon Auburn would be demanding, and expecting, to get *its* way, for a change.

Van Allen Plexico to David Housel, 2023

Was improving and expanding our stadium during the 1980s a big part of being able to move the Iron Bowl to Auburn?

David Housel

It wasn't just the Eighties.

You go back to Jeff Beard and Shug Jordan when they were in college, Auburn played all of its big games on the road, and most of the time, *all* of its games.

Coach Beard, who was the athletic director who hired Coach Jordan, they would talk about how, in their student days, it was their dream to have a stadium big enough to host our home games. To play our home games at home. *We're Auburn! We don't need to be going on the road.* So it was a dream among Auburn people, including Coach Beard and Coach Jordan, to play our games at home. But if you look at the size of the stadium, if you're wanting to play Georgia or Georgia Tech or Tennessee with a stadium that held 34,000, when you had Birmingham with a stadium that held 44,000, well, that's a lot of money. In those days, 44,000 times five dollars, it was a lot of money. They had to play in Birmingham because they didn't have enough seats and infrastructure.

Tennessee said there were not enough restrooms in Auburn. And I said, well, Texas came and Nebraska came and they didn't have any trouble finding enough restrooms. Does Tennessee just do that more than others - do they **** more than others?

143

Alabama is not so much the villain though they did fight to keep it for their own self-interest. But I think you can look at the Georgia game coming out of Columbus because it was so small. You can look at the Georgia Tech game. For Auburn, the Georgia Tech game was the biggest money game Auburn had. Georgia Tech could pay Auburn more money for coming up there (to Atlanta) than Auburn could make playing here.

Georgia Tech used to play Auburn and Clemson in Atlanta every year. *Every year.* Why? Because they could pay more money than Clemson or Auburn could make (at home). Coach Beard came up with a thing called stadium rental that let the home team make even more money. If you went to Birmingham, you had to pay stadium rental for the use of Legion Field. If you play the game in Auburn then *Auburn* gets the stadium rental and the cost of operating the game. Not the neutral site.

John Ringer

Was there a moment in the stadium work or stadium expansion, when they were raising the money, and you're talking to people and they were like, "If we do this thing—if we put up this upper deck—we can get Alabama here?"

David Housel

1987. It was the Monday or Tuesday after the Alabama game of 1984 when we lost when Bo ran the wrong way. Coach Dye was AD, Oval Jaynes was Associate AD and the Board of Trustees was going to consider a proposal to build the upper deck on the east side, where the first suites were. Auburn lost to Alabama and everybody was devastated, but the Board of Trustees (voted to build the East Upper Deck). Bill Nichols might have voted not to do it. Maybe he and one more. He just didn't have the vision that others had. He had legitimate concerns. But Oval Jaynes and Pat Dye said that was the most significant vote of confidence ever in Auburn's football program, when the Board of Trustees voted to go ahead with an expansion after having lost to Alabama. That was *the* vote that guaranteed that game would come to Auburn, that day.

144

Over the course of the next few years, Auburn continued to crank out powerful teams that contended for conference championships every year. After a win over the Tide in a storm-wracked Legion Field in 1983, the Tigers dropped two bitter and very close Iron Bowls to Alabama in 1984 and 1985, about which the less said the better. Both games came down to tiny mistakes by Auburn and miracle plays by Alabama. The Tide was managing to hold even with Auburn for a little longer, but it was obvious which program had pulled ahead, and it wasn't the one from Tuscaloosa.

Alabama's coach during those immediate post-Bryant years was a former player of his, by the name of Ray Perkins.

Upon Bryant's retirement in December 1982, Perkins, the New York Giants head coach and an old Alabama receiver that had played for the Bear—was hired for the job in Tuscaloosa. He took on the athletic director job days later when Bryant passed away, and he maintained his old coach's attitude with regard to the series and its venue. As far as he was concerned, the game would always be played in Birmingham.

When told by a reporter in 1984 that at least one Auburn trustee was going to "demand" the Iron Bowl be played in Jordan-Hare after the contract with Legion Field expired following the 1988 game, Perkins reacted strongly:

"Demand? That's pretty strong, isn't it? (But) I'm not going to worry about it. I've said in the past that the game traditionally has been played on neutral turf and that it should stay that way. ... They can demand anything they want, but that doesn't mean they are going to get it."

When asked about playing the game in Auburn sometime later, Perkins went so far as to state unequivocally, "It won't happen."

According to Creg Stephenson, Perkins asked for a show of hands from Auburn fans at the Montgomery Quarterback Club in November of 1986: "Do you want the Iron Bowl to be played in Jordan-Hare Stadium?" When nearly all of them raised their hands, Perkins said, "It won't happen."

Later he attempted to clarify: "I didn't say 'never'." He said he'd only meant the people of the state—presumably on both sides of the rivalry— "won't let it happen."

145

Van Allen Plexico
Riiiiiight, Ray. Right.

He was an arrogant, pompous guy and a perfect fit for that program. I'm not sure how great of a football coach he was, but in terms of acting like an Alabama guy and trying to push Auburn people around, he had the rest of it down.

David Housel
Ray Perkins. His personality inflamed that thing. I remember there was a joke going around in Birmingham, even among Alabama people: If Ray Perkins found out you were not pissed off at him, he would try to look you up so he could piss you off.

Connie Kinackus was a restaurant owner in Birmingham. He said that he used to have fun saying: "Coach Perkins, your table for one is ready!"

Ray was a devil-be-damned guy. He didn't care. But you have to respect that. But Ray did not have real good personal skills. And he just said what Alabama people wanted to hear and what he believed. "Never, it won't happen. Never."

And hey, if I'm an Alabama guy, I love that in my coach. I loved it when Coach Dye said, "It *is* gonna happen." If I'm an Alabama guy and hear Coach Dye say that, it flew all over him. But now I understand what Ray was saying. And I would have said the same thing. But he didn't have the political clout to keep it from happening. And Coach Dye didn't have the political clout to make it happen. It was those trustees.

Van Allen Plexico
Pat Dye was later asked what his reaction was to Perkins saying that. Dye reportedly replied, "He didn't have a choice." I take this to mean Perkins was speaking on behalf of a bunch of high-powered Alabama boosters who had no intention of letting the game move to Auburn.

But things were changing. Jordan-Hare Stadium's capacity when Pat Dye accepted the Auburn job was 72,169. It had only reached that number a year or so earlier, with the completion of the West

Upper Deck. Prior to the 1987 season, Auburn constructed a second upper deck, this one on the East side of the stadium. The capacity for games that fall would be 85,214. That was bigger than Legion Field, bigger than Bryant-Denny, bigger than any other stadium in the state.

Approval for the construction of the second upper deck was granted by vote of the Auburn Board of Trustees two days after the 1984 Iron Bowl. Unspoken but understood by all involved was that this was to place more leverage in Coach Dye's and Auburn's hands with regard to moving future Iron Bowls to the Plains.

Auburn also constructed a new hotel and conference center, just across South College Street from campus. The old constraints—not enough seats; not enough hotel rooms—were falling by the wayside.

It was understood by Auburn that the 1987 game would be the last "home" Iron Bowl that Auburn was contractually obligated to play in Birmingham. Knowing that, Dye and the Board of Trustees began to look at the practical aspects of getting the game to the Plains in 1989.

That year had an interesting, coincidental aspect to it. The Iron Bowl had come to a halt after the 1907 game and didn't resume for forty-one years. Bringing it to Auburn in 1989 would mean moving it *out* of Birmingham for the first time in the same number of years: forty-one.

In 1985, with construction about to get underway on the second upper deck, Dye told the *Birmingham News:*

> "Birmingham has been good to Auburn, but I just believe that when it's our home game we have the right to play where we want to play and Alabama has the right to play where it wants to play. ... It's inevitable. We're going to have one of the finest stadiums in the country and it would be foolish on our part if we didn't play Alabama at our place when we're the home team."

Bobby Lowder elaborated:

> "At one time, especially when Coach Jordan was starting out, Auburn felt like Birmingham was a fine place to be. There were a lot of Alabama folks there, but we felt like we had almost as many, and Auburn played a lot of games in Birmingham.

147

"(But eventually that feeling changed, and) we wanted to get the Alabama game to Auburn. We had voted to expand the stadium and put the suites in. We knew that the big drawing card on a season ticket basis would be to move the Alabama game to Auburn."

After the 1985 Iron Bowl—another frustrating, last-minute, heart-breaking loss in a stadium that increasingly felt foreign to Auburn people—the Auburn trustees voted unanimously to play Auburn's home Iron Bowls in Jordan-Hare, and authorized Dye as athletic director to "negotiate a contract with the University of Alabama to that end."

Alabama had no intention of going along with any of this.

Rather than allow Auburn to play its home game in its home stadium, Ray Perkins threatened to cancel the series entirely. The Tide wasn't getting its way, and preferred to pick up its marbles and go home rather than compromise. They wanted to play *every* Iron Bowl, *every* year, in the stadium of *their* choice. It was 1908 all over again.

The day after the Auburn trustees voted, Alabama's president, Joab Thomas, told an AP reporter that moving the game to Auburn "is not something we'll be acting on in the near future."

Van Allen Plexico

There it is. That's their university president's reaction. They didn't want to discuss it, they didn't want to consider it, they didn't want to think about it. It was a non-starter with them.

A quick aside about Joab Thomas at Alabama: I remember in 1984 Alabama ran a TV commercial for the school, where President Thomas held up a book in one hand and a football in the other. He looked at the camera and said, "Here at Alabama, we want to be as good at this (book) as we are at this (football)."

My immediate reaction was that he was admitting they were not good at academics. Right there on TV, on an ad Alabama was paying for, their president was stating that their academics were not up to snuff.

As that season wore on, and Alabama ended up with an underwhelming 5-6 record in football, I remember laughing

148

and thinking, "I guess this means you have succeeded, Joab. Alabama is now as good at football as it is at academics!"

Auburn won a thrilling comeback Iron Bowl in 1986 when Brent Fullwood hammered away at the Tide for four quarters, and then receiver Lawyer Tillman took a reverse and wove his way through traffic to score.

The 1987 Iron Bowl marked the last time the game was played in front of a 50-50 split crowd, with Auburn as the home game in name only. The Tigers, with a powerful defense, shut out the Tide, 10-0.

Van Allen Plexico

The 1987 Iron Bowl was my first one to see in person. I think it's important that the 1989 edition wasn't my first one, because I had a first-hand sense of what it had been like to be the home team in Legion Field, with the crowd split in half. Looking back, the difference was clear. Auburn had a huge day against Alabama in 1987. We won the Iron Bowl, shutting Alabama out in the process for the first time since 1957. We won the SEC outright. We got invited to the Sugar Bowl for the first time since 1983. And the crowd was... *ehhh*. The Auburn people who were there were happy, of course. But there simply weren't that many of us. And it was considered an Auburn home game, featuring a highly-ranked Auburn team! Compare that to how it felt to be in Jordan-Hare two years later, for the First Time Ever game, and that's really all you need to know.

Pat Dye discusses Auburn's negotiations with Alabama in his memoir, *In the Arena*:

"The first time we sat down and met with the Alabama athletic department about moving the game was in 1987. We met in Atlanta. I can't remember the hotel, but it was downtown. We were playing in the Southeastern Conference basketball tournament at the Omni. We met during the tournament.

"There was Hindman Wall, and our attorney Tommy Thagard, and myself. We met with their athletic director, Steve Sloan, and Jim Goosetree, and their lawyers...

149

"They made it plain they didn't want to move the game out of Birmingham. I didn't blame them... Playing there is an advantage for them.

"What was their alternative? They could have appealed to the Southeastern Conference. But if they took it to a conference vote, I had no doubt we would be allowed to play our home game in Auburn. (Alabama) could get out of the conference. They didn't want to do that. But we never had to take it that far."

Later in 1987, Auburn trustees Bobby Lowder, Mike McCartney and Morris Savage were appointed by university president Jim Martin to a committee that was to negotiate with Alabama over the location of future Iron Bowls. Lowder's counterpart on Alabama's committee was trustee Winton "Red" Blount.

Van Allen Plexico

Winton "Red" Blount is a fascinating figure. He was postmaster general during the Nixon administration, and led the transition of that office from cabinet-level within the executive branch to being an independent agency, the US Postal Service. He ran for the US Senate in 1972, and one of the volunteers who helped with his campaign was future president George W. Bush. (This later became a point of controversy during the 2004 presidential campaign, as Bush was accused by some opponents of going AWOL from the Texas Air National Guard in order to serve on Blount's campaign in Alabama.)

Blount and his brother founded a construction company that worked on the Louisiana Superdome and the Apollo 11 launch pad. That company was later sold for $1.35 billion.

Nearest to my heart, Blount and his wife, Carolyn, created (at a cost of over $21 million) the Blount Cultural Park in Montgomery, which includes both a museum and the beautiful theater that serves as home of the Alabama Shakespeare Festival.

Lowder and his committee traveled to Montgomery to meet with Blount's group to discuss moving the Iron Bowl.

Blount lived up to his name: He immediately and *bluntly* declared Alabama would *not* be going along with Auburn's plans.

Bobby Lowder describes what happened:

"We had a meeting in the old Capital City Club in Montgomery. We set a meeting for like 3 one afternoon. We went over there at 3 o'clock. We had a private room for the meeting, and they were about 30 minutes late. That's a negotiating tactic. They try to intimidate people by coming late to the meeting. We had already decided that, no matter what they said, we were determined that the game was going to get moved.

"The first thing Red Blount said is, "Let me make one thing understood right here and now. The University of Alabama will never come to Auburn and play a football game."

"I was trying to be respectful to an older man. Morris and Mike had said I could be the spokesman. I said "We appreciate you coming, but we intend for the Auburn-Alabama game to be moved to Auburn. It's going to be moved. We are going to decide when that is. I'm sure it will be a heck of a game, but if your team doesn't show up, they are going to forfeit the game."

"We went back and forth. They finally got up and left. They were madder than hell. It looked like we were going to go to court."

Van Allen Plexico

This reminds me of a scene in the movie "Recount," about the 2000 presidential election. At one point George Bush's people sit down in a little room with Al Gore's people, and both sides immediately declare it's their way or the highway, and they're only there as a courtesy, to work out the small details. Both groups immediately get back up and leave.

As an Auburn person, it seems absolutely intolerable. It makes me want to punch a hole in the wall—or in Red Blount. But you have to stop and think: It's really just posturing. Alabama wants to act all big and bad and tough up front, but they could see the future as clearly as anyone else. They knew that, no matter how badly they wanted to keep Auburn's home games in the stadium of Alabama's preference, they could never make that stand up in court, or with the SEC, now that it was finally starting to act like a real conference and make teams all play one another, play the same number of conference games, and so forth.

Blount and Alabama had to make their big stand, like George Wallace in the schoolhouse door at Tuscaloosa in 1963. Once that was done, the real negotiations could begin.

Things, however, would get worse before they could get better.

The City of Birmingham jumped into the conflict with a lawsuit, fearing the loss of business and revenue if at least half—and maybe all—future Iron Bowls were played somewhere other than Birmingham. They believed Auburn was contractually obligated to keep playing in Birmingham for quite a few years to come.

Auburn's legendary radio announcer, Jim Fyffe, comments on this situation in his own book, *Touchdown Auburn*:

"I remember talking about (playing Alabama in Auburn) back during some of the early talk shows I did before I became the Auburn announcer. I wasn't shy about saying that the game should be moved to Auburn. In those days nobody could envision that it would be. It was even controversial to discuss it. Frankly it should never have been an issue. If Auburn wanted to play the game in the middle of the Sahara Desert they should have been allowed to and the same with Alabama. The city of Birmingham be damned. Birmingham never did anything for Auburn. Auburn fans never had the true sense of playing at home when playing at Legion Field. There were some great games and some great memories, and the split crowd was kind of neat, but the time had come to go forward. Here was Auburn playing at Alabama in deteriorating Legion Field, with all its dilapidated surroundings, while this great stadium with more seating capacity sat empty in the middle of one of the most picturesque college campuses in the nation."

David Housel

"Think what it would do to our economy," they (Birmingham's leaders) said, never pausing to think what it might mean to the economies of Auburn, Opelika, Montgomery, and all of East Central Alabama. Thinking only of themselves, "Never" became the battle cry of Alabama fans and of Birmingham.

"Auburn isn't big enough to handle the game. The game was meant to be played in Birmingham."

Businesses in Birmingham sent threatening letters to Auburn as well. Ray Perkins made his infamous "It won't happen" statement. Even a member of the board of directors of Lowder's own bank took a stand against Auburn's wishes. He—a man with the incredible name of Young Boozer, Jr—refused to try to persuade Alabama to acquiesce to Auburn's wishes.

Bobby Lowder explains:

"Mr. Boozer was a really nice guy, (but) he had the same attitude. As good a friend as he was to my father and me, he always said "I won't come to Auburn. Alabama is not coming to Auburn." He never changed his attitude. That generation of Alabama folks thought it was beneath them to come to Auburn. We were treated like second-class citizens."

Eventually Alabama came to see that Auburn was determined to move the game. But it took time, and it wasn't easy. Lowder and Blount met many more times, hashing it all out. Auburn contacted the SEC office to get the conference's opinion, and was told they could play their home games wherever they wanted. Alabama screamed bloody murder. Auburn would not give in.

The last card up Alabama's sleeve was a document their president, Joab Thomas, suddenly produced in the eleventh hour, in May of 1987. A letter, hand-written and allegedly signed by Bear Bryant, it was supposedly a copy of an original sent to former Auburn athletic director Lee Hayley in 1980. In it the original agreement over where to play the games was amended to extend the series in Legion Field through 1991. "We are enclosing signed copy of extension of games scheduled for 1988, 1989, 1990, and 1991,"

153

Bryant wrote in the addendum to Hayley. "One copy of agreement is being retained for our files."

While Auburn issued no official reaction to this revelation, a "highly placed Auburn University source" was quoted by the *Montgomery Advertiser* that day as dismissing the new letter, and adding, "We plan to say we are going to play the game in Auburn in 1989. If they show up, fine. If not, we'll consider it a forfeit."

Van Allen Plexico

In the course of researching this book, one of our AU Wishbone patrons, Patrick Williams, sent in a letter his dad received from Auburn University president James E. Martin, dated December 2, 1987—right in the midst of all this negotiating, and two years to the day before the First Time Ever game would be played.

Williams's dad had written to Birmingham mayor Richard Arrington, complaining about the bus service around Legion Field on the day of the 1987 Iron Bowl, as well as the general bad treatment of Auburn fans by the stadium staff. Dr. Martin wrote back, acknowledging receipt of the letter, expressing regret over how things had gone for that family at the game, and noting, "Last year our Board of Trustees had an experience similar to yours of this year."

That to me is interesting. Over and over, we have read and been told that the Board of Trustees had a big part to play in moving the game—that they got on board early with the idea of pushing for it, and backing Coach Dye in his public efforts with it. Clearly, their receiving bad treatment at Legion Field would only contribute to their desire to make this happen.

Back to the letter from Dr. Martin. He concludes it with a final paragraph that must, in 1987, have hit like a bombshell:

"Auburn University is making plans to *host* the Auburn/Alabama game in Auburn in *1989*. We look forward to having our alumni and friends return for that historic event."

"To my knowledge," Williams says, "this acknowledgement of planning to host the 1989 game in Auburn was made prior to any public announcement."

Clearly, Auburn officials, as early as 1987 and all the way up to the president of the university himself, weren't just

154

hoping a resolution could be found and the game could be played in Auburn in 1989. No—they were "making plans" to that effect. A line in the sand, indeed.

A few months later, in January of 1988, the city of Birmingham sued both Auburn and Alabama. The city believed the contract extending the series in Legion Field through 1991 was "iron-clad."

Auburn rejected this entirely and maintained that the 1989 game would be played in Jordan-Hare.

More prominent Alabama boosters screamed and hollered. President Thomas of Alabama wrote a letter to Auburn's President Martin suggesting they simply stop playing each other entirely.

Alabama's threats did not ring entirely hollow. They'd ended the series twice before. Who was to say they wouldn't do the same again?

Not for the first time, it was 1908 all over again.

"It was contentious," Lowder said of this period of negotiations. "We took a lot of abuse. Of course, once we moved it here and Alabama saw how successful it was, they wanted to move their home games to Tuscaloosa."

In the meantime, Ray Perkins left Alabama for the Tampa Bay Buccaneers of the NFL (where he would later draft Bo Jackson as the number one overall pick in the 1986 NFL draft—and Bo would refuse to sign with the Bucs or play for Perkins).

Alabama replaced Perkins as athletic director with former Alabama player Steve Sloan, and replaced Perkins as head coach with Bill Curry, who had played alongside the Tide's Bart Starr at Green Bay, but was a former Georgia Tech player. It seemed to be an odd fit, right from the start.

As Alabama AD, Sloan briefly toed the company line on the Iron Bowl's location, then made the mistake of wondering aloud why Auburn couldn't play their half of the games where they wanted to. It made sense to him, as it did to most rational human beings. Of course, he'd been coaching at Duke for the previous few years, rather than marinating in the Alabama mindset. When he later lost his job, many pointed to this as his greatest failing: He allowed Auburn to move the game, and didn't put up a big enough fight. They felt he was too soft.

At that time, Sloan said:

"I just think the game is bigger than some feelings that we might have about our program. We're obviously going to negotiate hard about the things we believe and obviously we like playing the game in Birmingham. Everybody knows that. We'll probably keep playing the game in Birmingham even if Auburn plays their game in Auburn."

Curry was worse, as Alabama saw it. The former Yellowjacket never seemed a proper fit in Tuscaloosa, and he, too, couldn't find a realistic angle for how to force Auburn to keep coming to Legion Field. He would later get a brick thrown through his office window by his own team's alleged fans.

Looking back on that period, Curry later said, "There was a tradition of never playing (the Iron Bowl in Auburn or Tuscaloosa). Steve Sloan and I had talked about it many, many times. Of course, he represented Coach Bryant's position by being one of Coach Bryant's greatest players and greatest leaders. And I represented quite the opposite in the minds of a lot of people."

With Alabama having "found" the supposed contract addendum and demanding Auburn honor it, the rivalry that had moved from the football field to the meeting room now moved to the courts. No one could predict the outcome there.

Back on the Plains, Bobby Lowder could see how miserable it was making the Alabama people to contemplate giving in to Auburn on anything. He worried they might actually do the unthinkable and end the series entirely, rather than come to Auburn. But playing the 1989 game in Jordan-Hare had become a red line beyond which Auburn would *under no circumstances* venture. Almost anything else was up for discussion—but not 1989. It made for a serious impasse.

John Ringer

For so long, Alabama had gotten their way and had rigged the circumstances to their benefit. Now Auburn was using the legal process and the power the university had developed to push Alabama into a corner. I don't think they expected that could or would happen.

At last, in April of 1988, Lowder hit upon a face-saving gesture for the Tide contingent: Auburn would, in the words of Pat Dye, "throw them a bone." And that bone was the 1991 game.

Van Allen Plexico
What was going on politically inside the University of Alabama that made them feel like they *could* keep it in Birmingham? What made them think it was fair—or *did* they think it was fair? What was their mindset about all of this?

David Housel
They had a contract, and I don't know if it was a valid contract or not, that supposedly Coach Bryant had initialed, extending (the game being played in Birmingham) through 1992. Giving them the benefit of the doubt, which I think you have to, I think they really thought they had a contract extension.

Auburn didn't have any record of that. Lee Haley didn't have any record of it. So I thought there was a legitimate legal issue there. Of course, the city of Birmingham got involved. They wanted to keep the game in Birmingham. You know why. Because "God intended that game to be played there!" (Laughs.)

You have to credit Bobby Lowder, you have to credit Mike McCartney, on the board of trustees. Coach Dye gets all the credit, but he was the front man. That decision was made in the highest (levels of) power of the Auburn trustees.

I think Alabama fought it until they realized they couldn't win it. I remember (former Alabama and NFL quarterback) Scott Hunter calling me one night. I was driving back from Birmingham. I don't know if he took this upon himself or if he was sent as an emissary, because it was a substantial move on their part. He said, "David, the Alabama leadership knows they're going to have to come to Auburn. But you've got to give them something to justify it."

Van Allen Plexico
"Throw them a bone."

David Housel
That was Coach Dye's term. But, in negotiation, you've got to give them something they can hang their hat on. It's got to be a win-win.

John Ringer
They have to save face.

David Housel
Yeah. And (Hunter) said, "Alabama is willing to come to Auburn in 1991 if you'll play the 1989 game in Birmingham." And I said, "Scott, I don't know anything about that." So he said, "If you would, call some of the Auburn leadership and let them know Alabama would be (amenable) to that compromise."

So I called Mr. Lowder. I stopped at a phone booth coming back from Birmingham and told him what they'd said. And he was real quiet. Real quiet. And then he said, "Okay, I appreciate it. If you hear anything else, let me know," or something like that. As it turned out, thank God, Auburn's position became, "We've got to resolve this thing. We will play in Birmingham in 1991, but you're coming to Auburn in 1989, because that is so important."

Because of the fact that Auburn had said early on that "You're coming in 1989," if we had then said, "1991," it would've given the appearance that Alabama had won the argument. But the fact that Auburn had said, "1989 or you're going to forfeit," that gives for history the appearance that Auburn won the argument. And Auburn *did* win the argument. Playing in 1989 in Auburn is so significant. *So* significant.

"They finally tried to put off (the game being played in Auburn) until 1991. It had gotten to be such a thing that I said, 'This is what we will do: It's really important to our people (that the 1989 Iron Bowl happens in Jordan-Hare). (So) we'll play the 1989 game in Auburn. In 1991, we'll come back to Birmingham one more time.'"
—Bobby Lowder

158

"We threw Alabama a bone in 1991 and got forever. A bone in exchange for forever."
—David Housel, 2019

John Ringer

It was absolutely worth it. I would pay the price of giving up the 1991 game a hundred times out of a hundred for what we got for it.

But we shouldn't have had to in the first place. We gave up something just for their pride, but we shouldn't have had to give that up.

The settlement eventually agreed to by both universities and by the City of Birmingham hewed closely to Lowder's proposal. Included in the formal agreement was language stating that the two sides really, truly wanted to put the whole dispute behind them and never have to deal with it again:

This agreement is intended to resolve finally and permanently the issue relating to the right of each university to determine the location of its "home" game with the other university.

Van Allen Plexico

Part of the settlement included a requirement that Alabama play the 1992 and 1994 Iron Bowls in Legion Field. I find it interesting that the settlement only required Auburn to play there as the home team once more (1991), while it required Alabama to do so twice.

Alabama really did not get the better end of this deal at all. It's remarkable just how much they had to concede before it was all said and done. Think about it: the series would not end. Alabama *would* be coming to Auburn. It would be happening in *1989*, not 1991. And Alabama was now locked into playing in Legion Field through *at least* 1994. And all Auburn had been forced to give up was the location of the 1991 game. That was it.

I don't know who Alabama was using for lawyers at that time, but they folded up and capitulated like France in 1940.

A joint press release issued by the Auburn and Alabama boards of trustees consisted of three short paragraphs essentially saying they'd reached a settlement, had been working on one for a little while, and were happy they'd resolved it, "and that their respective campuses now could direct their full attention to other important matters." That was it.

John Ringer
That's so typical.

Van Allen Plexico
This is the greatest press release ever. It takes three paragraphs to say, *Okay, we've reached an agreement.* It gives no details whatsoever as to what that agreement might be. But it does add that part at the end, which essentially is saying, "How were we supposed to get any work done on our campuses while this Iron Bowl dispute was hanging over our heads? Thank goodness that's over! Back to work now!"

The settlement, agreed to by all three parties, locked in the fact that Auburn would get to play the 1989 Iron Bowl in Jordan-Hare. That was the main thing Auburn cared about, and they won on that point.

However, the "bone" thrown to Alabama was that Auburn agreed to return to Legion Field in 1991 to play one last "home" game in that aging venue. That gave Alabama something to feel good about, and it gave Birmingham one more Iron Bowl than they otherwise would have hosted.

Meanwhile, Alabama would receive a full home-game allotment of tickets for the 1988 and 1990 Iron Bowls, as if those games were being played in Tuscaloosa. The 1987 game was the last time the crowd was split in half.

Bill Curry, speaking years later, engaged in a bit of extremely selective memory:

"There was such a groundswell for (moving Auburn's home Iron Bowls to Jordan-Hare), I don't think anything would have kept it from happening. There was no one at Alabama that could have said "I don't think we ought to go over there." There was

160

only one person that could have made that statement, and he (Bryant) had passed away a few years before."

Van Allen Plexico

Curry's statement there verges on brain damage, as far as I'm concerned. Alabama had assembled an entire committee whose job was to say to Lowder's group, "We will *never* come to Auburn." Their previous coach had outright stated, *"It won't happen."*

Curry is right about the relocation being much more possible after the Bear passed away, though. Shug had said we'd need to have a few funerals first, and Bryant's was the main one.

By 1988, it seemed that everyone on both sides understood the Iron Bowl was coming to Auburn sooner or later. The only remaining question was when.

Van Allen Plexico

Alabama people had talked big, but—once that contract expired—they knew there wasn't really anything they could do about it, short of just not scheduling Auburn. And an SEC team refusing to play another SEC team was a proposition that was much harder to pull off by the 1980s. In previous decades, Alabama had gone forever without playing Ole Miss or Georgia, but they'd also played more SEC opponents some years than Auburn did, because we were still scheduling Georgia Tech.

That kind of thing became impossible by the 1980s. The SEC had begun to take a more direct role in how teams scheduled conference opponents, and everyone's schedules were more regular by then.

And, of course, radical ideas such as leaving the SEC outright, Alabama would never do. They knew Auburn would look like the winners and they would look like losers and cowards. They absolutely *had* to play *in* Auburn, if Auburn wanted them to, and that was all there was to it. The truly remarkable thing is that they made such huge fools of themselves for so many years, pitching fits and issuing threats and declarations, before they finally capitulated and accepted reality.

With that fact understood, if not actually spoken out loud yet, the controversy became much more about the 1989 game specifically, and where that one would be played. At that point, I think Alabama wanted to twist Auburn's arm and make them play it in Birmingham mostly as a face-saving gesture. They wanted to tweak their argument from "We will never play in Auburn" to "We won't play in Auburn *in the year* you want us to." Auburn's leaders, however, had made playing the 1989 game in Jordan-Hare an absolute red-line requirement, and would not back down from it.

There's a moment in the movie "Gandhi" where the Mahatma tells his friends that the British were still talking like they planned to dominate India forever, but you could tell that even the British didn't really believe it any longer. He says something to the effect of, "Their words are the same, but the feeling has gone out of them." That's how Alabama was at this point, I think. They were still talking big in public, but behind the scenes they were looking for an exit strategy from this impossible situation they'd painted themselves into.

The 1991 Iron Bowl was that exit strategy. It let Alabama and the city of Birmingham act like they'd gotten something off of us. That was fine, because we didn't care about it enough to make a huge fuss against letting them have it.

John Ringer

Even if Alabama had a convincing legal argument that the hand-notated contract the Bear had was a binding document and could take Auburn to court with it, the ultimate outcome would have been that the 1993 Iron Bowl would have been the First Time Ever game. It was inevitable—and on that point Auburn would never yield. So everything else was just negotiation over exactly *when*.

Van Allen Plexico

Let's pause for just a moment to talk about that 1991 game, because it's a fairly important historical footnote.

"It's our home game this year, but that's a bunch of bunk. It is an Alabama field, and the majority of the people of Birmingham are for Alabama."
—An Auburn fan, shown on the ESPN TV broadcast just before the 1991 Iron Bowl

Van Allen Plexico

I was there, at the 1991 Iron Bowl in Legion Field. It was a truly bizarre experience.

The electronic lights in the stadium, such as they were, had never been intended to appear orange or blue. So we got a sort of red and purple haze from them the entire game.

The end zones were painted to look like Jordan-Hare's, with "AUBURN" in one and "TIGERS" in the other. And there was a big "AU" logo at midfield. But on that ragged Legion Field astroturf, surrounded by a rickety, bare, chain-link fence, it all looked cheap and flimsy. Certainly it looked nothing like the genuine article; not even close. It made for something of a "Bizarro Jordan-Hare." It very effectively highlighted how much nicer our own stadium was, by comparison.

I do want to say, however, that while no one could have predicted, years earlier, that the 1991 Auburn team would have been significantly weaker than the 1989 team, it's a darned good thing Coach Dye and Bobby Lowder and company demanded the First Time Ever game be played in 1989. If we'd had to rely on the 1991 team to win the first-ever Iron Bowl in Auburn—and with all due respect to the players and coaches on that team—I'm not completely sold on the idea that they would have pulled it off. Alabama won that game, 13-6. The Tide had a very good defensive team, and the Tigers were having a hard time scoring points that year.

Auburn fans departing Legion Field afterward were disappointed, sure—but we were also feeling an enormous relief. It was like finishing an odd sort of community service sentence. We'd thrown Alabama a bone, playing as the home team in that awful stadium one more time. Now it was done. From that point on, every Iron Bowl in an odd-numbered year would be played in Auburn. That was what mattered.

"We're giving up this game today, and we're playing it in Birmingham, but we got December the 2nd, 1989. And no matter whatever else may happen in the history of Auburn, we've been to the mountaintop."

—David Housel, interview on the ESPN TV broadcast of the 1991 Iron Bowl

The issue had been settled at last, but there was still one Iron Bowl to be played before the First Time Ever game in Jordan-Hare. And it was a very important one.

Auburn came into that 1988 game with a record of 9-1 and ranked 7th in the country, with as powerful a defense as has ever prowled the Plains. Only a last-second, one-point loss at LSU back in October—in what has become known as "the Earthquake Game"—was keeping the Tigers from entertaining thoughts of a national championship. The SEC title was most definitely on the line, along with an invitation to the Sugar Bowl and traditional bragging rights as state champs.

Auburn won the 1988 Iron Bowl—and with it, back-to-back SEC championships, giving them three in six years. The Tigers had definitely become the dominant football power in the state by then.

It was a true Alabama home game, played in their preferred home stadium. Any pretenses of "neutrality" were gone. The tickets had been allocated to Alabama just like any other home game for them. Auburn fans represented only a sliver of blue in a sea of red.

For some Auburn fans, that's how it had felt, more often than not, all along.

Mike McClendon

It was a combination of things that caused the game to eventually get moved. Probably the biggest factor was doing away with the 50/50 ticket split. We started buying season tickets at Auburn in 1974 when I got out of the USAF. Even back then Auburn had a priority system. In a season ticket book you received a ticket to each Auburn home game and one Alabama ticket for every two season books. That was because Auburn could offer a lot more tickets for games at Jordan-Hare than they could at Legion Field for the Alabama game.

When Alabama started their ticket priority system, "Tide Pride," in the 1980s, they had to face the same problem that Auburn had been living with for years: They did not have enough tickets available for the Auburn game to be able to put a ticket in each book. Rather than ration the tickets, they decided it was better to do away with the 50/50 split and give their fans a complete book in years when it was their home game.

Once the 50/50 split was gone, the series became a true home-and-away game even though it was always played in Birmingham. That made it possible to make the argument that Auburn should play its home games wherever we wanted. I have always believed that eliminating the 50/50 split was the true catalyst that allowed Dye to move the game.

Also, somewhere in there the NCAA changed the recruiting rules. Up to that time, Alabama could treat their games in Birmingham as a home game and bring recruits to the games just like they would in Tuscaloosa. The NCAA changed that so that games played off campus had strict limits on the recruits. The idea was that recruiting visits were tied to the university, not the football game. So, when you weren't on-campus, their recruits were getting nothing to do with the actual university. This had a huge impact on Alabama's games in Birmingham because it placed limitations on the numbers of high school recruits they could bring to Legion Field.

Van Allen Plexico
The Bear would *never* have allowed that rule change to happen!

"Greed." (How he described the ticket distribution system, whereby Alabama received 10,900 tickets to the Iron Bowl in Jordan-Hare Stadium, while Auburn kept over 74,000 tickets.)
—Kirk McNair, editor and publisher of Bama Magazine, 1989

"That's the figure Alabama came up with." (Tennessee and Georgia each received 10,000 tickets when playing in Jordan-Hare—900 fewer than Alabama received.)
—Bill Beckwith, Auburn ticket manager

"I don't have to get into that. That's the way the (ticket) situation was (when he took over from Steve Sloan). I never look back on something like that. I just try to do the things I've got to do."
—Hootie Ingram, Alabama athletic director, 1989

Van Allen Plexico

When you start hurting Alabama's recruiting efforts, as well as telling their boosters they can't have as many Iron Bowl tickets as they want, you start seeing changes happening very quickly.

I'm not completely convinced of Mike's argument above about the ticket situation being the catalyst that most directly led to the Iron Bowl coming to Auburn, simply because, in my recollection, they didn't change the ticket apportionment until the year before the game came to Auburn. That doesn't seem like enough time for it to have made a difference. But the overall point is a good one. Certainly Alabama wanting to be able to offer their boosters more tickets than they were able to during the 50-50 split years had to have been a factor for them.

There's one more factor to consider there. Prior to the Pat Dye era at Auburn, Alabama fans were notorious for buying up every ticket to the game they could get their hands on. During the lean years, lots of Auburn fans would happily scalp their Iron Bowl tickets for quick cash, even if it meant putting more red-clad rear ends in seats. Consequently, Alabama didn't need quite so many tickets available to their fans up front, because they knew they'd end up with the vast majority of them before the day of the game.

But with Auburn's resurgence in the Eighties under Pat Dye, suddenly there weren't nearly as many Auburn fans willing to part with their tickets.

Alabama couldn't have Auburn fans outnumbering them at the Iron Bowl. They had to do something.

Their view on splitting the stadium down the middle changed very rapidly at that point.

At long last, the job was done. Cooler heads prevailed. Auburn's determination won through. The series was not canceled. The agreements, hard-fought but now secured—were in place.

Yes, Auburn would have to play Alabama in Legion Field in 1990, 1991 and 1992.

But the 1989 Iron Bowl *would* be played in Jordan-Hare Stadium. It *would* happen.

Now, all that remained was to *win* it.

-10-

"NEVER PROVED TO BE A VERY SHORT TIME"

"It was said that this day would 'never' come, but, as so often happens, 'never' proved to be a very short time.
—*David Housel, Auburn Football Illustrated, Dec 2, 1989*

"It was just part of my job as athletic director. But I didn't do it alone. I had the great support of the trustees and administration."
—*Pat Dye, interview with Creg Stephenson, 2019*

On December 2, 1989, Alabama—a school that had once shut down its entire football program rather than play an away game with anyone—played the one away game they had always vowed they would *never, ever* play.

Before that game happened, however, many things had to change.

Auburn had to expand its stadium to a capacity so large that the size of Legion Field could no longer be used as an excuse to only play in Birmingham.

Auburn had to build up its program and its credibility on the playing field to the point that it was truly relevant, its opinions mattered and its leaders would be listened to.

And Auburn had to hire a head coach and AD with the drive, ability and determination to look Alabama in the eye, not blink, and stare them down.

Each of those things had been accomplished by 1989.

In addition to expanding Jordan-Hare Stadium prior to the 1987 season, Auburn also constructed a brand-new athletic complex, further enhancing the program.

Up until then, most of the Athletic Department's offices and facilities were located inside Beard-Eaves Memorial Coliseum.

Van Allen Plexico

I never even knew there were offices and other rooms inside the Coliseum until my sophomore year, when I found out one of my classes was being held there. There's a whole maze, a labyrinth, inside the walls of that big brick hat box. The basketball arena inside there is only one part of it.

Obviously, the football staff wanted their own headquarters, and they got it. There wasn't enough room inside it for everyone, though. Some members of the football staff remained located in the Coliseum, and didn't get to move out until 2023, when the brand new and gigantic Woltosz Football Performance Center opened.

I used to play tennis on the courts they bulldozed to make room for the football complex, so I was sort of disappointed when they first built it. It made sense to put the complex there, though, because it was right across the way from Sewell Hall, the athletic dorm building, and had room for practice fields.

An 88,000-square-foot, $7.3 million facility located at the corner of Samford and Donahue, work began on it in October of 1987. It was occupied in June of 1989 and, as described in the 1989 Media Guide, housed "all football operations as well as various administrative offices of the Auburn Athletic Department." It originally included the 5,000-square-foot Lovelace Museum, just off the main lobby, holding many of Auburn's greatest trophies and awards. The museum was moved into Auburn Arena (now Neville Arena) upon that facility's completion in 2010.

Three practice fields were located outside the bottom level of the complex. That level contained locker rooms, training rooms and equipment rooms.

The second level included meeting rooms for various positions, an auditorium, the weight room, academic support offices, and a broadcasting facility.

The third level held offices for coaches, administration and staff, along with game analysis facilities.

Van Allen Plexico

I always thought they should name the 1989 football complex after Pat Dye. If there was any building on campus that should have his name, it was that one.

I think there was a ladder behind the head coach's office, so he could quickly descend to the practice field without having to go all the way through the complex to get down there.

Auburn's success on the football field during the previous decade, and the desire to continue that trend, led directly to the complex being built. In some ways, 1989 marked the culmination of a number of processes and trends that had begun way back in 1981, with the hiring of Pat Dye. The football program had become one of the best, if not the best, in the conference. The stadium had expanded with a second upper deck. The football complex had been completed and occupied. And now the First Time Ever Iron Bowl loomed at the end of the year.

Before that game could finally come to pass, however, an entire season's worth of games had to be played by both Alabama and Auburn.

Even before the season started, the excitement of knowing what was coming was having an effect on Auburn people. And sometimes those people were in possession of large quantities of *paint*.

Today the tiger paw at Toomer's Corner is a permanent part of the landscape, beautifully formed out of orange-hued paving stones amid the red brick of the intersection. In the summer just prior to the First Time Ever game, however, that intersection was as blank as it

171

had always been. The ancient oaks nearby notwithstanding, it was just another bland, nondescript conjunction of two roads.

But one man saw it not as a patch of asphalt but as a canvas for something greater.

The idea to cover the street in a giant tiger paw originated in the mind of Frank "Butch" Parsons, who in 1989 was the chairman of the Student Government Association's Spirit Committee. The same committee that, just a few weeks later, would begin stashing away a portion of the paper shakers allotted for each football game—saving them for a more, shall we say, *historic* use, come December.

Parsons and his committee had just spent part of the evening of August 19 refreshing the paint on the orange tiger paws that led from the I-85 exit at South College St to the stadium. They had permission to do that. What they *didn't* have permission for was what they decided to do afterwards.

It was still too early for many cars to be out, and they had a bunch of orange paint left over. "As the night went on, there was talk about trying to do something with more of a splash," Parsons told the *War Eagle Reader*. "Something to get more attention."

They made a splash, all right. They "splashed" a few coats of orange paint in the shape of a huge tiger paw, right in the middle of the intersection. Then they waved pizza boxes at it, to dry the paint as quickly as possible before cars started driving through and running over their new masterpiece.

Bryan Schreiber, one of the committee members involved in it, later described the complex thought process behind the decision to paint the giant paw: "It was like, 'Why the hell not?'"

As they were finishing the operation, the police rolled up. Stories differ on the details, but all agree the cops quickly figured out the painters had no official permission to be doing what they were doing.

For a short while, it looked like the members of the Auburn Spirit Committee might be doing some hard time in the pen. And because it wasn't immediately clear whether the city, state or federal government had ultimate jurisdiction over that particular intersection, it wasn't even clear *which* pen they would be doing that hard time in: county, state or federal!

"There were three or four (legal) lines we had crossed because of that intersection," Parsons explained later.

Fortunately, a few phone calls to various government officials (and lawyers and school representatives and parents) later, everyone decided to chill out about it. No charges were filed, and the kids were released with essentially a warning to use better judgment in the future—or at least to get permission first.

Once the various government entities concluded they were okay with the paw being there, and that it didn't cause a hazard to driving, the SGA officially got behind it. For the next two decades and more, the paw would be regularly repainted in a more professional manner.

Parsons, meanwhile, was bombarded with dozens of requests from other Auburn fans to paint a giant paw in their driveways. Then Auburn redesigned Toomer's Corner and the paw became immortalized in stone.

In the end, it all worked out well for everybody. But it all started with a renegade bunch of college kids, the cover of night, and a whole lot of extra paint.

Van Allen Plexico

I wanted to include this story here for a couple of reasons. Part of it is that I remember it all happening. I remember seeing the giant paw on the street right after they painted it, and then I either heard from someone in SGA or I read about it in the *Plainsman*, or both. I couldn't believe they'd done that—and gotten away with it! It was both hilarious and AUsome, as we say.

Second, I think it serves as another vivid example of just how fired up we all were that year, knowing the First Time Ever game was coming. I'm a lot less surprised this would happen at Auburn in 1989 than in almost any other year. We were all going a little nuts that whole year, just waiting for the arrival of Alabama. For some, it manifested itself in paint.

John Ringer

Van makes a good point here: This was the beginning of the buildup to the craziness that would arrive in December, an early symptom of the mania that would grip the entire town of Auburn like nothing else before... "They are coming."

Alabama was indeed coming, and at a time that Auburn was fielding some of its strongest squads in school history. The 1989 team, however—the team that would have to actually face the Tide on the field of play—was causing even the most hardcore Tigers fans a little concern.

Auburn's 1989 squad was very good from the beginning, but it was clear early on that something was missing. The teams the three previous years had been dominant at times, winning 29 games and two SEC titles and coming within two bizarre ties in 1987 of winning double-digit games three years in a row.

Of course, Auburn teams over the previous four years had featured superstars like Bo Jackson, Tracy Rocker, Brent Fullwood and Lawyer Tillman, as well as veterans such as Freddie Weygand, Walter Reeves, Ben Tamburello, Shan Morris, Nate Stallworth and Benji Roland.

The 1989 Auburn Tigers didn't feature a single player that might be classified as a "superstar." There were of course veteran standouts; seniors and juniors like quarterback Reggie Slack and running back Stacy Danley, receivers Alexander Wright and Shayne Wasden, linebackers Quentin Riggins and Craig Ogletree and kicker Win Lyle. The team had solid leadership—particularly after junior running back James Joseph stepped up into that role mid-season. Overall, though, this was not a team laden with 5-star phenoms. The 1989 Auburn Tigers arguably were the last of the great Pat Dye-assembled and coached Auburn teams; certainly the last of the Eighties. The last of his teams to win ten or more games, beat Alabama and win the SEC. But they were also a blue-collar bunch, giving extra effort and relying on experience at least as much as on any fabulous talent. This is not to slight them—not at all. On the contrary, it is to praise them for accomplishing so much, despite having no real superstar to lean on. They did it all with sheer determination, desire, and work—*hard* work.

Alabama, meanwhile, in their third season under Bill Curry, ran through their first ten games undefeated. They had a solid defense, coordinated by Don Lindsey, and a high-scoring offense, as guided by celebrated coordinator Homer Smith. After falling behind 21-0 at Ole Miss on October 7, that offense had exploded, ringing the Rebels up for 62 points, while the defense allowed only 6 more. Two weeks later they met undefeated and 6th ranked Tennessee at Legion Field and outscored them, 47-30. A week after that, they edged number 14 Penn State in Happy Valley, 17-16, blocking a Nittany Lions field goal attempt with thirteen seconds left to preserve the win. On November 11 they crushed LSU in Baton Rouge, 32-16. By the time of the Iron Bowl, they'd climbed all the way to second in the AP Poll. Their offense, defense and special teams had all shone and saved the day for them at different times in the season. They were a complete team, hitting on all cylinders, by the time the Iron Bowl rolled around.

Van Allen Plexico

For as long as I can remember, I've always kept at least one eye on Alabama all season long, since we generally end the season playing them. That year, of course, I gave them special attention, because I wanted to see what they would be bringing down to the big game on December 2. I wanted to know what kind of chance we had.

Prior to the season, I'd felt pretty good about things. Auburn was coming off a run of three dominant seasons, from 1986-1988. Our defense in particular was stellar during those years. But then we struggled a bit, at the start of the 1989 season.

Meanwhile, what I was seeing from Alabama, week to week, was frankly scaring me to death.

The Tide had been mediocre for most of the Eighties. Now they'd clearly turned things around. I remember wondering out loud many times that fall, "Why *now*? Why do they have to be this good *this year*, of all years?"

> "If beating Alabama in Auburn would be the greatest victory in Auburn history, beating Auburn at Auburn the first time the game was played there would be the greatest victory in Alabama history. It would spoil Auburn's greatest day. Nothing would be better for a true Alabama fan. The worm turns both ways."
> —David Housel, 1990

Indeed, Auburn was not having quite as successful a season as had been expected. Prior to the Iron Bowl, they amassed eight wins and two losses. They lost two games before the end of October; they'd only lost one game before Halloween in the previous three years combined.

Road losses to ranked teams at Tennessee (14-21) on September 30 and at Florida State (14-22) on October 21 had dropped the Tigers in the rankings from a high of 4 all the way down to 16.

Van Allen Plexico

The Tennessee loss was galling. It reminded me of the trip to Knoxville four years earlier, when we had Bo Jackson and were ranked number one in the country, and we ran into a buzzsaw. Coach Dye said of the 1985 game that the Vols "ambushed us." Once again, in 1989, it felt like Johnny Majors had gotten one over on us.

Auburn's emerging threat that season was the blazing-fast senior wide receiver, Alexander "Ace" Wright. Tennessee head coach Johnny Majors knew he didn't have anyone on his roster who could adequately cover Wright. Fortunately for Tennessee, it rained heavily the night before the game. The field was going to be much slower than normal. Majors, however, was not satisfied with this. He wanted even *more* water on the field. So he turned on all the sprinklers and let them run overnight before the game. By the time the two teams took the field on Saturday, Neyland Stadium was a quagmire. The slick and sloppy conditions caused Auburn to give up a safety on a punt attempt early on, muff a field goal attempt, and generally suffer issues all over the field. Alexander Wright was mostly held in check. He did score a long touchdown, but only one—and that wasn't enough, as Tennessee prevailed, 21-14.

Van Allen Plexico

The pop group Milli Vanilli had a hit at that time with the song, "Blame it on the Rain." Some of our friends who had traveled to Knoxville immediately christened this loss the "Blame it on the Rain Game."

Two weeks later, the Tigers exacted some much-needed revenge on LSU for the catastrophic "Earthquake Game" in Baton Rouge the year before. That loss, the only one Auburn suffered in the regular season, and by just one point, at the very end of the game, cost the Tigers a shot at Notre Dame in the national championship game. It was as costly a loss as an Auburn team has ever suffered, right alongside the Texas loss in 1983 and the Florida State loss in 2013.

In a grind-it-out affair, two teams with powerful defenses and limited offenses fought for three hours, resulting in Auburn managing a 10-6 victory.

The very next week, the Tigers traveled to Tallahassee to take on FSU in Doak Campbell Stadium. The Seminoles had won the previous two games in a series stretching back almost every year to 1983. Auburn had risen back to 11th in the polls after the LSU win, while Florida State was 14th.

The Seminoles got out to an early 22-3 lead, but Auburn attempted a comeback late. Trailing by 8 points in the final seconds, quarterback Reggie Slack scrambled on fourth down, deep in FSU territory, but was stopped just short. Florida State's win streak against the Tigers had reached three in a row. Auburn, meanwhile, stood at 4-2 overall and dropped in the rankings.

Alabama that same weekend scored their big upset over sixth-ranked Tennessee and climbed into the top ten. The Tide had passed Auburn in the polls on October 14, but the two teams had remained fairly close to one another, week after week, until Auburn lost to FSU. The following week, Auburn was 16th while Alabama was 6th.

Van Allen Plexico

The week after the FSU loss was the low point of the season, I think. We'd started out the year ranked ahead of Alabama, which meant we should be favored in the Iron Bowl—which was our main focus, all year long. But after Alabama won their big victory over Tennessee and then we lost to Florida State, they were suddenly ten spots ahead of us in the rankings!

I don't know about you, John, but I was about ready to push the panic button. Not that it would have done any good.

John Ringer

I was not ready to panic yet but I was starting to get a little concerned. I knew that Jordan-Hare would be a tsunami of emotion in December and I felt like this Auburn team was deep and talented enough to turn it around for the Alabama game.

Van Allen Plexico

We talked about it in our previous book, *We Believed, Volume 1*, but I was at the Florida State game. I remember our offense in particular just didn't look very impressive. We lacked a big-time playmaker. Alexander Wright had his moments but, in my opinion, we just didn't use him enough. We tended to stick to shorter, higher-percentage passes to guys like Shayne Wasden. Our running game, with Stacey Danley and James Joseph, was more of a grind-it-out, running-back-by-committee affair; neither of those guys, as solid as they were, ever felt like a breakaway threat in the Jackson/Fullwood mold. We really needed that home run threat at running back.

Which brings us to the Florida game.

Auburn went back to basics against Mississippi State on October 28—a game in which Dye had the Tigers focus on only three running plays in preparation all week, and barely throw the ball at all.

"We were not physical, and coach Dye wanted a physical team, so we went back to work."
—*Quentin Riggins, Auburn Linebacker*

The now-more-physical Auburn welcomed the Florida Gators to Jordan-Hare on November 4.

The Iron Bowl was less than a month away. It was well past time the team started to show improvement and put things together for the stretch run.

Unfortunately, for most of the Florida game, it looked like they had regressed.

Florida was a program in transition, having reached the end of a decade that had seen them prosper under Charley Pell and Galen Hall, and would a year later see them operating the Fun n' Gun of Steve Spurrier. In 1989, however, with interim coach Gary Darnell in charge, they had virtually no passing game to speak of. Instead, they leaned almost entirely upon the abilities of running back Emmitt Smith.

Van Allen Plexico

I've said it before: If Auburn had signed Emmitt Smith before the 1987 season, we would have won at least the 1988 national championship, and maybe more.

Some claim that his mother was unhappy with how Coach Dye had handled Brent Fullwood in his senior season, not "holding him accountable" when he skipped classes. Others argue that Emmitt's mom had simply told him he could go to college anywhere he wanted, as long as it was south of the Florida state line.

The final moments of this game I believe mark the turning point at last for the 1989 Auburn Tigers. Everyone knows how it ends, right? We can still hear the echoes of Jim Fyffe screaming!

Auburn fumbled inside their own 5-yard line early in the game, and Smith punched it in. Nothing else of note on offense occurred for either team. At the half, Florida led 7-0. Auburn managed a field goal in the third quarter, but by the time the game reached its final stages, the Gators still led, 7-3.

For as little offense as Auburn had managed, Florida did even worse. Their quarterback completed only one pass all night long, for a grand total of 6 yards. The great Emmitt Smith was held to 86 yards, meaning that in his three tries against Auburn, he never gained a hundred yards.

Van Allen Plexico

In fact, Auburn linebacker Quentin Riggins was awarded National Defensive Player of the Week for his 23-tackle performance against Florida in 1989, holding Emmitt Smith to just 86 yards.

Finally, with time running out, Auburn's Reggie Slack engineered a drive deep into Florida territory. It looked to have come up short, however. The Tigers stalled yet again, now facing 4th and 11 on the Gators' 25. A field goal would do them no good.

What came next may have turned the season around for Auburn.

Slack dropped back, saw Shayne Wasden running uncovered into the right corner of the end zone, and lofted a pass to him for the winning score.

As Jim Fyffe went memorably berserk on the radio, Auburn held on for the 10-7 win.

A 20-3 stomping of Georgia two weeks later seemed to confirm the idea that this Auburn team had finally found itself. A win in the Iron Bowl certainly wasn't guaranteed—Alabama, after all, was still undefeated and had risen to 4th in the country, soon to be 2nd—but the Tigers' chances appeared better than they had since early September.

John Ringer
That Florida game was a great confidence builder for the team and the home crowd, and I think it helped the team recover from the earlier losses and move into the last few games with a lot of confidence.

Van Allen Plexico
Auburn and Alabama both used to take the Saturday before the Iron Bowl off every year. Of all the years we didn't need an extra week to think about a game and get worked up over it, this was probably the year! Excitement was at a fever pitch. The campus seemed to pulsate with energy for days.

The rest of November passed excruciatingly slowly. It felt like the big day would never come.

The bye weekend came and went. On the Monday of game week, November 27, a few people dressed up in orange and blue appeared on campus, but not so many that one would especially notice. Then, on Tuesday, November 28, it became obvious that this was *not* going to be a normal game week.

John Ringer (to Mark Murphy of Auburn Undercover)
What do you remember about that week, the buildup during the two-week period before the game?

Mark Murphy

It was the most intense pregame buildup I've ever seen for any Auburn football game, even more than the national championship games out in Arizona (January 2011) and in California (January 2014), which were really crazy in their own way. Tickets were impossible to find. People started coming into town many days before the game. I think, by midday Thursday, the whole campus just basically shut down and it was like, forget about work. This is football, it's a party. Let's have a good time.

Van Allen Plexico

I remember walking from Haley Center past Parker Hall and there were already RVs parked there and people barbecuing, on Tuesday. *Tuesday!*

Mark Murphy

Oh, yeah, they didn't have all the rules back then (about where and when you could park). People in the Athletic Department told me they really believe there were 150,000 people there on campus for game day. Of course, a lot of them stayed outside during the game. But most of them went and found a television to watch the game.

That Tiger Walk was just enormous. I looked at it from above, from inside the stadium. It was just like a sea of humanity. It was a great Tiger Walk.

I remember, a couple of days before the game, having a meal with some sportswriters. And we said, "What else can we write about this game? We've written so much already." Back then, a lot of people said that the two weeks of buildup (before an Iron Bowl) was too much, because it gets crazy. But hey, I was glad it was a two-week buildup that time because it just was such a huge game, and so big in Auburn history. To me, it's always going to be the most important game in Auburn history.

And that's why there was a lot of pressure on Coach Dye and the players to win that game. Alabama had a really good team that year, a really good offense. Bill Curry ratcheted up all his nonsense about having Alabama fans come around, come there and "protect the team" and all this kind of stuff. It was just nonsense and insulting. He lost a lot of credibility as a coaching person for all that nonsense. And I think a lot of Auburn officials were very offended by it.

I can't remember the exact stuff he said, but he was implying it was going to be dangerous for his team to come down here. That the Auburn fans were going to be so hostile, which was absolute nonsense.

Clyde Prather was Auburn's Public Safety Director in 1989. His job was to figure out how Auburn would manage everything surrounding this massive event. It was complicated by the fact that Alabama fans had never descended on the Loveliest Village in such numbers before. And it wasn't helped by the way Bill Curry and other Alabama people were handling matters on their end.

Clyde Prather
When we knew the game was coming, we in Public Safety expected it to be a big game with a lot going on, and we formed a committee to evaluate our roles and how we would handle any situation. And of course, the funny thing about it is, the way we approached it was, if Auburn won then we had it made; all we would have to do was direct traffic. But if they lost, then we'd better get ready. Because all these (Alabama) people were saying, "We're gonna cut down trees at Toomer's Corner" and everything they'll do all over town. So we were a little bit edgy about it.

We had this committee, and we met and figured out what everybody might do, including the Auburn police, and the University Police were still around at that time. And so we tried to evaluate it. The two main people, the police deputy chief and the fire chief, had been involved in this committee, but they both had died. And so we couldn't get any ideas from them. But we did our planning, and we had everybody working that day. Everybody we could get in public safety was working that day.

I will never forget, when the Tiger Walk was starting, we were standing up at the top of the hill. I guess at that time the parking deck had not been built. It was kind of open. So from that walkway down that hill, and across the street all the way to the Coliseum, it was solid *people*. And of course our daughter was a cheerleader. And so she was down there in the (middle of it all in) Tiger Walk.

I remember some of the players saying with the Tiger Walk that, the further they got, the more they worried about being crushed, because the people were closing in on them, and they had to walk single-file. But they made it, and of course as the game turned out, it got better and better for us. We knew our life was going to be better after the game (because Auburn was winning). And things went really well for us after the game, because the Alabama people just bailed out and left. It calmed down pretty quick.

And so we had to start getting ready for the next time they came, (in case they) beat us.

Van Allen Plexico

What kinds of things were you concerned could happen, that you were having to prepare for?

Clyde Prather

We felt like possibly vandalism at various points, and possibly fights, with the jawing back and forth. Those were the main things, other than being able to get people out of town after the game.

John Ringer

Were the Alabama people concerned about the safety of their team and their fans? Did they exaggerate that? Did you have to work with them to reassure them that it was going to be okay when they came?

Clyde Prather

I don't think the Alabama people were concerned a bit. I think they felt like *they* were in charge, and they were going to do what *they* wanted to, and we would take it, and then they would go home. But no, I don't think they had any concerns about what the Auburn people might be planning or any retaliation or anything.

Van Allen Plexico

We've heard that maybe one excuse Alabama was using to not play in Auburn was, "Oh, we're worried about the safety of our fans. If they come down there to Auburn, you know, they might be in danger." (Laughter)

Clyde Prather

Well, yeah, they used that for years, before they were actually coming.

Van Allen Plexico

Mark Murphy told us that Auburn people were very insulted by Alabama people talking about (security in Auburn) that way. And I don't blame them.

John Ringer

Because we're very friendly to visiting fans here. That's part of the way we do things.

Clyde Prather

But Auburn didn't get a lot of respect from the Alabama people. You know, they had been so dominant and they just thought we were the little cow college that they were obligated to beat every year.

We really didn't know what to expect, and the general feeling was that we were going to lose. And so we didn't really know what to expect from the Alabama crowd.

We had the vice-president (Dan Quayle) visit a few years later, and we had people on top of the buildings and all around, but we had some of that for this game too, to just be able to monitor what might happen with groups at different places. (Mostly it was security people) being spread out and monitoring the different areas on the ground. And then the few things we did from the buildings above.

Van Allen Plexico

I mentioned to Mark Murphy that the official attendance for this game has always been listed as a hundred more people than capacity for the stadium. And he said, "Oh, there were probably 150,000 people." Was that your impression, that there were many more people, beyond just those in the stadium?

Clyde Prather
Oh, yeah. You know, at one time it looked like there were probably more people outside than there would be inside. It was unbelievable. You couldn't see anything. It's kind of like on the Today Show you look at those people going two blocks down. They couldn't see a thing. But I guess people just wanted to be there and say "I was there when" whatever happened.

Ken Ringer
It was a pretty exciting game.

Clyde Prather
Yeah, it was, and most folks didn't expect it to be that way.

John Ringer
What were your overall impressions of that day—before, during and after the game?

Clyde Prather
What I remember is being glad to get in the stadium, and be through with everything that was going on outside. Because we knew (once it started) we could sit down and watch the game without a lot of anxiety about the things happening. Which is exactly the way it went. As the game materialized, of course, Alabama fans slid down in their chairs a little bit, and we couldn't believe the way it was going. But the game went so well. And then we felt really good after the game, that we could handle anything that would come up.

Van Allen Plexico
Were you worried that, if they lost, the Alabama fans would get mad and (vandalize or start fights)?

Clyde Prather

No, we thought if they lost, they would just go home. And they did. Yes. But we felt like, based on (phone) calls that were coming in, and all that, that if they won, (some of them) were going to leave their mark. And that's what we were mainly concerned about.

Van Allen Plexico

Was it different from any other fan base coming to visit?

Clyde Prather

Well, we were kind of concerned that they were different; that they disliked Auburn a lot more than some of the other teams (that visit Auburn). And so we were concerned from start to finish about what might happen.

John Ringer

What do you think this game meant to you and to Auburn people?

Clyde Prather

I think it meant a lot. There was just a lot of satisfaction because we had put up with the Bear for so long and (he'd) just beaten our brains out. He'd gotten as many players as he wanted, and set them on the bench, to keep them from coming to Auburn. We just hated the way it was. And so to think we could turn it around and have our day, I think, gave most Auburn fans a lot of satisfaction. Because every year we went to Legion Field, and we said, "I can't believe we're doing this again." We'd go to the Auburn-Alabama game, and we'd be in the upper deck on the back row.

One time we were there and a tornado came through. It was terrible going to Birmingham.

Van Allen Plexico

How did having the game in Auburn compare with what you'd experienced in Birmingham?

186

Clyde Prather

Well, obviously we're partial, but I felt that we were more accepting to them and friendlier and welcoming to them coming to Auburn than you ever got in Birmingham. But in Birmingham, you were like an outcast if you were in the Auburn section. And there was just so much Alabama there. And at least a third of them were rednecks that didn't know where Auburn University or the University of Alabama were. But they were big Alabama fans. It was not a good situation up there. It was always awkward. We were worried about where we parked the car and what we were going to find when we got back to it.

Van Allen Plexico

You had a sense of what the Alabama fans were like in Birmingham. Did you get a sense of the ones that came here for the game in 1989? How would you characterize them? Did it seem like they were more faculty and staff and students? Or did it seem like a bunch of those Birmingham-type fans?

Clyde Prather

Generally, as I remember, I thought it was more the rowdy crowd than professors and alumni, but of course they were both here. It was just that the rowdies stood out and gave you that impression.

But they paid out the nose for their tickets, I remember.

Van Allen Plexico

Was there any other event in Auburn that you had to deal with that was more concerning than the 1989 game?

Clyde Prather

I was named Public Safety Director in 1982, and I don't remember anything, while I was in that position, that came close to this in terms of the Public Safety Department's concern and planning and all. And then we got a little relief before we had to plan for the Vice-President (in 1992).

It went so well that, when Alabama came down again in 1993, we came back with the same plans we had originally:

What are we going to do if Alabama wins? Because that was our main concern. We felt confident that if we won, it would be just like before, and they would load up and leave town. But our concern was always the first time Alabama won, and all the carrying-on they might do.

Van Allen Plexico
I was at the 1999 game when Alabama finally did win in Auburn. Were you still there, and how did things go? Did the Alabama fans cause any problems?

Clyde Prather
I was still there. No, everything we expected (and worried about and planned for) didn't happen. You know, they were good fans. I mean, there were a few little skirmishes and all, but, for the most part, they were happy, they loaded up, they may have gone to J&M (Bookstore) and bought a souvenir or something. But we didn't have any significant problems.

Van Allen Plexico
One of our friends said at the time that he'd heard rumors that Alabama fans were planning to roll Toomer's Corner with red toilet paper if they won. Did you hear anything like that?

Clyde Prather
We heard that a lot of times. They talked about it before the games. But then, when we won, we didn't have to worry about it.

Van Allen Plexico
I remember our friend saying that he and a bunch of other Auburn people went to the Corner (after the 1999 game) to protect the trees. He said it ended up that only one Alabama fan came up toward them with a roll of (regular, not red) toilet paper, ready to throw it, and Jody just took it out of his hand and said, "No!" And the guy turned around and ran off.

Clyde Prather

I'll tell you, you go to Toomer's Corner after the game, and if I was for the opposing team, I wouldn't want to get in the middle of it!

All week in Auburn, the atmosphere was surreal. No one had ever seen such a build-up for a football game before. Even the players took notice.

"Wednesday was almost like game day. So many RVs, jam-packed."
—Ed King, Auburn offensive lineman

Auburn's legendary radio announcer, the late Jim Fyffe, talked about it in his *Touchdown Auburn* book:

"That whole week, from when the RVs started rolling in as early as Tuesday, the tension and adrenalin became almost uncontainable. Of course my big fear was that Alabama would come in and beat the daylights out of us and laugh at us from now until the cows came home. Alabama fans would have liked nothing more. They whined all year about having to play in Auburn, as if it were sacrilegious. They said the Bear was turning over in his grave. Maybe he was. And then Bill Curry with all his junk about wanting Bama fans to come to Auburn, with or without tickets, and circle the stadium and hold hands. I'll never forget the remark of the late Bill Beckwith, who was the Auburn ticket manager at the time. Bill said, 'We don't want that trash down here.'"

John Ringer

I don't have a lot of distinct memories of the week before the game, other than, like most Auburn people, I was ready for kickoff by about Tuesday. I don't believe that was my best week of class during my time as a student at Auburn, as I'm sure my brain was fifty percent focused on the game every movement of every day. (As opposed to regular games when my brain was only twenty-five percent focused on football during the week.)

I remember the RVs all over campus, and I remember the first large group of Alabama fans walking on campus. They were on Thach Avenue and I was stunned to see them.

Van Allen Plexico

That week was just a blur. Trying to focus on classes and work and whatever, but the distractions were everywhere. All I could really think about was the game coming up.

And then I nearly missed it. We'll get to that soon!

"Tickets once cost $18. Now the asking price is upwards of $300, even $500—and maybe throw in a color television, too.

"It's the ticket to Saturday's Alabama-Auburn game, which will be played in Auburn's home stadium for the first time in the history of the cross-state rivalry."
—*AP wire story, Dec. 1, 1989*

Prior to the season, Auburn sold 75,000 season tickets. In the 85,214-seat stadium, this qualified as a season ticket sellout—the first one ever.

"I have never been involved in a game that's as exciting as this one. You can take all the Super Bowls and put them together and they're not as exciting as this."
—*Bill Curry, Alabama coach, AP story, Dec. 1, 1989*

On his radio show the week before the game, Curry said death threats were made against Alabama players and that he planned extra security to guarantee his team's safety. As Jim Fyffe mentioned, Curry also called upon Alabama fans to come to Auburn even if they didn't have game tickets, and surround Jordan-Hare. He felt doing that had helped his team defeat LSU earlier in the season in Baton Rouge.

Bill Beckwith, ticket manager at Auburn, suggested Alabama fans without tickets should stay home and watch the game on TV instead.

"He seems like he's trying to incite a riot," Beckwith said. "We don't need riff-raff surrounding our stadium. What good would it do for Alabama?"

"It's hard to imagine Auburn not wanting people to come and buy gasoline and candy bars and cold drinks. He's calling our fans 'riff-raff'?"
—Alabama sports information director Larry White

While plenty of fans of both teams did come to town despite having no tickets, there were plenty who did. Jordan-Hare Stadium that day was as packed as it has ever been. In fact, it went *over* its officially listed maximum capacity by exactly one hundred attendees!

Van Allen Plexico
From the time we expanded the stadium before the Texas game in 1987 until this Iron Bowl, the top attendance was always listed as 85,214. And then for this game, they listed 85,*314*, which became the record attendance for a football game in the state for many years. I always wondered how they squeezed that extra hundred people in there for the Iron Bowl.

Mark Murphy
I was told there were so many people in the stadium, it was actually over 90,000, but they couldn't say so because of the fire marshal.

"The two weeks leading up to the game were crazy. That's all the media wanted to talk about. We had twice the media we normally had. Everybody wanted an interview. It was on the front page of the newspapers. They were doing specials about it on TV. Everybody was calling you. I was getting fan mail. I was getting letters, personal pleas, 'You've got to do this for me.' It was nuts."
—Rob Shelby, Auburn offensive lineman

"What was remarkable about Coach Dye is that he remembered details about you and would share different stories on Thursday night and Friday night with the team and you would think, 'I didn't know that about Reggie Slack,' or 'I didn't know that about Craig Ogletree.' He wanted you to know that you were playing with a person, not just a jersey. He never wanted you to forget that there was a special person in that jersey."
—Quentin Riggins, Auburn linebacker

David Housel

A guy in North Alabama had written Coach Dye a letter. He was an Auburn guy, telling him about the importance of not forgetting who you are. And he told a story about some American prisoners of war during World War II. That they were beaten, they were starved. They were brutalized by the Germans in the POW camp. And he said, as a show of force to further embarrass them, they made all the Americans march through a wall of German soldiers and German people to ridicule them. He said the American soldiers were down, heads down, and said there was a Black guy, somewhere in the ranks. He said "You should raise your head! Don't you forget who you are. Don't you forget who you are. You're Americans. Don't you forget who you are. Get those shoulders up, get that head up!"

On Thursday nights, Coach Dye would meet with the team. On that Thursday, he read the letter to the players, and he was crying by the time he got through reading it. The whole team was crying by the time he got through. It was probably one of the more emotional moments (of the weekend). And he mentioned it after the game in his postgame press conference.

Van Allen Plexico

Stand by, folks, because this story is about to take a turn.

David Housel

I got home after the game and I had (missed) maybe six or eight phone calls from this guy. He said "Oh, David. Oh, Mr. Housel. Oh, Mr. Housel. Oh, David. Oh, David. Terrible, terrible, horrible." I said, "What?" He said "I made that story up. I'm an abuse counselor, and I use that story to tell alcoholics, 'Don't forget who you are.' And I wrote it to Coach Dye as if it was true. And Coach Dye talked about it."

And Coach Dye, when I let him know, he got mad. He got pissed. I don't know if he ever mentioned it again. I had already run down some information on it, but I didn't know the whole story. I don't know if Coach Dye ever mentioned that again. And the guy is dead now. I met him one time. Nice guy, old guy, down-to-earth guy, loved Auburn and was trying to help. But he stepped in more than he thought he was gonna step in there.

The national betting line for the game was even, with Alabama's perceived slight advantage in scoring counterbalanced by Auburn's defense and home field advantage.

One prediction that leaned the Tide's way, however, was made by a quite literally bird-brained prognosticator: "Ted the Rooster," whose owner, Dick Frymire of Irvington, Kentucky, often had the bird pick the winners of sporting events and elections.

The animal's accuracy was so renowned, he had appeared on the Tonight Show and Late Night with David Letterman.

"So far this year, Ted has an 83 percent accuracy rate," Frymire said.

Ted the Rooster picked Alabama to win by 3 points.

Van Allen Plexico
Clearly, that rooster was no War Eagle. He didn't understand the importance of the First Time Ever.

Although, weirdly enough, he would've been right on the money if the game had ended at halftime.

Maybe he didn't buy into the whole "sixty minutes" thing preached by Coach Dye.

David Housel
Auburn-Alabama has always been a clash of cultures.

Auburn people tailgated and still do. Today it is a commercial gig, it is corporate tailgating. But, (years ago), tailgating was just becoming popular on a mass basis. Auburn people loved to come here and eat cold fried chicken and that

193

kind of thing. Alabama people loved to go to Legion Field in Birmingham and then go eat at the restaurants. Tennessee (complained) that there were not enough restaurants in Auburn; Alabama fans said the same thing. Everything Tennessee said, Alabama said too. But the culture of Alabama, playing in Birmingham, they went to restaurants. Auburn people tailgated. And that was kind of a clash of cultures.

Van Allen Plexico

Alabama fans didn't want to have to stoop to the level of bringing their own food with them and eating outdoors before the game.

David Housel

One of my vivid images of (December 2, 1989 is this). I was driving from the office in the complex to the stadium parking lot by the press box. This Alabama man comes along with a big "Bama" shirt on and the little felt pants with "Roll Tide" on them. You know, a perfectly nice guy. He could have been a preacher, for all I know, or he could have been a devil, for all I know. He was crossing Donahue, and he was just looking around. He was so out of place. And he didn't know where he was. He didn't know where he was going or where to go. And I said, "Man, I love it!" The visual image of him being uncertain.

Van Allen Plexico

You can't go to any Auburn sporting event where there's not at least one person in Alabama gear. It's like they have a rule that they have to send one representative every time we ever play a sporting event. It's weird. But we had never seen a *crowd* of Alabama people in all Alabama gear on this campus ever before—maybe for basketball or something, but never *that* many; not for a football game. And I said back then that it was like Martians had landed. They looked like aliens from some other dimension.

David Housel

It was foreign.

194

On Friday afternoons, if we were playing a conference team or somebody I knew worked with the other team, I would always go over to the stadium when they worked out just to say, "Hello, welcome to Auburn, is there anything we can do for you?" Just doing unto others as you would have others do unto you. You know, that's just the Auburn way.

I remember going in the south end zone gate, going around on the east side and making that turn and then walking out on the field. Seeing those crimson warm-ups, it took my breath away! I thought, "They are really here. They are *really* here." I mean, I knew what was happening, but visually and emotionally it took your breath away. To come around and see them and think, "They're really here. They're really here."

I'll never forget that, and never forget one other thing.

On Saturday I would always go and welcome the opposing coach. Again, just being nice. And they had that bus screw-up. Bill Curry ordered the buses to come off the Interstate onto Wire Road instead of going around where all the law enforcement people were waiting. The state troopers and Montgomery Police and Auburn Police and Lee County Police, everything had been set up so there wouldn't be any problem with them coming through and getting to the stadium.

Well, Curry apparently thought this was a trap or something. So, out of the blue, he ordered the troopers to exit the highway onto Wire Road. And so they came up Wire Road, a little two-lane road. and they got to just before the Coliseum and they couldn't get through! Because then people were just lined up in a mass. That was a big screw up on his part.

Van Allen Plexico

This just drives me crazy. Auburn had everything set up to run smoothly, but good old Alabama paranoia causes Curry to deviate from the plan, and then they get stuck.

And you just know the Alabama people were complaining that it was somehow Auburn's fault—that we hadn't cleared out a path for them to get to the stadium—when they were the ones who intentionally took the wrong road!

David Housel

I like Bill very much. But I don't know what was going on in his mind. Maybe the (buildup for the) game had messed with him. But, at any rate, the team got there finally.

And (before games) I would always say, "Hey Coach, anything we can do for you?" and "Good to have you in Auburn," and the normal greetings. But on that day I was gonna be up there at the gate where they came in. And I did this the whole time I worked in Auburn, but this one, as you might say, was kind of special. I had already talked to the security people at the gate, I did my usual deal, and they (Alabama) came in. I had the padlock in my hand.

Because *I wanted to be the son of a bitch that locked the gate behind them. And I wasn't going to let them out until we kicked their ass.*

For me, it was the symbolism of being the Auburn guy who locked the gate behind them.

Van Allen Plexico

I love this so much. It's like the line in "Watchmen": "I'm not locked in here with *you. You're* locked in here with *me.*"

David Housel

On Friday night (the Auburn players and coaches) had a big pep rally on the baseball field. They had a flatbed truck. Coach Dye got the whole team up there. And there were thousands of Auburn people there. People are jumping around with energy. That whole team was doing that on that flatbed trailer. It's more common now, but that was not something you saw at that time in history.

After the pep rally, the Auburn team boarded buses and headed out of town for some peace and quiet.

"We did something unique... We didn't stay here (in Auburn) the night before the game. We went to La Grange (Georgia).

"The crowd came in early that week. Tuesday, Wednesday. It was unreal. We needed to get away."
—Craig Ogletree, Auburn linebacker

196

"We had to leave town that day. We had to go to a different state. We went to Georgia to stay the night and we came back."
—*John Wiley, Auburn defensive back*

"That's the first time I ever went away from campus the night before a game. We actually went and stayed in LaGrange and came back the next morning. You wouldn't believe all of the people who were in Auburn that day."
—*Corey Barlow, Auburn defensive back*

And so, with the Auburn players all tucked gently in their beds in La Grange, the Auburn fans—and some Alabama fans—asleep (or trying to sleep!) in their camper vehicles on campus and in hotel rooms all over the region, and the campus still fairly buzzing with knowledge of the excitement the dawn would bring, we take our leave of Game Week.

For now it was time for Game *Day*.

-11-

"IT WAS NEAR A FRENZY"

The sun dawned on a cool, clear Saturday. No rain in the forecast. Moderate temperatures all day. December 2, 1989 would be a perfect day for football.

Students arose much earlier than normal, got ready and headed toward the stadium.

Van Allen Plexico

Even with the dreaded "Jefferson Pilot 11 am time slot of death" games, you still could sleep in a little. Seating in the student section was more-or-less general admission, or first-come, first-served, but it's not like you'd be fighting for the best seats to see Louisiana-Monroe or something. For a game starting at 1 pm, normally we wouldn't have left our little rental house until like 10 or 11.

But this day was different.

Not only did we want to get the best seats possible, we also just wanted to be there, at the stadium, around all the other students and fans, soaking it all up for as long as possible. I think about students nowadays camping out in tents outside the Arena before a big basketball game. It was sort of like that. I think if the First Time Ever game happened now, we probably would have camped out at the stadium.

Of course, for a while on Friday, I didn't think I'd be able to go to the game at all.

I've told this story before, but it was such an important part of my experience that weekend, I have to tell it here:

In the fall of 1989, as a senior at Auburn, I lived in a small rental house on Ross Avenue that I shared with two roommates. The day before the game, I drank some juice from a carton in our refrigerator. I should have known better than to eat or drink anything in our house. These guys were great friends at the time, but they had incredibly bad skills at keeping house. They would do things like scrub mud off their shoes in the kitchen sink, using the dishwashing brush, and then put the brush back. I just didn't trust that any food in the house would be safe at all times. I mostly ate out the entire year, because greasy fast food seemed a lot safer than anything kept in that house. But I made the critical mistake of buying that juice and storing it in our fridge.

Apparently one of them had helped himself to some of it, the day before, then left the carton sitting out all day. Eventually one of them put it back in the fridge. Then I got it out and drank it.

Oh man. I got so sick. I mean, *horribly* sick. To the point that I wasn't able to drink that particular variety of juice again for *seventeen years*. Even the smell of it used to make me queasy.

If you've ever had food poisoning, you know it just makes your entire body feel like garbage. Aside from the more obvious symptoms, it's almost like you have the flu. It's hard to move your muscles at all. You just want to lie there and moan, until the next time you have to crawl to the bathroom. It's terrible.

My roommates had no interest in helping me. I asked one of them to please get me a bottle of water from the store nearby, and he refused. They both left. I had to call my girlfriend in Sylacauga and ask her to please come down early. I also told her I wasn't sure I'd even be able to go to the game. You can imagine how sick I must have been, if I was seriously considering missing this game. I made bold statements like, "I'll be there even if I have to carry a barf bag!" But in all honesty, that wasn't going to happen. Either I was going to feel better on Saturday morning or I was going to miss the most important game in Auburn history.

My girlfriend drove down and brought me water to drink and made soup for me, and basically nursed me back to health that evening. The next morning, I was fine. That's the other weird thing about food poisoning: It comes on suddenly, you feel like death, you sleep, and then it just goes away.

My girlfriend and I left the house about 7 am. We met up with some other friends and walked to McDonald's for breakfast, then made it to the stadium's student gates about 7:30, where we rendezvoused with John and his girlfriend and roommates. As early as it was, quite a few other students were already there. Nobody was exactly "in line." We all just sat around on the concrete outside the stadium gates, in little groups, playing cards and chatting. Occasionally someone would start a cheer and we'd all join in, then get back to our card game or whatever. We had hours and hours to wait. But the excitement—the fabled "electricity"—was palpable even that early in the morning. A lot of anticipation, a little bit of dread, and a ton of energy bundled up and waiting to explode.

On the way to the stadium, we passed the little building where one of the fraternities had hung their banner that read, "It won't happen." —Ray Perkins, 1985. "It happened." And their fraternity name.

For a lot of Auburn people, it wasn't just about winning the game and beating Alabama. It was about sticking all those years of lording it over us right back in their faces.

I think Alabama people understood it would be that way, and that was yet another reason they didn't want to come to Auburn.

Speaking of signs, our friends debated making a sign and carrying it into the stadium. Of course, Auburn has never been big on having signs up. They didn't even allow advertising inside the stadium for many years.

Our friend Kristin took a bed sheet and, knowing CBS was airing the game, painted on it:

Can
Bama
Survive?
I don't think it lasted long inside the stadium.

John Ringer
I remember it was a chilly morning. We sat on a blanket outside the student gates and played cards. We were in the first few hundred students there, so we knew if we held our spot we could get our choice of seats. We normally sat in the upper half of the student section, above the walkway, and close to the regular seats—so in section 27 or so. We sat five or six rows up from the walkway so we could see over the people walking back and forth.

At 9:30 on the morning of the game, Auburn officials unveiled a bronze statue of a soaring War Eagle on the concrete front concourse of Beard-Eaves Memorial Coliseum. A plaque on the base read, "Dedicated Dec. 2, 1989, on the occasion of the first Auburn-Alabama game played in Auburn," along with the first four lines of "War Eagle."

John E. Davis, Jr., an architect and former Auburn quarterback, came up with the idea for the statue, designed the base on which it rested, and led the successful effort to raise the $140,000 to have it constructed.

He passed away of a sudden heart attack on Thanksgiving, just days before the game.

"Working on that statue was a labor of love for my father," his son, John Davis III, said. "I'm not sad that he won't be there, because for him stepping back and looking at a finished work was nice, but it was bringing the project to fruition that he really enjoyed."

The statue remained in front of Beard-Eaves Memorial Coliseum for only twenty-two years, until 2011, when the new student activities center was built in the space formerly occupied by the Coliseum concourse. During construction, the statue was removed, but Auburn officials had no idea where it should be moved to, or even what to do with it in the interim. The statue was eventually placed into storage for four years while officials tried to figure out what to do with it. During that time, apparently, no one at Auburn thought to ask the opinion of the family that donated most or all of the money for it. In 2015, it was moved to the top of the scoreboard of Jane B. Moore Field, the softball facility.

In 2016, Everett Duke, a former AU Libraries development officer, spoke with the family. Tom and Jane Fickling told him it had been intended as a gift to Auburn's College of Engineering, but that they'd unanimously agreed that it could be placed at the Coliseum so all students could appreciate and enjoy it, including using it as a meeting place: "Meet me at the War Eagle!" They were unhappy with its treatment in the years since 2011 and with its ultimate placement on the softball scoreboard, and were upset no one ever contacted them about it. They had raised the issue with the University but there had been no follow-up on the part of Auburn.

Van Allen Plexico

I remember seeing the eagle statue there the next week, and assuming it had been unveiled the day of the game. I didn't learn it had been moved until we started working on this book.

They constructed a new building all the way along that street in front of the old Coliseum, and the eagle was just in the way.

We missed the unveiling by being in line at the stadium so early. Of course, the other thing we missed was the thing people still talk about to this day: *Tiger Walk.*

For many Auburn people, one of the most memorable moments of the day would turn out to be the short trip made by the players from their dorms to the stadium.

Tiger Walk, when Auburn's football players and coaches walk from Sewell Hall to the gates of Jordan-Hare, had been happening for some time prior to 1989. It was simply never the phenomenon it has become in more recent years. Many would argue the moment that changed was December 2, 1989.

"Anybody who was on our 1989 team who walked down Tiger Walk that day from Sewell Hall to the stadium will tell you that, by far, that was the best thing about the whole season. The 1989 Alabama game was one we were playing for other players—the

Zeke Smiths of the world, who didn't get a chance to play this game at home against Alabama, guys like Tucker Frederickson and Freddie Smith, all of those outstanding guys."
—Quentin Riggins, Auburn linebacker

"The day of the game, and seeing the crowd for Tiger Walk, and going through Tiger Walk, it was over. The game was over that morning at Tiger Walk. It wouldn't have mattered who we played. If we played the Dallas Cowboys that day, they were going to be in for a run for their money."
—Stacey Danley, Auburn running back

In place of the usual lines of fans on each side of the street, a crowd estimated at some 20,000 was packed in to witness the team make the short journey—and to offer encouragement. It took three times longer than normal to make the walk.

Mark Rose, a senior offensive lineman for Auburn, described the scene from the team's point of view:

"You had people crying, and you could just see it in their eyes—you know, just hugging and shaking their hands. Man, those people just wanted the game here so long, and they were tired of suffering and being treated like second-class citizens."

"There were men and women crying. That could've been me standing there, pleading with somebody for payback. That was a real emotional time."
—Rob Shelby, Auburn offensive lineman

"Walking single file down the line in Tiger Walk. We'd never done that. It was just in the air that night.
"We knew Alabama was No. 2 in the country at that point, but there was no way they could have beaten us that game. No way."
—Corey Barlow, Auburn defensive back

"The fans, the look in their eyes, some people were crying with joy that we had gotten that game there finally, and what it meant to the Auburn people."
—Win Lyle, Auburn kicker

"The Tiger Walk seemed like it took an hour to get from Sewell Hall to the stadium. When we got onto the field it was just awesome."
—John Wiley, Auburn defensive back

"Wednesday was almost like game day. So many RVs, jam-packed. The Tiger Walk, it was like a tunnel. It was so tight. Tiger Walk was so pumped up. It was like a pep rally. I remember Coach Dye telling us, 'Keep it down, keep it down, not yet,' because we were ready. We had to go through warmups and by kickoff, I remember Coach Dye saying, 'It's going to be alright.'"
—Ed King, Auburn offensive lineman

"It was near a frenzy. It was a lifetime experience walking down the street that day. We had to walk in single file and Auburn fans of every nature and every social status—you saw them all. From people that had no money to people who had lots of money, older people and people holding up babies and children everywhere. It was a one-of-a-kind thing. There won't ever be another one like it."
—Pat Dye, to Tom Green, 2019

Patrick Ringer (John's brother)

Tiger Walk that day was very memorable for me. We tailgated in between Sewell Hall and the baseball field all through the Eighties. I was just a kid and the people who tailgated with us and around us felt to me like the originators of Tiger Walk.

As soon as the players would start to come out of their dorms, we would walk up to the side of the road and Buddy Edwards would hand us these homemade, hand-painted signs. For all the games I can remember leading up to that, there was always a ton of space. Room everywhere. Plenty of elbow room, if you will.

On that day, December 2, 1989, I could not believe how many tens of thousands of people there were, where we usually were in our small numbers. It was overwhelming. It also made me realize that maybe I hadn't quite grasped how big this was to some people. I started getting even more excited/nervous about the game.

Two other things stood out to me. One was the paper shakers and the "haze" from them. Every single seat got a shaker. An orange and blue paper shaker. And by the time the game kicked there was absolutely a haze drifting over the field from the 60,000 or however many of them that were being shaken as fervently as one could shake.

The other thing I remember was people talking about ticket prices. Scalpers were getting a thousand dollars per ticket. Or at least that was the word. This seemed insane but also made me realize how lucky I was to be there at that moment. I wanted to explore this idea while we were sitting in our seats in the pregame.

"Dad," I asked, "would you sell your ticket for a thousand dollars?"

"No," he said without thinking.

"Two thousand?"

Same quick response: "No."

"Five thousand?"

He wasn't budging.

"Ten thousand?"

He paused. He was thinking. What was he thinking? This was going to be interesting.

He turned directly towards me. "Pat, for ten thousand dollars I would sell *your* ticket."

John Ringer

Pat was getting ready to go to college (at Auburn) in a couple of years. That ten thousand dollars could have paid his full tuition! And room and board and books!

Patrick Ringer
I was in the same seat for the First Time Ever game (in 1989) as I was for Kick Six (in 2013).

Van Allen Plexico
That is just mind-blowing to me.

In his column in the *Auburn Football Illustrated* program for the 1989 Iron Bowl, David Housel waxes philosophical on the day that was about to dawn.

Interestingly, he attempts to look at the game's move to Auburn from the perspective of *Alabama* fans:

I am man enough to admit that, had I been born an Alabama man, had I been raised on the tradition of Wade, Thomas and Bryant, I would have loathed this day. I would have opposed my team coming here at almost any cost. Had I been born an Alabama man, I too would have probably said, "Never..." because it would not have been in the best interest of my school's football program to come to Auburn.

As an Alabama man I would know that as long as we could dictate to our cross state rivals where they played their home football games, we held the upper hand. We held the higher ground in image if not in fact. The cross state rival could never be equal to us as long as we could dictate the terms on which we played.

And there are Alabama people here today who are man enough or woman enough to admit that had they been born an Auburn man or an Auburn woman, had they been raised in the tradition of Heisman, Meagher, Jordan and Dye, they would have felt exactly as Auburn people did.

As long as our cross state rival could dictate where we had to play our home games, the rival held the upper hand, the high ground. There was no equality.

Today, for the first time, there is equality.

That is what I, as an Alabama man, would have loathed. It is not in Alabama's best interest to have Auburn as an equal. But equality is what I, as an Auburn man, have longed for. I owe it to my school to accept nothing less.

For Alabama, it was a matter of advantage. For Auburn it was a matter of principle. For both, of us, it was a matter of pride.

... We know you didn't want to come and we understand the reasons why. We appreciate your loyalty to your alma mater and your support of its football program. We applaud you for your commitment to Alabama and what is best for its football program. Had we been in your position, we would have felt the same way.

We hope you can put yourselves in our position and appreciate the qualities in us that we appreciate in you.

Perhaps therein we can find the common ground this rivalry so desperately needs.

Forty years from now historians will look back at this day and wonder what all the hoopla was about. Our game site issue—as real and intense as it has been to both of us—will seem as silly to them as the reasons for Auburn and Alabama not playing for 40 years seem to us—a disagreement over whether to have 22 players at a per diem of $3.50 or 20 players at $3.00.

The day we have loathed or longed for has come. It has not only come. It has come to pass.

Van Allen Plexico

I definitely understand what David was saying in that 1989 column. I'm just not entirely sure I would have had the attitude he describes, had I grown up an Alabama fan. But then, it's hard for me to imagine myself as an Alabama fan, and having *any* of the attitudes they tend to have. I'd like to think I would have been better than that; that I would have been fairer towards others—even towards our most bitter rivals.

But I suppose I'll never know. And that's something I'm very grateful for.

Meanwhile, with emotions running so high all around, others were concerned that things should not get out of hand.

"My greatest desire is that all those who go to watch or just to be a part of the hoopla surrounding Alabama's first visit to Jordan-Hare Stadium will keep their heads and not do anything crazy."
—*Phillip Marshall, Montgomery Advertiser, Dec. 1, 1989*

Pat Dye was only one of many who noticed the blue-purple haze already floating above the stadium—a haze that would only grow thicker as the game played out.

It seemed the Spirit Committee—remember the kids that painted the big tiger paw in the middle of the Toomer's Corner intersection?—had held back a portion of the orange and blue paper shakers that were normally distributed in the student section each game. By the time of the Iron Bowl, they'd saved up not the usual 20,000 shakers, but more like 60,000—enough for nearly every Auburn fan in the stadium to have one.

That image of a purple haze stuck with nearly everyone who was there.

David Housel

I remember when the Auburn team came on the field. There was a blue haze over the South endzone. I'm not bragging but I was the first one to write that. And I don't know whether anybody else saw it and just picked up on my observation. But there was a blue haze all over the stadium (from everyone) shaking those shakers.

Van Allen Plexico

It seems to be the one memory everyone shares about that day. (See Appendix 3!) I've always said we probably all got lung cancer from it, but it was worth it.

"I looked around, and my buddies and I said, 'We ain't losing this one today; you can forget that.' We were just going to do whatever it took, because it was a once-in-a-lifetime deal. It was special…. It was just an electric atmosphere and just pure emotion for three hours."
—*Mark Rose, Auburn lineman*

209

Bill Curry was always looking for ways to motivate his players. Sometimes it worked out, and sometimes it didn't.

On the Thursday before the game, Curry played Whitney Houston's "One Moment in Time" for the team, and then presented each of them with a cassette tape copy of it.

A short while later, he had to go and ask them each to give the tapes back. Turned out it was an NCAA violation.

"It didn't seem to work for us," said Alabama center Roger Schultz. "It didn't work for me. I get what he was trying to do. I understand the motivational tactic.

"It was one moment in time all right. And then we lose the game."

Before leaving for Auburn on Friday, Curry took the team through the Paul Bryant Museum for inspiration. Then they all drove down to Montgomery to spend the night. Along the way, Curry was amazed by the number of Alabama fans that turned out to see them go by.

"It was unbelievable. They were incredible. It was one of the most inspiring moments of my life. There were Alabama people all along the way, on almost every bridge. Even on the freeway. They were standing on tops of buildings, on overpasses, all the way to Montgomery.

"I don't know how many thousands there were on the way out of Tuscaloosa. Just thousands and thousands. They lined the road. It was very emotional."
—Bill Curry, Dec. 2, 1989

Arriving in Auburn, the Alabama coaches and players visited the stadium. Curry was as impressed as he'd been during his previous visit, saying, "I was last here in 1986. This is a fantastic stadium. It's beautiful. This is a beautiful place, isn't it?"

After that walk-through, the Tide traveled to Montgomery, where they went out to dinner, then to see a movie.

"I don't know what the movie is tonight. I'm scared to ask. I just go with them, sit there with my daughter and kind of (cover my eyes).

*"What it is is two hours where the whole team is together...
It's offense and defense mingling, laughing and enjoying a movie.
It has been priceless for us."*
—*Bill Curry*

As often proved to be the case with Curry's messaging, it was muddled with regard to Alabama's fears for the safety of its players. Some had reportedly received death threats earlier in the week, and word was that the coach was demanding extra security—if not for fear of violence, at least out of concern that the players might be harassed in their hotel. The day of the game, Curry denied this, saying he knew of no extra security being added for that reason.

"I've never been in a hotel where they didn't do a good job," he said. "I've been in a couple of places where other teams stayed and tried to make noise. Frankly, that didn't bother us much."

Before the game, Quentin Riggins was asked about the animosity between Auburn and Alabama fans, and if it spilled over to the players as well. Not at all, he said:

*"There is a lot of respect between us. There are players here
and there who might dislike each other, but not many. A lot of
our players will go out with their players after the game.*
*"It's gotten to the point where the fans dislike each other so
much it's ridiculous."*
—*Quentin Riggins, Auburn linebacker*

The day before the game, Pat Dye was asked how good Alabama really was. "I don't know," he responded. "Do you? To be ranked number 2 in the nation, you've got to be a great football team. You can't be pretty good. Does that tell you anything?"

*"Their offense puts more pressure on the linebackers. If you
hesitate for one second, they've got you.*
*"I think (Hollingsworth) is a poised quarterback. I know his
arm is not the strongest. I guess that's why he throws the short
passes. He's real poised. He'll sit back there. He's got sort of a
quick release. When the pressure does get there he'll just step up.*

I've seen him do that many times, just step up and make a great throw."
—*Craig Ogletree, Auburn linebacker*

"The strength of this (Auburn) team is that we've been through the deal. We've been in the pressure cookers. We've been ahead and we've been behind, but the thing is, we've always been hungry in the fourth quarter and we've always had a chance to win."
—*Reggie Herring, Auburn linebackers coach*

"Alabama has the most physical front five we've played against. And McCants is in a league by himself. They gamble and attack you in the vulnerable spots. You have to read that gamble at the snap."
—*Neil Callaway, Auburn offensive line coach*

One unnamed Auburn assistant coach was asked about the pressure on Auburn's players before the game. "Pressure?" he responded. "This isn't pressure. We were feeling more pressure at the *beginning* of the season, when everybody expected us to be undefeated and we didn't even know how good we would be. Everybody expected (Alabama) to be 7-4 by now. No, the pressure is on *them* now."

"Homer Smith was Alabama's offensive coordinator and Alabama had an outstanding offensive game plan, an outstanding scheme, in which the tight end and the fullback were the leading receivers. Everything looked the same. We couldn't cheat. We couldn't line up and expect a run out of this formation or a pass out of that formation. We had to beat them straight up. We ran a lot of 52 with cover three behind it and just lined up. We didn't blitz. We just tried to beat them man to man.

"I remember the student section and how we fed off that energy. I remember Alexander Wright making the big early catch on third down and Reggie Slack just putting the football downfield perfectly. I remember the poise that Slack had. He

would always come to the sideline and say, 'Defense, just give us a three and out and we will get it right.' It was just a confidence that he brought to the team.

"I remember watching Shayne Wasden catching a little seam route from Slack. If it wasn't for Keith McCants running him down from the backside he would have scored, but we just started feeling the momentum from that point. Siran Stacy couldn't get going. He was frustrated, yelling at his offensive linemen. We just got after them.

"It was the most intense atmosphere I have ever played in. We could see things in Alabama's first score. We saw it coming, but we were just out of position. We should have made the play. Once we stopped them, we felt like they couldn't move the ball on us. We were just absolutely confident that they couldn't move."

—Quentin Riggins, Auburn linebacker

For those watching on television, as 1 pm central time rolled around at last, the CBS Sports coverage of the Iron Bowl began with a short video feature narrated by Jim Nantz:

"From the cradle to the grave, football borders on religion in the state of Alabama. This timeless phenomenon solidified some seventy years ago. It was during the Depression of 1929 and on into the Thirties when the hopeless Alabama citizens looked with pride towards the great Crimson Tide teams. In this era Wallace Wade and Frank Thomas won four national championships, soothing the desperate times.

"When America rebounded, Alabama football continued to be the toast of the upper crust. The state's doctors, lawyers and bankers sent their children on to Tuscaloosa to be educated. Auburn University was an agricultural and engineering school, attracting the state's middle class. Auburn always felt it was being shunned by the University of Alabama followers, and Auburn knew the one place to gain respect from Tuscaloosa was on the football field.

"For the past forty years, these social wars have been settled on a battleground in Birmingham. These two teams have met on the last weekend of their seasons to settle 364 days of impassioned arguments over who has the better team, and the better way of life.

"When Alabama and Auburn play, the goal is to win. But the fear is of losing, and having to tolerate your arch rival fans and their incessant torture for an entire year.

"People said it would never happen. Today it will happen. Second-ranked Alabama against 11th ranked Auburn—in Auburn, for the first time ever."

—*CBS Sports voiceover, prior to 1989 Iron Bowl*

Then Bo Jackson appeared, with a word of warning for viewers at home:

"You better buckle your seat belt because it's gonna be a show to watch. You'd better tie your TV set down if you're gonna stay at home and watch it, because it may just jump right off the stand."

—*Bo Jackson, CBS intro to the 1989 Iron Bowl*

After that, they cut to game announcer Jim Nantz standing atop Haley Center, with the North End Zone of Jordan-Hare Stadium visible behind him, as he introduced the telecast. He explained for the national audience all the various things that were on the line— none of which held much import for Auburn fans at that moment, beyond simply *winning the game.*

"A full spectrum of football heroes from Bear Bryant to Bo Jackson have been a part of this glorious series, yet many of them never would have believed that this game would one day shift to this site.

"Good afternoon, everybody. I'm Jim Nantz, and welcome to the southern plains of Alabama where, for the first time ever, the Alabama Crimson Tide comes in to challenge the Auburn Tigers. Clearly today the objective for these teams is to win the state

title, but there is certainly much more at stake than just that. In fact, by the end of the day, the Southeastern Conference title will be finalized, as will the conference representative in the Sugar Bowl in New Orleans.

"Now, Alabama can win the conference outright and go on to New Orleans undefeated with a victory today. However, Auburn could spoil those plans, and we could even see a three-way tie by the end of the day if Tennessee can claim victory against Vanderbilt. The national championship picture is also in focus here. The Crimson Tide, ranked second in the country; however, obviously needing a victory today to keep any hopes at all alive of winning the national championship.

"Yesterday, Alabama made its first journey ever from Tuscaloosa to Auburn, and many of their fans tagged along. They went through the towns of Centreville and Maplesville they all came; 160 miles they traveled to a new world.

"Meanwhile, here at Auburn all week, it's been a celebration."
—Jim Nantz of CBS Sports, 1989 Iron Bowl broadcast

Around that time, the Auburn Network went on the air with the Voice of the Auburn Tigers, Jim Fyffe:

"Some said it would never happen. There have been lawsuits, arguments, discussions and fights over moving this game out of Birmingham, where it's been played every year since 1948. And where some said it would always be played.

"How wrong they were.

"Because today history is being made. And the biggest crowd this school has ever hosted is on hand to watch the fifty-fourth edition of football's hottest rivalry.

"The nation's second-ranked team, the Alabama Crimson Tide, brings an undefeated record into Jordan-Hare Stadium, needing a victory over eleventh-ranked Auburn to keep alive its hopes of a national championship.

"The Tigers meanwhile are playing this game for a share of their third straight SEC Championship, and looking to extend their streak of wins over Bama to four straight.

"Hello again everybody and War Eagle! This is Jim Fyffe with Charlie Trotman... Never in the history of this storied series have emotions run as high. Maybe it's because the game is being played on Auburn soil for the first time. Perhaps it's because of Bama's great season. Maybe a combination of both, and other reasons that we haven't even considered. Whatever the case, you can almost see the sparks flying this afternoon in Jordan-Hare Stadium.

"Weather will not be a factor. Weather conditions are nearly perfect for today, a high in the low sixties is predicted; no rain is in the forecast. This one is rated by the oddsmakers as a toss-up. It has all the trappings of a classic matchup today."

—Jim Fyffe, radio broadcast

Not everyone was thrilled with the game being played in Auburn, however. And having a rational argument to make wasn't necessarily a requirement.

"The reason I'm opposed to (playing Auburn in Auburn) is they didn't have any money when we started playing them. They were almost bankrupt. We made 'em. Now they got a little money in their pockets and they want to run us around. It kind of irks me. I'm not going down there. This will be the first Alabama-Auburn game I've missed."

—Grafton Hocutt, Alabama fan who had attended Tide practices for 63 years

Van Allen Plexico
If you've read this far, you know that pretty much everything that guy said is false.

Shocking, yes, I know.

Some Alabama fans that didn't object outright to the game being played in Auburn took refuge in the idea that it was all really no big deal, or that the crowd wouldn't have any effect on the game.

"I don't believe it will be any different from playing at Tennessee and LSU."
—*Alabama executive athletic director Jim Goosetree*

"Realistically, you know the crowd is there. Once you focus on the game, that takes the crowd out of it. I don't see this stadium being any different from some of the others we've played in."
—*Willie Wyatt, Alabama defensive lineman*

Others saw things in a different light:

"It's a dream come true."
—*Evelyn Jordan, widow of Ralph "Shug" Jordan*

Reynolds Wolf, friend of the AU Wishbone and meteorologist for the Weather Channel, as quoted in our *We Believed* book, said this about the time just before kickoff:

"Alabama, coming onto the field, came through—if memory serves—the south end zone, and they split in two and they paraded around the sidelines in this weird formation, as though they were giving the middle finger to the Auburn people. They came up each sideline and it was like they thought they owned the place."

Van Allen Plexico
The Alabama players did do that. And it was indeed strange—and a very "Bill Curry" thing for them to do. Maybe he thought it would intimidate the Auburn fans or players, or fire up the Alabama fans.

If so, you can be the judge of how well it worked.

And with that, and as we switch verb-tenses for the duration of four quarters of description and discussion, the game begins.

- 12 -

THE FIRST QUARTER: "A FUNNY THING HAPPENED ON THE WAY TO THE FARM"

Jim Nantz and Pat Haden are the CBS commentators. John Dockery is the sideline reporter.

Auburn wins the toss and, in an unusual move for the defensive-minded Coach Dye, elects to receive.

Phillip Doyle kicks off to Alexander Wright, who returns the ball to the Auburn 32 before being hammered down.

Auburn's starting lineup on offense: Reggie Slack at quarterback, Alex Strong at fullback and Stacey Danley at running back. The receivers are Alexander Wright and Greg Taylor.

The Tigers begin in the I-formation that they will stick to for most of the game.

Slack rolls to his right and passes to Taylor for 12 yards and an initial first down.

Alabama's defense features star lineman Willie Wyatt at nose tackle, in between George Thornton and Thomas Rayam.

Behind them, John Sullins and Keith McCants— "the great one," says Jim Nantz—are at linebacker, along with Steve Webb and Spencer Hammond.

John Ringer

Keith McCants was the latest in a long line of Terminator-level linebackers that Alabama rolled off the assembly line. Cornelius Bennett. Derrick Thomas. And now McCants. He was huge, he was fast, and he was a real problem for Auburn.

On the second play of the game, with Alex Strong in as the single back, to block for Slack, Auburn's quarterback passes to Wright for 6 yards. Two plays in, and the Tigers are already at midfield.

Van Allen Plexico

The "mic man" cheerleader can be heard starting a *"Reggie Reggie Reggie"* chant. There had been some negative talk about Slack earlier in the season, and the Tigers made a real effort to show support for him and encourage the crowd to do likewise.

I think he was a very underrated player and deserves a loftier spot in the ranks of our former players than he probably occupies with most people.

John Ringer

You will recall that Auburn went "back to basics" in the second half of the season and got tougher at running the ball. So I am sure everyone in the state thought Auburn was going to come out and establish the run. But Auburn's offensive game plan fooled everyone. We knew we needed Reggie Slack to have a good day for us to win, so they opened the game up by letting him throw the ball. It was very different the first few series from what anyone had seen from Auburn so far that season, but it worked and had Alabama on their heels.

Auburn's offensive line is anchored by John Hudson at center, along with the great guard Ed King and Brad Johnson. The tackles are Anthony Brown and Rob Selby, who has been battling injuries this season. The tight end is Victor Hall.

Van Allen Plexico

John Hudson was in one of my classes when I taught at Auburn. As befits a center, he sat at the front and center of the classroom. He was a very cool guy and I enjoyed talking football with him here and there. He was either with the Eagles still or had just finished his NFL career and was back in school.

On second down, Stacy Danley runs up the middle for 1 yard. He's stopped by Willie Wyatt. "Bill Curry says you can make a case for Wyatt being our MVP this year," says Jim Nantz.

On third and 5, Auburn goes to a split backfield with everyone blocking as Slack lets it go deep.

Jim Fyffe, on the Auburn Network broadcast:

"Reggie Slack needing five yards on third down, is gonna throw long to Alexander Wright—oh, a great catch over the shoulder, inside the ten, down to the seven yard line, as he beat Efrum Thomas who made the tackle down at the seven. Reggie Slack threw a beautiful pass and Wright took it over his left shoulder as he raced down that eastern sideline."

Auburn Network Color analyst Charlie Trotman:

"Reggie Slack... saw that Alabama was playing man-to-man in the secondary. They were in a blitz situation; they had Keith McCants coming toward the quarterback. Auburn's offensive line needs the credit. Great pass by Reggie, great catch by Alexander, but the pass protection was there that allowed Reggie to get the ball off."

Reynolds Wolf

They had this great quarterback, Hollingsworth, who seemed to do no wrong, and Bill Curry had these guys firing on all cylinders—but there was something about that day. You could feel it just wasn't going to be their day. Especially after Reggie Slack stepped up to drop a laser beam down the sidelines, hitting Alexander Wright, and I can still see Wright running to this day. And just the eruption! The party started then and never ended.

"Receivers coach Larry Blakeney said (Auburn was) going to throw the ball six times deep to Alexander Wright," says Pat Haden, the CBS color commentator.

The Alabama cornerbacks are John Mangum and Efrum Thomas. Safeties are Lee Ozmint and Charles Gardner.

Nantz helpfully points out, "Bill Curry is looking for his first win over Auburn."

After an incomplete pass, Auburn drives to the 1 on a strong run by Danley.

Haden tells us: "Stacy Danley says of himself that 'I'm a power runner. I don't dip and dodge much. But you give me a little crease and I'll find it.'"

On third and goal, Auburn lines up in what Dye called the "full house backfield," with no receivers out wide. Three backs are lined up horizontally behind the QB, like something out of the Notre Dame playbook circa 1932, with Danley to the right and Joseph in the center. A third back—either Alex Strong or Darrell 'Lectron' Williams, about whom more later—is on the left. Three powerful weapons stand behind Slack, and the Alabama defense has to decide very quickly which one to focus their attention on the most.

They choose poorly.

Slack gives the ball to James Joseph, who dives in for the touchdown.

The crowd goes berserk. The CBS camera mounted on the end zone stands is bouncing up and down in stomach-churning fashion as Win Lyle kicks the extra point.

Sideline reporter John Dockery notes that, the previous week, Notre Dame had been bothered by the crowd in the Orange Bowl stadium against Miami. He says Alabama had hoped to avoid that same thing happening to them by striking early to take the crowd out of it. "That hasn't happened here." Clearly Dye was wise to change up his usual methods and receive the kickoff instead of deferring to the second half.

Auburn 7, Alabama 0

Jim Von Wyl kicks off for Auburn. It's returned for only a short distance by Pierre Goode.

Alabama's offense takes the field for the first time ever in Jordan-Hare. They are led by redshirt junior quarterback Gary Hollingsworth, a tall, lanky quarterback from Hamilton, Alabama.

Assistant Coach Rocky Felker recruited three quarterbacks for Ray Perkins and Alabama in 1986. Big things were expected of two of them: Jeff Dunn and Billy Ray. The third one was Gary Hollingsworth, an afterthought. Sometimes things don't work out the way they're expected to.

"While the date of Dec. 2 has been circled gleefully in red by Auburn fans, most Alabama followers cringed at the thought of journeying to Jordan-Hare Stadium.

"Some people feared Dec. 2 would hold the same meaning as Dec. 7: a day of infamy.

"But a funny thing happened on the way to the farm: the fortunes of the two football teams changed dramatically.

"When quarterback Jeff Dunn went down against Kentucky, Alabama fans wondered if the team could recover. But under Gary Hollingsworth, the Tide not only recovered, but flourished to an undefeated season and No. 2 national ranking."

—Paul Finebaum, Dec. 1, 1989

"The conventional wisdom was, you lose Jeff Dunn and you won't win a game. We didn't know the gold mine we had in Hollingsworth. He had decided he was going to give up football and play baseball. But I got him in the office, locked the door and said, 'You ain't quitting.' ... He changed his mind, thankfully, and stayed out there."

—Bill Curry, Alabama coach, on quarterback Gary Hollingsworth

Van Allen Plexico

Hollingsworth had an All-SEC season in 1989, and then played one more season under new head coach Gene Stallings, in a completely different offense.

In 2018 he was diagnosed with throat cancer and received treatment. Two years later, he was cancer free.

"(Hollingsworth) uses a lot of receivers and that makes it tough. And their line and backs do a good job of giving him time. We've got to have pressure on him, or he'll find an open man and hit him.

"I think in a hyped game like this, we can put pressure on him and make him do things he doesn't want to do."
—Corey Barlow, Auburn cornerback

"That's just the way they (Auburn's defense) play. They line up and say, 'Here we are.' Hopefully with the number of things we do, we'll be able to keep them off balance, and they can't just sit there and dominate us.

"I think it would be stupid to change (the offense) right now... We have been doing the same things all year long and we're 10-0.

"We know it's going to be a war. They get a lot of pressure on the quarterback and they have good coverage in the secondary, which makes it tough. We're going to try to do the things we've been doing all year and see how it works.

"They have a good defense. That's no secret. I know at times they're going to stop us. That's just the way football is. But we can't get discouraged by that. We just have to keep plugging."
—Gary Hollingsworth, Alabama quarterback, Dec. 1, 1989

Behind Hollingsworth at quarterback, Alabama starts Kevin Turner and Siran Stacy at running back. Marco Battle, the team captain, and Craig Sanderson are the starting wide receivers.

Alabama's offense uses a great deal of pre-snap motion in this game, as they have all season. The objective is to confuse the defense and cause them to either misread the play or at least be delayed in getting to the ball carrier.

Stacy runs for a short gain on first down. On the next play, Hollingsworth hits tight end Lamonde Russell for 15 yards and a first down.

Richard Shea is Auburn's starting nose tackle, with Lamar Rogers and Fernando Horn on either side of him. Linebackers are Darrel Crawford and Quentin Riggins inside, Craig Ogletree and Eltin Billingslea outside.

Kevin Turner runs up the middle for 3. On second down, Auburn's David Rocker—brother of the famous Tracy Rocker—has rotated in, showing just how much substitution the Tigers plan to do today. (A lot.) Rocker pressures Hollingsworth into an incomplete pass.

Alabama has started their dependable workhorse, Roger Shultz, at center. Chris Robinette and Trent Patterson are the guards. Vince Strickland and Terrill Chatman start at tackle. Lamonde Russell is the tight end, and comes in as the top receiver on the team.

Hollingsworth lines up in the shotgun on third down. The extra distance back from the line of scrimmage doesn't help him here. He is sacked by backup lineman Mike Campbell. Auburn is rotating a lot of linemen already.

Alabama's Bill Smith punts the ball away. Shayne Wasden makes the fair catch at the Auburn 24.

Commentator Pat Haden says Bill Curry told his offense after that first series, "Hey, guys, we can move the ball but we have to stop stopping ourselves. We have to quit making mistakes and letting this crowd affect us."

Good luck with that, Coach.

Teapot Brown comes in at fullback for Auburn. He will play a little bit in this game, but the bulk of snaps involving a fullback for Auburn will feature either Mark Strong or James Joseph lining up in that spot.

Stacy Danley at running back plows up the middle for 5 yards. The hitting by both defenses so far is vicious. Neither wants the other team's offense to impose its will. Neither wants to be seen as backing down.

"Jim, I really believe this is going to be a fifteen-round fight," Haden says, "and the first round clearly goes to Auburn. They've done just about everything they had to do, running and passing." He notes that Auburn tight end Victor Hall does a good job of blocking

Keith McCants and keeping him away from the play so that Danley can gain yardage.

On second down, Joseph lines up at the single back but only serves as an extra blocker for Slack, who rolls left to pass. His intended target, Greg Taylor, is well covered, so he throws the ball deep out of bounds.

Slack gives the ball to freshman Darrell "Lectron" Williams on a draw, and he promptly fumbles. Alabama recovers. Alabama's nose tackle, Willie Wyatt, makes the play, charging up the middle. He is already becoming a force to be reckoned with, and will have a lot to say about the outcome of this contest.

Alabama takes over on the Auburn 21-yard line. They do a lot more pre-snap motion from the I-formation. Siran Stacy gets the ball and cuts back to his right, taking it down to the Auburn 4. But then he loses 2 yards on the next play, thanks in part to the efforts of free safety John Wiley, who has a great game this day. With four Auburn defenders blanketing the tight end, Russell, Hollingsworth has to throw the second down ball out of bounds.

During that play, David Rocker's right knee is injured. He retreats to the sideline to have it wrapped up, but eventually he has to give up on playing any more this day. Instead, we see him sitting silently on the bench. His disappointment is obvious and overwhelming, and who could blame him?

On third and goal at the Auburn 6, Alabama lines up in the I-formation. Hollingsworth executes the play-action fake, rolls to his right and throws, but misses his receiver, Marco Battle.

Now facing fourth down, Curry plays it safe and sends out Phillip Doyle to kick a short field goal. (It is his 21st of 23 attempts on the season, setting an Alabama record.)

Auburn has dodged a bullet after the turnover at their own end of the field.

Auburn 7, Alabama 3

Meanwhile, Alabama fans are going crazy in the crowd. You can tell they feel the intensity of this day just like Auburn fans do. To pull off the win would be huge for their program. Despite being undefeated and ranked second, while Auburn isn't even in the top 10, the game was rated even by the Las Vegas bookmakers. They

225

understood just what an advantage Auburn would have in the stadium today. Alabama wanted nothing more than to ruin the party.

Jim Nantz explains that if Auburn wins and Tennessee beats Vanderbilt, there will be a three-way tie for the SEC title, and conference officials (17 of them!) will have a conference call to decide who goes to the Sugar Bowl.

It could very well come down to who gets the most "style points," regardless of the winner.

Alabama kicks off. Alexander Wright brings it out to the Auburn 29.

CBS shows us a snippet of an interview with Bill Curry recorded earlier.

> *"I can be walking across a shopping center parking lot in July, and I can have an eighty-year-old matriarch walk up and say, 'Coach, I would just like to hug you—I'm an Alabama fan,' and of course I say, 'Fine, that's wonderful, I appreciate it.' And then she whispers in my ear, 'Beat Auburn. You've just got to beat Auburn.'"*

On first down, Slack hits Joseph for 14 yards, whereupon he's corralled by Keith McCants. This won't be the last time Alabama's star linebacker is heard from.

Haden points out how the Auburn team was struggling earlier in the season to find a leader, and Joseph was one who has emerged in that role, lending the team his tough, physical personality.

Next Slack throws to Shayne Wasden on a crossing route for 18 yards. Wasden goes out of bounds at the Alabama 40. Joseph stayed in as the single back in the formation, helping protect the quarterback. Auburn is leaning on the passing game a lot here.

Van Allen Plexico

All this passing seems very uncharacteristic of a Pat Dye team. But Dye knew what he had in this team—Slack's arm and some good receivers—and what he *didn't* have. What he lacked was that dominant power rushing game he'd had in years past. He would occasionally try to force Stacy Danley and James Joseph into that role, and they absolutely did the best they could. But he knew he also had to open up the passing game for this team to be successful on offense.

Haden notes that Auburn is throwing almost every pass to the *outside* now, because the Alabama corners are taking the inside away.

On first down, Danley slips and falls for no gain.

Haden points out that Reggie Slack is not as impressive on film when you first watch him, but the more you watch, the more scared of him you get.

On second and 10, Slack audibles to maximum protection and fires a pass toward Wright that goes over his head. The following play, with four receivers in, Joseph bobbles and drops a short pass. The drive has stalled and Auburn has to punt for the first time. Richie Nell boots the ball down the field, where it's collected by Alabama's Gene Jelks, who makes very little on the return.

Van Allen Plexico

Gene Jelks is an interesting story that I want to pause here to address.

In 1985 he exploded onto the scene and into Iron Bowl history by outrushing senior (and Heisman Trophy winner-to-be) Bo Jackson, helping carry Alabama to a 25-23 win. In 1989 he was still on the team, but his role seemed much diminished. And somewhere in there, he contributed to getting Alabama put on probation. It's quite a story.

He played two years at running back for Ray Perkins, and seemed like a natural at that position. When Bill Curry's staff took over, however, they felt he was not big enough to make it in the NFL as a running back, and moved him to defensive back. He would go on to play three more years at that position, while also returning punts. (Presumably he took a medical redshirt after a knee injury early in the 1988 season, because he has stats for all five years.) As William Thornton of AL dot com put it, "For a generation of Alabama fans who came of age after Bear Bryant but before Nick Saban, Gene Jelks' life summed up much of that era— a flash of speed that hints at greater things, just before a harsh reality and a bitter finish."

227

Saying his "heart just wasn't in it," Jelks finished out his career at Alabama at defensive back. After a failed attempt at pro football, he came out to the media with claims that Alabama had offered him a car and cash payments during his recruitment. The subsequent investigation revealed more trouble surrounding star Alabama player Antonio Langham, and suddenly Alabama found itself on probation.

After that, many Alabama fans felt about Jelks similar to how many Auburn fans feel about Eric Ramsey.

This *First Time Ever* Iron Bowl was his next-to-last game for Alabama. Jelks spiraled down into alcohol and drugs, and ended up homeless on the streets of Atlanta, before slowly making his way back toward redemption and respectability about a decade ago, founding a youth ministry and hosting football camps.

Jim Nantz points out that this is the fifty-fourth meeting between Auburn and Alabama. Forty-seven of those games were played in Birmingham, four in Montgomery, two in Tuscaloosa and now one in Auburn. (We have endeavored in this book to make it clear why the games were played in those locations!)

Alabama turns to the run game and their star back, Siran Stacy, to start this drive. He manages 2 yards on a handoff, then 6 more on a draw, up to the Alabama 20.

To this point, Auburn has outgained Alabama, 96 yards to 35 yards. A lot of that, of course, came on the big pass to Wright.

Stacy takes the pitch on third down and converts, reaching the 26—but he loses the football. Auburn linebacker Eltin Billingslea comes up with it, but the referees rule Stacy was down. Haden says it should have been called a fumble, and when they replay it, he is shown to be correct. Stacy clearly lost the ball well before he was down.

Van Allen Plexico

Siran Stacy fumbled and Auburn recovered it in Alabama's red zone. The refs gave it back to Bama. File that away for later.

Alabama continues to lean on Stacy. Hollingsworth tosses a short pass to him on first down. Then Alabama calls timeout.

During the break, we are shown a prerecorded video of Alabama DB John Mangum saying, "When you're 0-3 against Auburn, it means everything. It's our last shot at redemption, I guess you'd say. And going down there makes it all the more special."

Haden notes: "We talked to the Alabama players, and they say, 'We think about Auburn 365 days a year, and if there were more days, we'd think about them more.'"

Van Allen Plexico

And file that last little statement away for the next time an Alabama fan tries to tell you Auburn *doesn't* live rent-free in their heads!

After a short gain on second down, backup running back Derrick Owens-Lassic, who will be a featured player in the future for the Tide, dives up the middle, and is hit hard by Ogletree and Riggins. He makes the first down by millimeters.

Nantz notes that Auburn continues to shuffle through defensive linemen. This was something Pat Dye's defenses were always known for: using a lot of linemen to keep them fresh for the fourth quarter. Sixty minutes indeed.

Hollingsworth throws incomplete to the left side on first down.

CBS points out the yards per pass attempt so far: Alabama 3.6, Auburn 10.1. Hollingsworth has passed for 18 yards in total.

After a short gain on second down, Hollingsworth from the shotgun hits the tight end, Russell, on a deep ball down to the Auburn 34. Now the Tide is in business.

Another short run, followed by another long pass to Russell. Auburn's defense is penalized for a late hit afterward. That puts the ball inside the Auburn 5-yard line.

On first and goal, Alabama uses pre-snap motion to flex to the I-formation. Siran Stacy loses 2 yards running left.

A second down pass intended for Prince Wembley is broken up by safety John Wiley. Pat Dye meanwhile is screaming at the refs that Alabama's offensive line is holding. That's not a recent phenomenon.

On third and goal, Hollingsworth overthrows Russell in the end zone. Meanwhile Marco Battle is wide open in the middle of the field. File that away for later, as well.

On fourth and goal at the Auburn 5, Bill Curry decides to get cute. The Tide players line up for a short field goal, but the holder jumps up and throws the ball into the end zone. Auburn breaks it up.

John Ringer

The big thing that happened in this series after the "fumble" was that David Rocker, who had been injured and removed from the game, tried to come back in but was ineffective. He was one of Auburn's better defensive linemen so this was big.

"It was a stupid call by the head coach. Actually, it would have been a good call had we executed it. We just didn't execute in the moment. And that was the fake field goal. It was my call. We had studied and studied and studied it. We expected it to be a walk-in, but one of our guys didn't execute it. So, there you are."
—Bill Curry

Van Allen Plexico

It's totally like Curry to place the blame fully on his players for not executing, rather than on himself, for gambling when he didn't have to, and not just making the first down.

One Eric Ramsey is name-checked as among the defensive backs who contributed here. To this day, it's hard to hear that name called and not feel weird about it. Who in 1989 could've imagined that, three years later, Ramsey would have essentially brought down the entire Dye regime and left us with probation, two years of no post-season play, and one year of no television? And all because he told Dye his child was hungry. And because his wife apparently thought they could make a buck off of it. It's all so depressing.

On first down, and having to be very careful because they're starting out on their own 5-yard line, Auburn sends Stacy Danley up the middle for no gain.

On the sideline, reporter John Dockery shows off the special Iron Bowl ticket and a t-shirt with the ticket image on it.

Van Allen Plexico

Students didn't get the commemorative ticket. I've never owned one. We just had our one little yellow pass for the entire season, and the ticket-takers at the gate to the student section would punch holes in it for each game. I shouldn't complain, though, because it was a *season* ticket, and it only cost me four dollars per game, including the Iron Bowl!

I still can't believe I paid *four dollars* to get into the First Time Ever game. Some people paid *thousands*.

The clock expires on the first quarter. Auburn leads Alabama, 7-3, and has stopped what looked to be a strong drive by the Crimson Tide. But the Tigers are now deep in their own territory, at their 5-yard line. Meanwhile, what started out as almost a shootout has turned into a defensive struggle. Both teams have enjoyed big plays and both have made mistakes.

There's a lot of football left to be played, and Auburn is starting out the second quarter deep in the hole.

- 13 -

THE SECOND QUARTER: "IT STARTED WITH A DREAM"

"I have never seen so many people so passionate about a single game. We cover a lot of games, a lot of rivalries, but I have never seen so many people passionate about it."
—*Pat Haden, CBS commentary*

As the second quarter begins, Auburn faces second and 10 from their own 5-yard line.

As Stacy Danley runs for 4 up the middle, Pat Haden notes that Auburn used three different players to try to block Keith McCants. The star Alabama linebacker is causing problems for Auburn's run game.

On third and 6 from the 9, Slack rolls right and passes to James Joseph for 8 yards and a first down.

Now at the 17, Slack hands the ball to Joseph, who runs for five more, to the 22. On the next play, however, Auburn's offensive line moves before the snap, and has to give up the 5 yards they just gained. Replaying the down, Slack drops back and throws for Dale Overton, but the pass falls incomplete.

Haden points out that the crowd noise forced Slack to use hand signals for an audible there. "This is a very loud Jordan-Hare Stadium."

Auburn calls timeout, then huddles up as they face third and 10 from their own 17. The Auburn brain trust has clearly decided it's time to try Alexander Wright deep again. Slack's deep ball is almost intercepted, though, and then goes through Wright's hands and to the ground.

Richie Nell is summoned again, and punts to midfield.

Now Auburn turns to the defense to step up. Ricky Sutton, yet another lineman rotating in, does the job. He drops Hollingsworth for a massive sack and a loss of 5 yards.

Alabama comes out in a split backfield but then motions into the I-formation, as they've done quite a bit so far, and will continue to do. From that formation, Siran Stacy runs up the middle for a negligible gain.

On third and 12 from Alabama's 48, Hollingsworth stands deep in the shotgun, but it affords him little in the way of pass protection. Linebacker Craig Ogletree, unblocked, charges at Hollingsworth and wrestles him down.

Alabama punts the ball to Shayne Wasden, who catches it at the 18 and runs to the 24. Now the Tigers have better starting field position than they'd had previously.

CBS shows a clip of Pat Dye talking about the game today:

"This is the last brick in our building. It started with a dream fifty years ago. Our stadium is fifty years old this year. Jeff Beard and Coach Jordan through the years, that dream was to give Auburn the kind of home schedule that we've got now. The history of that to me is more significant than looking back twenty-five years from now and who won or lost this football game."

Van Allen Plexico

I understand what Coach Dye is saying there. In terms of continuing to play the Iron Bowl every other year in Auburn after this, I agree—that matters more than who won or lost the first one.

But when it comes to this particular game—the first game against Alabama ever played in Auburn—I think it did matter who won. I think it mattered a great deal.

We'll talk more about that later.

Danley runs up the middle for 3 on first down. On second down, Keith McCants blasts his way through Danley, who makes a vain attempt at blocking him, and crushes Reggie Slack for a huge sack. But there is a flag on the play! It's a facemask on McCants, who clearly grabbed the quarterback's mask in his huge mitt. It's called "inadvertent" and results in just a 5-yard penalty on Alabama.

Now only second and 2, Danley dives into the middle of the formation for 3 yards and a first down. He has 8 carries for 22 very tough yards so far.

On first down, Slack calls another timeout. Haden notes that it's unusual for a team to call timeout on first down, especially just as they're gaining momentum.

We learn during this little break that Dye has suggested to Pat Sullivan, the passing game coordinator, to maybe use two tight ends to block McCants, and also to use fullback Alex Strong more in that way, as well.

CBS takes the opportunity to point out that Georgia first came to Auburn in 1960; Georgia Tech followed in 1970; Tennessee came to the Plains in 1974; and Alabama in 1989. The headline of the graphic they display reads, "WE'LL NEVER GO TO AUBURN."

Van Allen Plexico
(The point is, they all did.)

Coming out of the timeout, Auburn goes to a hurry-up offense, presumably to try to shake things up and also to keep Alabama from substituting on defense.

Danley manages only short gains on back-to-back runs. Facing third down and 4, Danley runs it up the middle one more time, and the officials' measurement shows he made the first down—barely.

To start the next set of downs, Auburn puts Danley at single back, adds a second tight end, and has Slack fake a handoff before rolling to his right. He narrowly avoids being sacked and scrambles for nine yards.

Disaster strikes on the next play.

It's second and 1. Time to try something daring. Slack throws the ball downfield, but it is deflected by Spencer Hammond and falls right into the waiting arms of one Keith McCants.

Alabama takes over possession on their own 37, after the second turnover by Auburn.

Van Allen Plexico

We'd thought after the first quarter that it might come down to which team made the fewest mistakes and which team made the most. At this point, it looked like Auburn was definitely making the most.

John Ringer

Turnover, turnovers, turnovers. This was the only thing keeping Alabama in the game. Auburn was shooting itself in the foot and handing the ball back to Alabama. We were not capitalizing on our chances and that was worrying.

John Wiley steps up from safety and stops Siran Stacy on first down, allowing him only a yard. On second down, the pass is almost intercepted by Auburn's Frankie Stankunas, but Stacy somehow manages to grab it and gain 9 yards.

At this point, CBS shows us Auburn lineman David Rocker on the sideline, looking sad. John Dockery tells us he spoke to him and they taped up his ankles and he tried to go back out there but he just couldn't. It's the biggest game of his career and he has to sit and watch it. He's obviously very sad and dejected and it's no surprise whatsoever.

Hollingsworth meanwhile dives over center for the first down.

Now Alabama tries to get cute, but it blows up in their faces, too. They give to the tight end, Russell, on the end-around, but he's brought down 4 yards behind the line of scrimmage by Billingslea.

CBS informs us that Tennessee has come from behind to beat Vanderbilt. Thanks to their win over Auburn in the "Blame it on the Rain" game, the Vols now have earned a share of the SEC title—*if* Auburn wins.

The Tigers have just gained many thousands of passionate supporters in the area of Knoxville.

Kevin Turner, the fullback, catches a 10-yard pass on 2nd and 14. Then Hollingsworth runs a bootleg and keeps it for a nice gain and the first down. Alabama is now set up on Auburn's 36.

An illegal shift penalty backs them up to the 41, and then Fernando Horn nearly sacks Hollingsworth, whose frantic pass falls incomplete.

CBS tells us Auburn has the second-stingiest defense in the country, behind only Miami. Auburn this season averages giving up 10 points per game. Miami gives up 9; USC 11; Penn State 12.

The total yards in the second quarter so far: Auburn 43, Alabama 19. But mistakes have held Auburn back.

Siran Stacy fumbles on his next run, but Alabama recovers.

John Ringer
Auburn was robbed here. We should have been awarded the ball after this fumble by Stacy.

They make the first down on the following play when a pressured Hollingsworth finds Derrick Owens-Lassic and gets it to the Auburn 23. Alabama keeps him in and runs him up the middle for 3 more, to the 20, and then again for another short gain.

Now it's third and 5, and Alabama at last cashes it in. Hollingsworth finds Marco Battle open in the middle—remember, he'd missed the same receiver, also wide open, in the first quarter—and Battle weaves his way through traffic for the touchdown.

The extra point is good. Alabama leads for the first time.

Auburn 7, Alabama 10

That was only the second touchdown against the Auburn defense via the pass all season.

Haden agrees with us that Battle had been open the first time they ran that play, in the first quarter, and they came back to it here.

Sideline reporter Dockery questions the legality of the pick route Battle used.

Alabama kicks off; Auburn's kick returners run into each other and drop the ball at the 12 yard line. They're lucky to recover it quickly but gain nothing from the return. Suddenly it feels like the game is sliding Alabama's way.

On first down, Slack throws a wide screen to Alexander Wright, but he can't get away from Keith McCants, who tackles him for a loss. The game is definitely sliding Alabama's way.

The great offensive lineman, Ed King, steps up on the next play and opens a hole for Danley, who carries the ball up the middle to the 24 yard line for a first down.

Slack then attempts his third bomb to Wright, but the pass is just a bit too long.

Danley is tackled behind the line of scrimmage on second down. Willie Wyatt leads the charge that brings him down.

Now it's Alabama's turn to call timeout, with just 24 seconds left in the half. They want to stop Auburn on third down and get the ball back.

James Joseph runs left for 3 yards, and Alabama calls another timeout. There are 13 seconds left until halftime.

Pat Haden points out that both defenses have played well in the second quarter.

On fourth down, Richie Nell punts the ball deep. Gene Jelks catches it at the Alabama 38, with no return.

Hollingsworth executes a shovel pass to Siran Stacy, who makes it to the 41, but at that point the clock expires and the half is over.

Auburn scored on their first possession, thanks mainly to the long pass to Wright, but have done very little on offense since then. The defense has kept Alabama mostly in check, but the Tide lead the game, 10-7.

Pat Dye, depending as always on Auburn's depth and conditioning, tells Dockery, "We're gonna come back and try to run basically what (we've been) doing. Hopefully we can go into the fourth quarter with the game as close as it is now, and then we'll have a chance."

"When we got in the locker room at halftime, we made some little adjustments. The coaches said, 'When you see this formation, they are going to run the little pick plays. Just pass it to the next guy.' And that is what we did."
—*Quentin Riggins, Auburn linebacker*

"We went to halftime and I think we were down 10-7, but Coach Dye gave us the most electrifying, run through that wall talk, and in the second half, we rolled up 20 points."
—Ed King, Auburn offensive lineman

Van Allen Plexico
Actually, 23 points, Ed.

John Ringer
The Alabama band performed at halftime in Jordan-Hare before the Auburn band, another first that was a surprising sight to many Auburn fans.

I remember some marching band performances over the years that I have enjoyed, but I have no memory at all of this halftime. For many fans at the game, the tension of the buildup and the first half was huge, and halftime was a chance to breathe deeply and recover before the second-half plunge.

-14-

THE THIRD QUARTER: "WE DECIDED TO GO FOR THE BIG PLAY"

Auburn having won the pre-game toss and electing to receive the opening kickoff, we start the third quarter with Jim Von Wyl kicking off to Alabama.

Gene Jelks returns the ball to the 32, where he is tackled by Eric Ramsey.

Van Allen Plexico
Good heavens. Jelks and Ramsey together. Possibly the two players disliked the most by their own fan bases.

CBS reminds us that Auburn turned the ball over twice in the first half, leading to all 10 of Alabama's points. Alabama, meanwhile, did not turn the ball over.

Auburn did have seven tackles for loss, however. Alabama had only one.

Passing yards by quarter: Alabama 72 and 69. Auburn 91 and 2.

Yes, Auburn had only 2 yards passing in the second quarter.

That long pass to Alexander Wright on the opening drive remains the biggest play of the game for Auburn, other than maybe breaking up the Tide's fake field goal attempt.

On first down, Lamar Rogers stops Siran Stacy on an inside handoff for no gain. On second down, Alabama stays in the shotgun and Hollingsworth connects with Marco Battle for 14 and a first down.

Now Alabama goes no-huddle. On first down at their own 44, the pass falls incomplete. But on the next play, Hollingsworth audibles and hits Battle down at the Auburn 39. Battle is becoming a problem for the Tigers.

With that pass, Hollingsworth has set the Alabama single-season passing yardage record.

The commentators note that it has gotten very loud in the stadium. After an incomplete pass, Stacy takes the second down handoff and rumbles to the left for 9 yards.

Now all Alabama needs on third down is a yard. Once again, however, Bill Curry decides to get cute. He has Hollingsworth execute a play-action fake handoff and then throws incomplete. He very likely could have run for that one yard and a fresh set of downs. This is Alabama's second missed opportunity, coming after the fake field goal that blew up on them earlier in the game.

Facing 48 yards for the field goal, *now* Curry decides to try the kick. The usually reliable Doyle misses it short. The score remains 10-7, Alabama.

Van Allen Plexico

Bill Curry was the kind of head coach that makes decisions I can't stand. When all he needs is a yard for a first down, and he has Siran Stacy and Derrick Owens-Lassic and a good offensive line, that's when he decides to get cute and try some funky trick play. But when he's 48 yards away from a field goal, that's when he decides to send in his great kicker. His decisions make no logical sense to me.

About that third-and-one decision, Curry later remarks, "We had a chance for a big play against a great short-yardage defense. You

242

don't get many chances for that against Auburn. We decided to go for the big play."

Of the incomplete pass to Turner, Quentin Riggins later says, "That was the biggest play of the game. That's when we grabbed the momentum."

He continues, "You have to give our coaches credit for that one. We watched miles and miles of film, and they had us prepared for that play. We knew Hollingsworth was going to fake it and try to throw, and since Turner was the only one going out for a pass, we knew Hollingsworth was coming to him.

"Here they've got Siran Stacy, who's been running the ball well, and Martin Houston, who runs the ball well in short yardage situations, and they pass. I don't know why they did it."

Taking over after the missed kick, Auburn appears to wake up at last. Following an incomplete pass on first down, Reggie Slack throws to a wide-open Shayne Wasden on the right sideline. Wasden takes off down the middle of the field on what looks like it will be a touchdown run, but the dreaded linebacker, Keith McCants, somehow catches him and slaps his ankle to bring him down on the Alabama 12.

John Ringer

Shayne Wasden was one of the smallest players on Auburn's team. This reception and long run may have been the single biggest play of the entire game. And no one but McCants could have caught him and the fact that McCants *did* catch him had NFL general managers making a note as they watched the game: *Draft this McCants guy early!*

After Joseph runs for no gain on first down, he catches a rollout pass from Slack and carries it down to the Alabama 1, for a first-and-goal. But then right guard Brad Johnson is flagged for a false start, backing the Tigers up to the 6.

This time, with Joseph at fullback, Stacy Danley slashes his way to the 2.

Now all the fans in the stadium are on their feet—except one person we see in the press box, typing up the play-by-play on an electric typewriter, as it happens.

On 2nd and goal, Joseph dives into the end zone for his second touchdown of the game. Auburn is back ahead.

Auburn 14, Alabama 10

"I had two touchdowns, by the grace of God. We got down there and they called my number."
—James Joseph, Auburn running back

Offensive lineman Rob Selby limps off the field with an ankle injury before Win Lyle kicks the extra point. The Tigers have scored on their opening drives of each half of the game, and lead, 14-10.

Up in the press box, reporter Dockery is chatting with Auburn's David Housel about what this game truly means for Auburn. Housel tells him, "We're equal. For the first time in 50 years, we're equal."

Jim Von Wyl kicks off. Gene Jelks returns the kick from the goal line and is stopped at the 23.

Siran Stacy from the single-back set rips off a 5-yard run on first down.

CBS offers us a quarterback comparison to this point in the game:
Hollingsworth: 12 of 22 for 172 yards, 1 TD, 0 INT
Slack: 9 of 18 for 161 yards, 0 TD, 1 INT

Van Allen Plexico

Neither quarterback is setting the world on fire here, but the numbers favor Hollingsworth at this point in the game—though not by a tremendous margin. The interception of Slack's pass was a fluke deflection. Alabama has run a few more plays, thanks mainly to Auburn's two turnovers. The issues Auburn is having are all correctible.

That said, the game seems remarkably even thus far. Auburn's turnovers are balanced out by Curry's bad coaching decisions.

On second down, Hollingsworth throws out of the I-formation and hits the tight end, Russell, who makes it to the Auburn 40. The Tide are on the move again.

Stacy runs for 3 yards next. To this point he has 14 carries for 53 yards, after five straight 100 yard games coming in. Meanwhile,

Auburn's defense, over the past few years, has prided itself on denying even the best backs in the SEC 100-yard games. Something has to give.

Quentin Riggins gets pressure on Hollingsworth on second down, and he throws incomplete.

Haden, the color analyst, says that Riggins told him before the game that he reads the hands of the offensive linemen. If they're leaning their weight on their hands, it's going to be a run. If they're not, it's a pass.

Hollingsworth completes a third-down pass to Russell for a first down. It's looking like Alabama is cooking up a serious scoring threat with this drive. But then disaster strikes for the Tide.

Hollingsworth dumps a short pass to the fullback, Kevin Turner, who makes a nice run—but then Quentin Riggins, continuing to make a mark on this game, knocks it loose. The ball is recovered by Dennis Wallace for Auburn at the Tigers' 26 yard line.

"Kevin and I had played against each other when I was at Robert E. Lee (High School in Montgomery) and he was at Prattville. He was just an outstanding player. All the years we played against each other, I never remember him turning the ball over or fumbling.

"They ran a great play... I was dropping into the hook zone, and out of the corner of my eye I could see Kevin coming out of the backfield and running an angle under route. When I saw it, I screamed 'Oh, you-know-what.' I got my left hand and caught the very end (of the ball) and ripped it out. (Dennis Wallace) recovered it, and that was the start of us making the run."

—Quentin Riggins, Auburn linebacker

Van Allen Plexico

Good old Quentin Riggins, who would one day be president *pro tem* of the Auburn Board of Trustees. Coming through for us again.

And this begins a great tradition of Alabama fullbacks fumbling passes in Jordan-Hare! (I'm thinking specifically of the ending of the 1997 game, and Ed Scissum.)

Auburn has the ball back now, and on first down, Dye dials up the fourth long pass attempt to Alexander Wright of the game. This one works, despite Wright being shoved way out of bounds as he ran along the left sideline. He makes his way back onto the field just in time to catch the ball and be tackled for a 60-yard completion.

A penalty on Alabama's defense is declined in favor of the outcome of the play. Auburn now has the ball on the Alabama 14.

Joseph plows ahead on first down to the 11, then Danley is stopped for no gain. The Tigers are feeding the ball to these two backs, giving Alabama a steady dose of power football, and wearing away at the Tide's defense.

CBS tells us that the yards-per-completion stat is now heavily in Auburn's favor, thanks to the two long completions to Wright:

Yards per completion: Alabama 14.1, Auburn 22.1.

Slack scrambles to his right on third down and 8. He makes it to the 5, a yard short of the first down. Dye calls timeout, then sends the dependable Win Lyle out to knock through the short field goal. He's now 14 of 17 on the year, and Auburn has extended its lead.

Auburn 17, Alabama 10

CBS informs us that not only is Lyle a good kicker—he is carrying a 3.66 GPA in Pre-Med. Additionally, that kick broke Al Del Greco's field goal record at Auburn.

Van Allen Plexico

I remember that it was sort of odd how we ended up with Win Lyle as our kicker. We'd struggled just a little bit with our kicking in the previous couple of years, starting with Robert McGinty missing the field goal that would've beaten Alabama in 1984. By 1986, Coach Dye was casting about for a more dependable guy, and somehow he found Lyle, who really exploded onto the scene in his first season in 1987, kicking a 55-yarder in Knoxville against Tennessee. He settled in as a very reliable kicker for the next three years. I remember it being mentioned that a technical detail had caused one of his years of eligibility to be used up, so he could only play for

246

three years total. That meant this season was his last hurrah with the Tigers. Kickoff man Jim Von Wyl would get promoted up to all-around kicker the next year.

Gene Jelks returns Von Wyl's kick to the 16 yard line.

Siran Stacy is stopped for a 1-yard loss on first down, and illegal procedure is called on the play as well.

The crowd is fired up now. They can sense momentum shifting yet again. Dockery states, "This is the loudest I've heard a stadium all year."

Once again, the tight end, Russell, bails the Tide out. He gains 13 yards on a short pass to the Alabama 25. On the next play, Martin Houston dives up the middle for the first down.

Two plays later, Derrick Owens-Lassic catches a pass and takes it to the Alabama 36. Hollingsworth receives a real shot from the pass rush as he throws the ball. On the next play, he throws incomplete.

Haden points out that Alabama is going to have to make some adjustments on offense. He says they need to throw the ball deeper downfield.

Alabama's 45-yard punt rolls dead at the Auburn 20.

On first down, Danley slices up the middle for 9 big yards. After an incomplete pass intended for him on second down, Danley on third down dives up the middle again for the first down. The Tigers are starting to lean on Stacy Danley to be their workhorse here in the second half.

After a 5-yard penalty for delay of game, Danley gets the ball again on 1st and 15, but manages little gain over left guard. Now the Tigers go back to the air. Slack executes a nice play-action and then hits Herbert "the Weapon" Casey on the left sideline for 16 yards and a first down.

With the Tigers on the 45 now, into the game comes Darrell "Lectron" Williams at running back, his fresh legs spelling Danley. He manages a yard on the right side, but that's all.

Slack goes to the air again and finds Alexander Wright open for a relatively short gain for him of about 9 yards, to the Alabama 45. Haden notes that Alabama is giving Wright a big cushion in their coverage, trying to stop him from making the long catches down the sideline, so Wright responded by breaking off his route early and finding himself wide open. The fear of the big play is allowing Auburn to make some shorter ones here.

Joseph dives for the first down, then Williams gets stopped for a loss at the Alabama 43. And with that, the clock expires and the third quarter comes to an end.

During these preceding fifteen minutes, Auburn has come from 3 points down to 7 points ahead, 17-10. But with fifteen minutes left to go in this Iron Bowl of Iron Bowls, it's still anybody's game.

-15-

THE FOURTH QUARTER: "LET THE CELEBRATING BEGIN"

Pat Dye's strategy was always to have the deeper and better-conditioned team, so that he could win in the fourth quarter. That's what he meant by "sixty minutes." It's about who's able to execute late in the game, and who's not.

Sideline reporter John Dockery notes that, indeed, Auburn has substituted all game long more freely than has Alabama, and Jim Nance notes that this is especially true on defense, so Auburn should be fresher at the end.

The Tigers begin the final frame facing second and 14 at the Alabama 47.

Reggie Slack takes a deep drop and launches a 14-yard pass to Alexander Wright for a first down. It's Wright's sixth catch of the game, and he has 123 total yards so far.

On the next play, Danley gets loose from the I-formation, breaking tackles, and plows through the defense for 20 big yards, all the way down to the Alabama 13.

James Joseph is stopped for only a yard gain, but on the next play—the 13th play of the drive— "Lectron" Williams takes the pitch from Slack and blasts his way around right end for the touchdown.

Williams and the crowd both go crazy, years before another "Williams" at running back for Auburn will "go crazy" and score.

With Lyle's extra point, the Tigers have now extended their lead to 14, and momentum feels as if it is securely on Auburn's side. Of course, these things have a way of changing very suddenly and dramatically, and the Iron Bowl has never been immune from that.

Auburn 24, Alabama 10

Van Allen Plexico

As a freshman in 1989, Darrell "Lectron" Williams seemed poised to become the next big Auburn running back. What went wrong?

A 2016 video report by station WPMI describes him as a "high school football legend in Mobile and at Vigor High School. At Auburn, a nagging knee injury forced him to end his football career. Now he is a successful personal trainer."

He tore a knee ligament as a junior in high school, and never fully recovered.

"When I tore my knee up," he said, "even though I came back, I knew I was never back the way I was before. As hard as I worked and ran the sand dunes, I wasn't the Lectron who did all that stuff before."

The first player in Alabama to be named Mr. Football and the Gatorade Player of the Year, he ran for 5,000 yards at Vigor, helping them win back-to-back state championships in 1987 and 1988, "and the ESPN national championship in 1988, the only high school team in Alabama to win one."

He ran for 1,000 yards as a senior in high school, after the injury, and then did what he did at Auburn. Eventually, though, the knee injury caught up with him, and his football career ended.

John Ringer

This is a great Auburn "What if?"

Medical technology was not nearly as good in the late 1980s as it is now. What if Lectron had benefited from modern surgery and rehabilitation techniques? Would he have continued to play and gone on to be an elite running back at Auburn?

Now down by two touchdowns, Alabama has to find a way back into this game, or they might lose more than just the Iron Bowl. They still need to impress the Sugar Bowl committee enough to take them even with a loss today. They know they have to rally, and they have to do it quickly.

Unfortunately for the Tide, things are about to get even worse.

After Pierre Goode returns Von Wyl's kickoff to the Alabama 25, Hollingsworth takes the first-down snap from the shotgun and throws a bad pass that is almost intercepted by Auburn's Darrell Crawford, who pounds the ground in frustration with both empty fists after he fails to snag the ball.

But wait! The referee has seen something different! He motions that Auburn now has possession. It was an interception after all!

"I asked the ref, and he said I pulled it in. He started counting: one-thousand-one, one-thousand-two. Back then, the ground couldn't cause a fumble. From his angle, it looked like the ground caused the fumble, where really I just had it on my hip and pulled it in. Today, that would have never been called an interception. But as coach Dye said, 'It's an interception in the record books, so we're going to leave it that way.'"
—Darrell Crawford, Auburn linebacker

Anyone watching on television, and especially after seeing the slow-motion replay, can clearly tell that Crawford dropped the ball. But the Tigers aren't complaining. They take over inside the Alabama red zone.

On first down, whistles and flags stop the play. Auburn is backed up. Once things have been sorted out, Danley runs to the 26 and then to the 21, making a first down.

Van Allen Plexico

Auburn is really leaning on Stacy Danley now. I remember Coach Dye saying at some point back then that

Danley was "the best-conditioned athlete on the team," and it's showing, as he's getting better as the game goes on.

CBS points out that Alabama has the current longest win streak in football. Their most recent loss was the previous Iron Bowl.

Nantz and Haden discuss which team will go to the Sugar Bowl. Auburn, with two losses, is a long shot. Haden notes that Auburn was chosen over LSU last year because, despite tying for the SEC title and despite LSU's head-to-head win, Auburn had the better overall record. The same is likely to happen today, with regards to Alabama—unless things get out of hand here.

Auburn is doing their best to help things get out of hand for Alabama.

On first down, Williams rushes for 2 yards to the 19. On second down, he runs left to the 17. It looks like the coaches are hoping to duplicate what happened on the previous possession, but Lectron is finding the sledding is tougher this time.

Danley comes in for the third down play, needing 6 yards, but is stopped up the middle for no gain.

There are 10 minutes to go in the First Time Ever Iron Bowl.

The ever-dependable Win Lyle comes out and knocks through the field goal.

Auburn 27, Alabama 10

Alabama led at halftime, but they have not scored in the second half. They are now down more than two scores.

Van Allen Plexico

I think this was the point where a lot of us started to relax and assume the game was in hand. The Auburn players were whooping and hollering on the sideline. I was breathing a bit easier.

But nothing like this can ever come easy. There was a lot of football left to be played.

In addition to being a plague and a pestilence, I always describe Alabama as being like the monster in the horror movies—you can't just trust that they're dead. You have to ram that wooden stake through their collective hearts!

252

CBS reminds us this game carries state championship, SEC championship, Sugar Bowl, and even national championship implications.

Von Wyl kicks off; Goode returns it from the Tide's 4 to the 26.

Alabama narrowly avoids a disaster so great it might have knocked them out of the Sugar Bowl entirely. On the very first play, Hollingsworth nearly throws yet another interception to Auburn. This time it's linebacker Eltin Billingslea, coming across the middle. The ball falls to the grass, incomplete.

With that, Alabama's players seem to gather themselves, find their composure, and settle down. What ensues is a drive that likely keeps them in play for the Sugar Bowl.

On second down, Hollingsworth dumps it to fullback Kevin Turner in the left flat for a short gain.

Now it's third and 8. The stadium is extremely loud.

Hollingsworth, from the shotgun, finds Turner over the middle for 15 yards and a first down.

On the next play, he hits Craig Sanderson down to the 34. A facemask penalty on Auburn tacks on 5 more.

Hollingsworth on first down feels the pressure of the Auburn pass rush and scrambles to the 25.

The clock goes under eight minutes remaining.

After another first down pass, Hollingsworth connects with Marco Battle in the back right corner of the end zone for their second touchdown of the game.

Doyle makes the extra point kick, and Alabama has narrowed their deficit to 10. The drive consumed only one minute and forty-five seconds.

Auburn 27, Alabama 17

Momentum has swapped its blue jersey for a red one. The question Alabama faces now is whether there's enough time left for them to come all the way back. A better question is, can Auburn widen that gap again?

Doyle kicks off to Dominko Anderson, who returns it to the Auburn 25. A penalty against Auburn on the return moves the ball back to the 12.

Now the Alabama players, coaches and fans can surely feel the excitement growing. They've just scored a touchdown in less than two minutes, and they've got Auburn pinned deep. Force a punt, get a decent return, and they could well be within 3 to 7 points of Auburn with a good five minutes left to play.

Auburn has to rally again. The Tigers have to reach deep inside and find something—anything—on offense, to move the ball, keep possession, and keep that clock running!

Coach Dye is being conservative. In the I-formation, Slack gives to Danley, who crashes into the line for 2 yards.

On second and 8, the Tigers go back to the "Alexander Wright" well once more. Slack finds the speedy wideout over the middle instead of down the sidelines for a change, moving the ball out to the Auburn 32.

Pat Haden notes that this call was an unexpectedly daring move by the coaches. "Give Pat Sullivan a lot of credit for calling that play," he says.

Joseph gets the handoff and loses a yard. One would think the Tigers would want the clock to continue running, but Auburn calls timeout.

Facing second down and 11, Slack leaves it with Lectron Williams, who gains a yard on a cutback run to the middle of the line.

Now it's third and 10 at the Auburn 32. Slack tries to connect with Wright again, this time on a crossing route, but the pass falls incomplete. The Tigers have to punt.

CBS informs us that, with regard to the Auburn offense in the second half, they have gone "Touchdown, field goal, touchdown, field goal, punt."

Gene Jelks returns the punt to the Alabama 31 yard line. The crowd boos, wanting a clipping call on Alabama. They don't get it.

On first down, Hollingsworth tosses a screen pass to Turner, who takes it to the Tide 38. On the next play, he connects with Sanderson for 11 more, to the 49.

John Wiley, Auburn's safety, knocks away a pass over the middle. Haden notes what a great game Wiley has had.

Van Allen Plexico

Watching this game again, John Wiley really did play well against Alabama.

I remembered his name, mainly because my roommates and I had a friend freshman year with that same name, who hung around our apartment a lot. But I'd forgotten how much he—the football player one—contributed to this game. He was everywhere, breaking up passes and making tackles.

With 4:09 to go, Hollingsworth takes the snap from the shotgun, executes a nice play-action fake, then runs the bootleg in the opposite direction for another first down.

It's at this moment that Jim Nantz helpfully informs us all that Hollingsworth grew up an Auburn fan, attending several games a year in Jordan-Hare as a kid, before ending up in Tuscaloosa.

Hollingsworth connects with Marco Battle again, down the right sideline for 9 yards. Auburn fans are understandably nervous now.

Van Allen Plexico

This game was not over yet. We had a seeming eternity still to suffer through.

And Marco Battle was scaring me to death.

Siran Stacy catches a short pass and makes it out to the 35 for a first down. Then Hollingsworth rolls to his left and hits Battle yet again.

The Alabama quarterback who grew up an Auburn fan is now 27 of 43 for 342 yards, with 2 touchdowns and 1 (very questionable) interception, against his old favorite team. And the Homer Smith-coordinated Tide offense is moving down the field again.

After a Kevin Turner run up the middle, Alabama is mere inches short of a first down. The clock goes under three minutes remaining.

Hollingsworth fires a pass over the middle, intended for a Tide receiver at the Auburn 2 yard line, but it's incomplete. CBS's announcers question if pass interference should have been called.

On fourth and 1, Curry finally stops overthinking things and sends Houston into the pile for the first down to the Auburn 9.

At this point, linebacker Quentin Riggins calls Auburn's last timeout. The defense regroups.

First and goal: Hollingsworth passes into the end zone. The ball goes just beyond the outstretched fingers of Marco Battle. One bullet dodged.

Second and goal: Back to basics. Houston runs up the middle to the 5, where he is tackled by Riggins.

The game clock goes under 2 minutes remaining. Alabama is still down by double-digits, but they're knocking on the door.

Third and goal: Hollingsworth fires a pass over the middle, but nobody's home to catch it.

Now it's fourth and goal from the 5. Curry knows he needs points. Even just 3 points, this trip. He sends Phillip Doyle out to kick the field goal.

Now the game is down to a single score: Auburn 27, Alabama 20.

A minute forty-nine remains to be played. Alabama has all three of their timeouts left. Auburn has none.

We all know the onside kick is coming. Alabama sends backup kicker Alan Ward out to do the honors. Frank McIntosh, the backup quarterback, recovers the ball for Auburn.

CBS points out that Alabama has outgained Auburn in total offense, 428 yards to 410.

Van Allen Plexico

That's remarkably close. The game has mainly come down to Auburn being able to punch it into the end zone more often when they reach the red zone. Auburn's defense has stopped Alabama when they absolutely had to. And both teams have made critical mistakes and have benefited from questionable calls.

For me, the difference in the game at this point comes down to a couple of things: Auburn quit turning the ball over, and Curry made coaching mistakes early on. If Alabama had gotten the first down and the touchdown on the drive where they tried the fake field goal, just as one example, it would be a different game.

The Tigers are flagged for illegal motion before they can even snap the ball. They start from just past their own 48. Slack takes the snap and pitches the ball to Danley, who runs to his right and goes out of bounds at the Alabama 42. This stops the clock, which is not the ideal outcome, but at least Danley got close to the first down marker. CBS informs us that he has now gone over 100 yards for the game. In his three games against Alabama in his career, he has run for a total of 366 yards.

On second and 5, Danley runs up the middle for the first down. Alabama has a very good defensive front, but the Auburn offensive line is handling them well enough. Alabama burns its first timeout of the half.

Danley runs up the middle again on first down, fighting his way for 14 yards to the Alabama 20 yard line. The clock has run down to 1:29 remaining. Alabama calls timeout again.

The Auburn seniors of 1989, CBS points out, have beaten Alabama four times in a row. That won't happen again until the senior class of 2005—followed by the seniors of 2006 and 2007. Alabama, as of the 2022 game, has not beaten Auburn four times in a row since Bear Bryant's 1981 team.

These Auburn seniors have won 38 games, and their bowl win will make it 39. They have won the SEC Championship three years in a row, something no other Auburn team has ever done. They have lost one — *one!* — SEC home game in four years. (That loss was to Georgia way back in 1986, on a controversial call by the referee on what should've been Brent Fullwood's winning touchdown run.)

Van Allen Plexico

In fact, between their November 13, 1982 loss at home to Herschel Walker's Georgia and their October 26, 1991 loss to Mississippi State, Auburn lost just 2 home SEC games: No. 2 Florida in 1985 (10-14) and the 1986 loss to Georgia (16-20). That's two home conference losses in the better part of a *decade*.

Pat Dye joins three other coaches who have won three straight SEC titles: Neyland at Tennessee, Dooley at Georgia, and Bryant at Alabama. Later Nick Saban would accomplish the feat from 2014-2016.

Auburn sends Danley into the line yet again, and he's stopped for no gain. Alabama burns its final timeout.

At this moment, Jim Nantz tells the television audience about the letter Pat Dye received from a 73-year old World War II veteran and former POW, Jim Fidell from Trinity, Alabama, who wrote about teamwork and fellowship and adversity. Nantz says Dye read the letter to his team on Thursday and it brought tears to the eyes of many players. Dye promised to take the man to the bowl game.

The CBS announcers don't know it yet, if they ever did, but—as noted previously—David Housel will later find out the letter was a fake.

Danley grinds out 3 more yards on second down from the Alabama 20. Short of an utter disaster, it's getting hard to see how Alabama can win this game, or how Auburn can lose it. But Auburn people understand what can happen when you least expect it—especially in football and especially in the Iron Bowl. Everyone keeps on holding their breath and saying their prayers.

On third down, with Alabama out of timeouts and Auburn just needing to run the clock out, hearts leap into throats as Slack passes the ball. Alabama's Spencer Hammond reaches up for it and gets his fingers on it, but he can only bat it down.

The clock stops yet again. Haden and Nantz, along with everyone else in the stadium and most people watching at home, are in shock that Auburn threw the ball in that situation.

It's fourth down, and Win Lyle trots out to attempt another short field goal.

"I don't need to tell you the magnitude of this Lyle field goal of 34 yards. Angled to the left, the ball will be placed down on the nearside hash mark by Dickinson. There's the kick, kick is away, kick is... good! Thirty-three seconds to go. Let the celebrating begin!"

"Win Lyle has been—he's my player of the game—he really is. He's been perfect today. He's been in pressure situations and I'll tell you what, he's come through like a champ."
—Jim Fyffe, Auburn Network broadcast

"Even though it wasn't the most pressure kick I'd ever had, that was by far the most satisfying kick I'd ever had to ice that game and put it out of reach. Then the celebrating began."
—Win Lyle, Auburn kicker

"The Auburn sideline is celebrating. They've just brought out the Gatorade jug and they've doused Coach Dye. He's soaking wet."
—Charlie Trotman, Auburn Network broadcast

Auburn has extended its lead to double digits once more.

Auburn 30, Alabama 20

This score will not only win the Iron Bowl, it will prove to be the biggest winning margin in Auburn's favor in the Iron Bowl for the next twenty-eight years, not broken until the 26-14 win in 2017. It ties the 1987 game for the biggest margin of victory by Auburn in the Iron Bowl for 48 years, dating all the way back to 1969.

First, of course, the win has to be secured—which means running out the last few seconds of the game clock.

Derrick Warren returns Von Wyl's kickoff to the 25.

CBS announces its Players of the Game: Alexander Wright and Keith McCants.

"I think Alexander Wright was probably the key for us offensively," says Pat Dye afterward. "I'm so thrilled for him. He's a kid who's probably scheduled to graduate on time. He's a fine, fine youngster, and football hasn't come easy for him.

"To be honest with you, he hasn't been easy to communicate with. But we made a commitment to each other and we finally came together. He's not far from being a dominating football player."

Van Allen Plexico

I might have given the Player of the Game award for Auburn to Slack, or to Danley, or to Riggins. But Alexander Wright's early catch did set the tone, and he went on to make several more very big ones.

Wright went on to play for the Dallas Cowboys and other NFL teams. Later he worked in coaching, and then became a minister.

Keith McCants totally deserved to win the Alabama half of that Players of the Game award. He made 19 tackles to go along with one big interception. And he drew way more attention from Auburn's blockers than one guy had any right to expect. The other player that maybe deserved consideration was Marco Battle.

Battle had a big day for the Crimson Tide, scoring both of their touchdowns. After the game, he tells reporters, "It really hurts bad to come this far and lose. We beat them in '85 when I was redshirted, but the next four years, we just couldn't beat them. It's really disappointing.

"Ten and one sounds great, but everybody will leave with a bitter taste in their mouth."

The Auburn sideline, meanwhile, is going nuts. Players are holding up four fingers.

On third down, Hollingsworth is intercepted by safety Dennis Wallace. Auburn picks up a celebration penalty for their reaction.

Auburn takes over the ball. Slack takes the snap and downs it. The last few seconds tick away. It is over.

"This one, my friends, is history.

"We're gonna let the crowd count this one down. Two seconds to go. One second. That's it. Game's over. Auburn wins. Auburn wins. Final score, Auburn 30, Alabama 20. And the Tigers have captured a share of the SEC Championship with their fourth consecutive victory over archrival Alabama."

—Jim Fyffe, Auburn Network broadcast

Auburn players and coaches on the field and the sidelines celebrate joyously. Auburn fans in the stands celebrate deliriously. Nobody rushes the field. Nobody *attempts* to rush the field.

The First Time Ever has happened. Alabama has come to Auburn to play the Iron Bowl, and Auburn has beaten them. Auburn has won.

Pat Dye had said that just playing the game in Auburn was far more important than who won it. To a certain degree, he's correct. And part of his job is managing expectations. He wanted this day to seem like a victory even if the Tigers lost the game on the field. And it would have.

To a degree.

Jordan-Hare Stadium, however, is at that moment filled with 85,314 people—not counting the Alabama fans that have already left—and the vast majority of those people are very, very glad the home team won.

The *home* team. A team playing in its *own home*, finally.

Finally.

-16-

"YOU WERE PREPARED
FOR THE TASK AT HAND"

"In 1989, when Alabama visited for the first time, the noise never stopped. It was the loudest I have ever heard a stadium from the start of a game until the end of the game."
—*Phillip Marshall, 2023*

Despite all the pre-game talk of how just playing the game in Auburn was a victory, the fans always wanted and demanded more. They wanted to *win*. And while losing the game would've been bad enough, what they most definitely did *not* want was *Alabama* winning it.

The fans were not alone in that. After the game, it quickly became clear just how much winning that day meant to Pat Dye and to his team.

"There was a lot on the line for us and we knew what was at stake. Everyone in the Auburn family knew what was at stake."
—*Reggie Slack, to AL dot com, in 2019*

Coach Dye, emotional as he's ever been, addressed the Auburn players in the locker room after the game. His words have been replayed and reprinted many times in the years since. They remain as powerful now as they were that day.

"Tonight's what our program's all about. I want you to think about it and let it sink in deep.

"This is the reason we work you in the summertime and in January and February and the spring. It's the reason we push you beyond what you think you can do. To experience moments like this.

"Ain't no easy way in life, and it wasn't easy out there tonight. But you were prepared for the task at hand.

"Every one of you players, there ain't no way—I ain't smart enough to tell you how I feel about you. Because it's family. Every one of you. I mean, you know it.

"Sure, I'd like to be 11-0, but I'm gonna tell you something. I wouldn't swap this year for any year that I've been at Auburn. I wouldn't swap it, men, because I've watched you struggle and I've watched you wrestle with them angels and, and, but I've watched you grow up and become men. I've watched you become men."

—Pat Dye, locker room after the 1989 Iron Bowl

Asked about the effect of playing the game in front of a home Auburn crowd, future All-American offensive lineman Ed King said, "I think it made a lot of difference. I know the Alabama fans would start chanting 'Crimson Tide' or 'Roll Tide' and our fans would come in and smother them with 'Auburn Tigers.' It helped us."

"There was no way in hell we were going to lose that game. That's just the bottom line. Whatever it took, that was our motto that day, whatever it took."

—John Wiley, Auburn defensive back

"Resilience. That '89 team had a great group of leaders. We were trained by some great leaders on that '88 team. Just a great

time, the Iron Bowl, awesome time. A great game that day, Dec. 2, 1989. We didn't realize the ramifications of that game or the impact it would have on the Auburn family, but whenever I look back, it was a great time in history, one that I will never forget. The excitement building up to it, the moment, and now 30 years later, it's still alive."
—*Craig Ogletree, Auburn linebacker, 2019*

"After the game in the locker room, it was really interesting hearing the fans yelling, 'It's great to be an Auburn Tiger!' My only regret is that we didn't go back out on the field to thank the fans, but you could just hear them. It was just a tremendous feeling."
—*Quentin Riggins*

"(Alabama) had a good football team. That No. 2 ranking wasn't out of order, at all."
—*Pat Dye*

Bill Curry was asked after the game what he would have done if Alabama had recovered the onside kick and gone on to score a touchdown. At that point in the game, the score was 27-20. Would he have gone for two and the win, or kicked the sure-thing extra point and taken the tie?

"It was one of the toughest decisions I ever had to make," Curry replies, as if he'd actually been in a position to have to make that decision. (Spoiler: He wasn't in that position, and he didn't have to make that decision. Auburn recovered the kick.) "I didn't tell our players (what I'd do). I just said I'd decide (during) the game if it came down to that.

"When a tie will give you a conference championship outright, you take the tie."

Van Allen Plexico

It's mind-boggling to me to think that this game could have ended in a tie, and that Curry would have gone that way with it if he'd had the opportunity. This game—the First Time Ever game—ending in a draw? It's simply unthinkable.

It's also funny to think of Auburn tying a rival in an SEC game, and the opponent isn't Johnny Majors and Tennessee.

Imagine the reaction by fans on both sides if Alabama had recovered the ball and scored, and then Curry had sent Doyle out to kick that extra point.

And, honestly, Pat Dye wasn't in much of a position to fault him, given his own track record of ties, including Syracuse in the Sugar Bowl, and of course Tennessee twice.

Curry did get one thing right about the game, when he spoke to a reporter afterward:

"It's not difficult to describe what happened. We got beat by a better football team. That's obvious.

"I hate all losses. My job is to teach people how to win and win all the time. I certainly detest losing to a coach our teams have never been able to beat.

"This is a great stadium, a great place to play football and a great crowd. But the crowd didn't beat us. The guys in blue shirts are the ones that beat us."

—Bill Curry, after the game

Knowing Pat Dye's preferences and tendencies, Alabama's defensive game plan was to stop the run and force Auburn to go to the air. They felt they had a better chance in the game if Auburn was forced to depend on the arm of Reggie Slack. This was stymied immediately when Auburn came out throwing on first down, and was successful at it. Hitting big plays early in the passing game shook up Alabama's defense and opened up the run.

"They just outplayed us. We wanted to shut down their running game and force them to throw. They came out throwing and kept us off balance running and throwing. They made more big plays than we did and they won. When they had to come up with a big play, they did. You can't give up many big plays and expect to win.

"We knew (Alexander Wright) was a great receiver with great speed. He made some big plays in some key situations."
—*Willie Wyatt, Alabama nose guard*

"He (Wright) had some success (with big plays) and that hurt us. We didn't want to give up the big play, but we did. You've got to give them all the credit."
—*John Mangum, Alabama defensive back*

"Reggie Slack was incredible. Great players rise to the occasion in games like this, and he did that today."
—*Bill Curry*

"Our offense was rebuilt in the Mississippi State game, and I think it has come a long way."
—*Reggie Slack, Auburn quarterback*

"This was a very special game for me. Because it was the first time Alabama has ever come here and the first time that I've ever played in it, this was tremendous. This game will always be remembered and I was a part of it."
—*Victor Hall, Auburn tight end*

Mark Murphy

Alabama was really good offensively, and they had some major talent on defense. The big thing about that team was they could really score and move the ball. Auburn had struggled on offense that year, and in typical Coach Dye fashion, his solution was to get physically tougher.

They really got after it in practice, and started running the ball and running the ball until they got good at it. Of course, they also had a really talented quarterback in Reggie Slack and world-class football speed in Alexander Wright, and they were going to take advantage of that. When they hit that early pass play to Wright in front of the student section, it was like, "Oh boy—game on! Auburn is ready to play ball!" But, to me, the biggest thing was how much more physical that team got from the start of the year to the end of the year.

They were just struggling on offense and getting in sync and everything, but the players knew how important that game was. And they were on a mission to win that game.

Van Allen Plexico

How were they able to raise their game? Was it just emotion? What factors do you think went into them being able to play above their heads like that?

Mark Murphy

First of all, there were a lot of good players on that team. They had a lot of confidence because they'd won the SEC the two previous years. And the year before (1986) that might have been one of the all-time best defenses Auburn had, and that 1987 team was really good on defense, too. So the big issue on Coach Dye's teams was, could they throw the ball effectively? Because they almost always could run the ball. But the 1989 team was having some problems running the ball, and Coach Dye talked a lot about how they just needed to get tougher.

"Coach Dye did a great job of recruiting us. A lot of us weren't five-star, can't-miss players. He found different pieces that fit, and he made us a team."
—Quentin Riggins, Auburn linebacker

"People really came to the game expecting to see Alabama beat us. That seemed logical, I guess. They were undefeated and we'd lost two games. What they didn't realize was how much better we'd gotten over the course of the season."
—Pat Dye, 2019

"Everybody always asks me what is the most memorable game I ever had at Alabama — it's that game. It's not the best memory, but it was a memorable experience. Obviously, I wish the result was a little different.
"It was the loudest game we ever played. I can remember looking at Trent Patterson, who was the guard — I was yelling at

Trent. We couldn't hear each other. The fans had the paper pom-poms, so there was a blue and orange haze that kind of hung over the stadium. You could feel the vibration on the field. Kudos to the twelfth man. They definitely took advantage of their opportunity."
    —Roger Shultz, Alabama center

"Some Auburn people were openly fearful as the season unfolded. Alabama was rolling and Auburn was struggling. But Saturday, supercharged by the noise, the emotion that filled the air, Auburn did the rolling."
    —Phillip Marshall

"Probably because of my NFL background, I always thought I could turn that (environment) to our advantage. And I wish that I had been better at that. I wish I had done a better job of convincing my guys that 'not only are we not going to be intimidated, we're going to feed off this energy.' Nobody says we can't experience a rush every time the crowd goes crazy, even though they're cheering against us. Within those three-hour battles, we seemed to be getting better and better at that. But not nearly enough that day. I don't think Auburn won because of the crowd. I think Auburn won because they had a better team that day."
    —Bill Curry

Van Allen Plexico

Auburn fans today like to say "there was no way Alabama was going to win that game."

I vehemently disagree.

They had every chance to win. It was purely by the monumental efforts of the players and coaches that we won.

Similarly, we like to say the fans willed the team to victory.

Yes, if there was ever game where that *could* ever be the case, it certainly was *that* day and *that* game. And the home field advantage Auburn enjoyed that day was *tremendous*. But it wasn't the *fans* that defended Hollingsworth passes or wrapped up Siran Stacy, and it wasn't the *fans* that hit Alexander Wright with that long pass or plunged into the Alabama end zone from the one.

The fans did everything they could, there's no doubt.

But the *players* and the *coaches* won this game, just like they did any other game—by creating a great game plan and executing it on the field.

And they deserve to receive the credit for it.

"Coach Dye got us in a position where we were winning football games. (Just to play the Iron Bowl in Auburn), it was like a war had been fought and a victory had been won. To top it off, we won the game."
—Bobby Lowder

Pat Dye noted, "It was fifty years ago when they had the last tri-champion (in the SEC). It was fifty years ago when this stadium was built." It was also when Pat Dye was born, though that happened on November 6, 1939, not December 2.

"Something this big and this important, it's hard to come up with exactly the right words.

"What you saw out there was the combined effort of a lot of Auburn people, going all the way back to Dr. Funderburk (the former Auburn president).

"I was encouraged after looking at the films and knowing our team like I know it. I was hoping the home-field advantage would make a difference, and it did.

"I don't think you can say we are a great talented football team, but I'd say our team can play with anybody in the country.

"I wouldn't say this win is any bigger than any other Alabama win, except that it was so important to Auburn people."
—Pat Dye, after the game

It was important, yes. And it was bigger.

-17-

"THE PROMISED LAND"

Playing the game in Auburn *at all* was, as Bobby Lowder said, tantamount to winning the war. Winning the football game itself was like winning a battle in that war—though a very, very *big* battle.

Late in the evening of December 2, 1989, with both the battle and the war won, Auburn people celebrated. *Oh*, did they celebrate.

> *"It's the most special thing I've ever been a part of. I had my nephews with me and took them to town after the game. There were people everywhere. Toomer's Corner was solid white. I know Coach Jordan, if he could see it, was tickled with that one."*
> —*Larry Blakeney, receivers coach on the 1989 team*

Van Allen Plexico

We celebrated in the stadium for a bit, then headed straight for Toomer's Corner.

When we got there, it looked like the entire stadium had beaten us there. I'd never seen so many people there before, and I haven't since. It wasn't just the corner. The crowd extended out from the intersection in all four directions. Toilet paper was everywhere. The oaks were white domes. The traffic lights were streaming with it. Trees of every size and shape, all the way down College Street away from downtown, were covered. If it was stationary, someone had rolled it. I'm pretty sure I saw a dog run by, covered in TP—he must have sat still for a second and gotten rolled like everything else!

There wasn't an Alabama fan in sight. If we ran into any, I don't remember it. Nothing but a vast sea of humanity, all of them Auburn fans, all joyous beyond words; finding expression only in hurling more and more toilet paper onto everything in sight.

Not long after the game, downtown Auburn looked as if a blizzard had come through. There were acres of paper; paper everywhere. And every piece of it, every bit, represented some fraction of the utter happiness the Auburn Family was experiencing that night.

At some point we must have gone home, but I don't remember much about that, either. I'm not sure how I was able to sleep at all, other than out of sheer physical and emotional exhaustion.

"I've never seen anything like that day. It was unbelievable."
—Pat Dye, 2019

The Iron Bowl had always been big. Auburn had just demonstrated to Alabama people how it could be so much bigger. Playing it on a *campus*, instead of in downtown Birmingham, made for a huge part of that. Alabama would put it off a bit longer for various reasons, including simply needing to build up their own infrastructure the way Auburn had. Soon enough, however, they did what everyone had always known they would do: They moved their home game to *their* campus, too.

"Alabama didn't like (traveling to Auburn). But when Alabama folks came down and saw the atmosphere, and the tailgating and things going on in and around the stadium, I knew that they would have to take the Auburn-Alabama game to Tuscaloosa.

"You couldn't do it in Birmingham because they didn't have the same set-up for tailgating and that sort of thing in and

around Legion Field. But... now they've got, not only for the Auburn-Alabama game, when it's played there, but for every other game that they play there, they've got a great atmosphere in and around the stadium at Tuscaloosa, just like we have."
—*Pat Dye, 2019*

In 1989, however, Legion Field was still a good bit larger than Bryant-Denny Stadium. Consequently, Alabama renewed its contract with the city and agreed to continue playing three of its home games there starting in 1992. That included the Iron Bowl in even-numbered years.

By 1998, Alabama had expanded their stadium to a capacity of 83,818, making it competitive with Legion Field, though still a few thousand seats smaller than Jordan-Hare. They welcomed Tennessee to Tuscaloosa for the first time the following year. The year after that, Auburn returned at last. It had been 99 years since the Tigers had played in Tuscaloosa.

Auburn had won the only two ever played in Tuscaloosa prior to that, in 1895 and 1901. After winning in 2000, the Tigers went on to win in 2002, 2004 and 2006. Until Nick Saban's first home Iron Bowl in 2008, Auburn was undefeated in Alabama's home stadium across *three centuries*.

In 2019, Pat Dye told Creg Stephenson that while a number of Alabama supporters over the years had "lamented the game leaving Birmingham," he figured by then even the most hardcore of Alabama fans had "come around" to playing on the home campuses.

"All the Auburn people ever wanted was to be able to look Alabama in the eye and know that we had a chance," Dye later told Tony Barnhart. "The move was good for Auburn. But it was also good for Alabama."

Van Allen Plexico, to David Housel, 2022
I knew some Alabama fans that had never been down here before the 1989 game. And I remember, after the game, there was an older guy whose son was in high school, who was all set to go to Alabama, who said to me, "I don't like that we have to go down there now. But, seeing that stadium, I can see why they wanted to have the game down here."

They understood.

David Housel

Yeah. The good ones did. The bad ones aren't *ever* going to understand. I remember Coach Dye saying that would be one good thing. He said, number one, all the riff raff won't be able to get tickets if Alabama was going to have 10,000 tickets. And only their good fans, your money people, your season ticket holders, only they would be able to get the tickets. .... But he said only the *good* fans are coming.

He said when Alabama people come down here and see what Auburn is, and what Auburn *has*, they're going to be amazed. He said most of them have never been here. They think of Auburn as being like Troy State or Livingston or Jacksonville State. Admittedly our town might not be as big as what they would like. But when they come to our campus and they see what we've got, they're going to be amazed. And he was right.

John Ringer

What does the 1989 Iron Bowl mean to you?

David Housel

The First Time Ever. The most emotional day in Auburn history.

I remember the first time I ever heard that phrase, "The most emotional day in Auburn history." It must have been on a Sunday. I was over in the Complex. Coach Dye was there. Normally there would be a pot of coffee brewing in the room but there wasn't that day. So he and I drove over to McDonald's. You remember how Coach Dye was: He'd either talk or he'd be real quiet. Well, after we got our order and started back, we got to the intersection of Tiger Drive and Thach Avenue, at the corner of where the old fieldhouse was. And he got real quiet. And all of a sudden he just blurted out, "You know it's gonna be the most emotional day in Auburn history." We hadn't even been talking about the Alabama game. So I asked, "What do you mean, Coach?" He said, "When they come here." And I knew what he was talking about. And he was so right.

I believe I said this on TV that day: Auburn people that day made a journey they never thought they'd make. *Never* thought they'd make. And that was *home*, to play Alabama. And it was like coming to the Promised Land. That scene has been reenacted twenty or more times since then, but the Children of Israel walked into the Promised Land only *one* time for the *first* time. That's what that day was. I'm not trying to minimize the struggles of the Jews or anything like that. But for Auburn people, they made a journey that day they never thought they'd make.

We were told, "*Never.*" We were put down. "We'll quit before we'll play you." All that stuff. And it was more than Ray Perkins that said that. But, for Auburn people, that was entering the Promised Land.

"Dye at the time compared it to the falling of the Berlin Wall, which happened less than a month prior to the Iron Bowl that year. Housel likened it to the children of Israel 'entering into the promised land for the first time.' Those analogies may seem ridiculous to some, but it'd be difficult to otherwise encapsulate how much getting the Iron Bowl to Auburn meant to the city, the team and its fans.
—*Tom Green, AL dot com*

David Housel

If you aren't an Auburn person, you can't understand what that day meant. Now, television, they tried to say (what it all meant), but if you were not an Auburn person, you could not understand the emotion, the heart, the anguish, the embarrassment of being forced to play your games in Birmingham. Being belittled by parking lot attendants and all those concession people wearing Alabama caps.

But, you know, I don't begrudge them. They're in Birmingham. It was and still is an Alabama town. If you look at it objectively, you can bitch, gripe and moan all you want to. But Coach Bryant did a wonderful job of cultivating Birmingham and the people of Birmingham and the political forces of Birmingham. He did a masterful job. And when we were talking about getting out, coming to Auburn in the late

Sixties, he was talking about bringing *more* games to Birmingham. The city of Birmingham—the Parks and Recreation board—they had a good, strong relationship with the University of Alabama. So I can see how it happened. And I don't begrudge them.

I'm gonna tell you something else: If I'd been an Alabama guy, I'd have fought like hell to keep them from having to come down here (to Auburn). So why am I gonna begrudge them, get mad at them, for doing something I would've done? Alabama had an advantage as long as that game was played in Birmingham. We all know that.

The Kick Six? Had that happened in Birmingham—well, we all know it wouldn't have happened in Birmingham, because that sideline would've moved in... (Laughter).

In my younger days I was full of vim and vigor and spite, and I really hated Birmingham and Legion Field and so on. But they were just doing what I would've done if I'd been in their shoes, so why should I get mad about that?

"If you're having to play a team 'away' all the time, they don't respect you. There's some dissatisfaction about being unequal. On Dec. 2, 1989, we gave Auburn people who had wanted that equal footing — we gave it to them. That will always be special to me."
—Quentin Riggins, Auburn linebacker

"I think it leveled the playing field for the Auburn-Alabama game, that game did. I don't think that's an overstatement."
—Charlie Trotman, former Auburn QB and radio analyst

John Ringer

The thing I remember about the game is that, I think, a lot of times in history the crowd at Jordan-Hare has influenced the outcome of a game, but never like that game. The will of the crowd in the stadium just carried into the team.

David Housel

I agree with you about the crowd. And I think the crowd built up the whole year and in particular that week.

I'll tell you how I felt about it. I remember this coming to my mind walking from Sewell Hall back to the athletic complex, looking over at the stadium. My great fear was that Alabama would come in and win the game. But suddenly it occurred to me, walking back from the athletic complex, I said to myself, "It's not going to happen. They are *not* going to win. The Ghost of Auburn Past—everything that has ever been Auburn—is going to rise up."

Notre Dame talked about shaking down the echoes and cheering her name. Well, I had the same sensation, but the Ghost of Auburn Past—you know, all the great players—the Ghost of Auburn Past was going to rise up and (Alabama) will not prevail. They will *not* prevail. We're not gonna let this thing happen.

And I think people in the stands, I think everybody (felt that way). I think there are times when the spiritual world touches the mortal world. I think that was one of those times.

You might think that's crazier than hell, but that's what I believe. That's what I feel. There are moments. And everything that's ever been Auburn came up that day, and Auburn was going to win. I think there's a tremendous spiritual aspect in it. And I think it was much bigger than Pat Dye. It's much bigger than Reggie Slack and it's much bigger than all the players on that team and it's much bigger than the fans. I think there was a wellspring of whatever it is that Auburn is. It was *all* there that day.

You can't win with emotion. Emotion won't play for sixty minutes. But it damn sure can have an effect.

Van Allen Plexico

It's better than the lack of it sometimes. Alabama was being more businesslike (about that game).

David Housel

Yeah.

Van Allen Plexico
Ever since that game, Alabama has always given the excuse of, "Well, we could never have been expected to win in an environment like that." That's what I always hear from Alabama fans. It's like they all memorized this phrase.

David Housel
That may be true. It may well be true.

John Ringer
I agree with that statement. I don't think there's anything they could have done to win the football game.

David Housel
I think it would have been a fluke, I really do.

Van Plexico
We'd have had to turn the ball over a bunch or something.

David Housel
We would have had to have had an Ed Sessions fumble.

And this may sound strange, but in the year 2000, when we finally went over there (to Tuscaloosa for the Iron Bowl), they were having a bad, terrible year, so they were not going to be very high anyway. But it was cold, snowing and raining. And I never thought I'd say this, but I kind of hate it for them that they didn't have the same opportunity to have that experience of your number one rival coming in and all your colors and your happiness and a beautiful day. I think we would have still beaten them, but I kind of hate it for them.

But I don't hate it *too* bad.

In the years since the First Time Ever game, generations of Auburn fans have been born, grown up, and come of age in a world where Alabama—without complaint or threat of legal action—travels down to Auburn to play the Iron Bowl in Jordan-Hare Stadium every single time Auburn is the home team.

Because of course they do. How else could it be? Who today could conceive of a different scenario?

278

But it all started somewhere. There had to be a *first time*.

"There's no way, no way people of this generation can understand what having that game meant here in 1989."
—David Housel

"Three decades removed from the event it may not seem like a big deal to a generation of fans who have known nothing else. But trust me. It was a big deal. It was simply the most emotional game I've ever attended in my 44 years of covering college football."
—Tony Barnhart

John Ringer
Looking back now, all these years later, why is it so important—especially for the younger Auburn people, who don't understand what happened and why?

David Housel
Well, thank God these younger Auburn people don't understand. Thank God they don't, because if December 2, 1989, had never happened, they'd still be going to Birmingham and they'd still be ridiculed. They would still be made fun of. Still be seen as second-class citizens.

But December 2, 1989, *happened*. All of a sudden, we are first-class citizens now. Not better than anybody, but not below anybody. And these kids don't know what it means to (be able to) play Alabama here in Auburn. And every year we play them, it will be more the routine thing.

We don't really think about having to play Georgia in Columbus, or Tech in Atlanta. Because December 2 happened, they don't have to hear what we had to put up with.

Thank God they don't have to.

Van Allen Plexico
They've grown up seeing us on an equal footing with Alabama their entire lives.

They've seen us win a third Heisman and a national championship and almost win another. And they see Alabama come to Jordan-Hare every time we are the home team, with no complaints.

Perhaps, to them, it's just uncomfortable to think there ever was a time it *wasn't* like that.

But there was.

Until there wasn't anymore.

John Ringer

What does this game mean now? At that time, we knew what it meant. But, looking back, what is the legacy of that game? What does it mean for Auburn people?

Mark Murphy

There could never be a do-over of that game. The first time at Auburn, Auburn won the game, which was really important to Auburn people. Just incredibly important. That's why the intensity was what it was. And it was just like, "I'll never be at another sporting event as intense as that one was." Nothing has even come close.

We had a beat Bama Bama party at our house the night before. And we had a lot of people there. We had 150-200 people. And that was the most fired up group of Auburn people I've ever seen. They were like, you know, like the Blues Brothers: They were on a mission. Whatever it took to win that game, people were doing it. And people just desperately wanted to win the game because Auburn people felt that Alabama people looked down on Auburn, and Auburn people didn't like that at all. And I think that's part of the reason why this was such a big deal.

Van Allen Plexico

Did it change the program? Elevate how we are seen? How this institution, this program is seen nationally?

Mark Murphy

I think it certainly helped. But I think the whole of the Eighties changed the scenario too, because Auburn had so many good teams, and they became so relevant on the national stage. But yeah, that game—the third straight SEC championship, winning a really big spotlight game like that and doing it against Alabama. All that just made it a monster game. And you know, the 2010 National Championship game was really big. But I think to Auburn people it was more important to win that 1989 Alabama game.

John Ringer
I think so too.

Do you think it changed how Auburn people view themselves, the football team, and our relationship with Alabama?

Mark Murphy
I don't think it really changed our relationship with Alabama fans, because I've always thought Auburn people considered themselves better than Alabama folks. No ifs, ands, or buts about it. But they liked to win the football game and remind their Alabama friends about it 365 days a year.

David Housel
For the first time, Auburn was equal. For the first time, nobody could tell us where we had to play our home games. So for the first time in history, we were equal.

But I think by being equal it also takes away excuses. You know, as long as you can say, "Well, we had to play in Birmingham, we got our ass beat in Birmingham." That (1989) game took away all the excuses Auburn ever had. You know, that's a risk and a reward thing. And Auburn had to have that game here. Otherwise, we could always have a crutch to come back on.

Auburn has no crutches now.

Van Allen Plexico
You can't say you're a top flight program, but then still have something that you can point to as an excuse.

David Housel

That's exactly right. For the first time in history, Auburn was in control of its own program. We were in control of our destiny. No excuses anymore.

Van Allen Plexico

It's hard to imagine it took until 1989 for that to be the case.

David Housel

Well, nobody was pushing it.

Van Allen Plexico

Yeah, and the Bear was so dominant for so long. What he wanted was going to happen.

David Housel

And Birmingham had so much political power.

At some point—you can go back in the history of Alabama, and I don't know when it was, but—they redistricted the legislature. There was some big federal court case where I think (the state legislature) was reapportioned. The Senate was reapportioned based on population. That's when Birmingham's political power began to go down.

But the bottom line is that Auburn's stadium was not big enough to even talk about it until 1960. It still took twenty-nine years. Coach Jordan said it will happen sometime, but there's going to have to be some real prominent funerals. He was talking about Bryant, but it wound up that he was one of them, too.

The First Time Ever Auburn team has been honored multiple times in the years since 1989. Gene Chizik had some of the players participate in Tiger Walk before the 2009 Iron Bowl to commemorate the 20th anniversary. The 25th anniversary was celebrated prior to the homecoming game against Louisiana Tech in 2014, and the university hosted a gathering for the players on the night before that game. The team was recognized again during the 2019 Iron Bowl, on the 30th anniversary.

Van Allen Plexico

It's too bad we can't just retire the jerseys of that entire team. Or make a statue of them as a group.

Hopefully this book will help commemorate their accomplishment as well.

After the 1989 Iron Bowl, Alabama still had a shot at winning a share of the national championship. To do that, they needed to beat Miami in the Sugar Bowl, but they lost to the Hurricanes, 33-25. They were the only one of the three SEC co-champions to lose their bowl game.

Six days after that loss, on January 7, 1990, Bill Curry resigned. Two days after that, he was named the new head coach at Kentucky.

His overall record at Alabama was 26-10. Possibly more importantly, as the Alabama head coach, he was 0-3 against the Auburn Tigers.

Van Allen Plexico

I agree with David Housel that there's a lot to like and respect about Bill Curry. But there are also plenty of things he's said and done, many of them documented here, that leave me scratching my head, at best.

Let's leave it at that.

And then there's Patrick Fain Dye.

Coach Dye would go on to coach the Auburn Tigers for three more seasons before retiring after the 1992 Iron Bowl. The reasons for his retirement are controversial. His health was deteriorating, but other issues were involved as well.

It's hard to imagine today that this would turn out to be the *only* Iron Bowl he would get to coach in Auburn. And the *last* Iron Bowl he would win.

Van Allen Plexico

Coach Dye finished his career 6-6 against Alabama, losing his first one, two in the middle he absolutely shouldn't have, and then the last three. Eleven of the twelve Iron Bowls he coached for Auburn were played in Birmingham. When he and Bobby Lowder threw Alabama the bone of the 1991 game,

283

they didn't realize they were giving away the other half of Coach Dye's opportunities to coach Iron Bowls at home.

"Coach Dye returned Auburn to national relevance in the 1980s and helped make it the tradition-rich program that it is today. He helped bring the Iron Bowl to Auburn and most importantly helped shape the lives of hundreds of men that played for him. I wouldn't be the person I am today without Coach Dye."
—Bo Jackson

Coach Pat Dye passed away on June 1, 2020.

In 2005, he was inducted into the National Football Foundation's College Football Hall of Fame. That same year, the playing field at Jordan-Hare Stadium was named for him.

The playing field where, on December 2, 1989, he led the Tigers to victory over Alabama in the *First Time Ever* Iron Bowl in Jordan-Hare Stadium.

The Promised Land, indeed...

-18-

CONCLUSIONS

After many months of research and reading and watching videos and digging through old newspapers and interviewing people, and then discussing and analyzing all of it, we can state the following:

Going all the way back to the first two meetings in 1893, Auburn was the dominant football power in the state. Alabama was not as invested in football during that era as Auburn was. The few games Alabama managed to win were all tainted by some degree of accusations of foul play on the part of the Tide.

After the 1895 game, Alabama demanded that all future Iron Bowls—home and away—be played in Tuscaloosa. When Auburn refused to go along, the series ended for five years. It was restored in 1900 mainly due to the outrage and protests of Alabama students and fans, demanding the university return to playing normal home and away games against prominent programs.

After the 1907 game, Alabama demanded that Auburn agree to Alabama's terms on player expenses and on which referees were acceptable for future games, among other issues. When Auburn refused to go along with all of Alabama's demands, the series ended for forty-one years. During that time, Auburn de-emphasized football just as Alabama began to emphasize it.

The series was restored in 1948 only after threats from the state legislature and discussions between the presidents of the two universities, as well as the extraction of promises from the state for additional funds for infrastructure on both campuses.

By that time, Alabama had become the dominant side of the rivalry. The series resumption agreement included playing the Iron Bowl in Birmingham temporarily, but then "temporarily" became permanent.

Alabama gained certain advantages, thanks to coaches like Wade, Thomas and especially Bryant, and was reluctant to part with them. That included playing the Iron Bowl where Alabama wanted to play it.

In the mid-1980s, when Auburn people began to raise the issue publicly, Alabama refused to allow Auburn to choose where its future home games in the series would be played. Their representatives categorically stated that Alabama would "never" come to Auburn to play the Iron Bowl. When Auburn balked at this, Alabama threatened to end the series yet again. The series was saved only through the efforts of leaders from both universities, who were able to work out a compromise that allowed Alabama to save face by publicly twisting Auburn's arm one last time.

The fact that this could be accomplished at all was nearly miraculous. It took transcendent figures such as Pat Dye and Bo Jackson to elevate Auburn football to a place where it could challenge Alabama's will. It took visionary and determined leaders such as Bobby Lowder and David Housel and Hanly Funderburk and the Auburn Board of Trustees to provide the infrastructure and the leadership necessary to push through to victory.

Until the early 1980s, Coach Paul "Bear" Bryant held such sway over the state that moving the game was nearly unthinkable. The fact that he had a signed agreement with Auburn to continue playing in Birmingham for a few more years only helped Alabama's position. (How long that agreement was good for, of course, is a separate and still-contentious issue.) Once Bryant was gone from the picture, however, Alabama slowly accepted reality and had to back down from thinking they could dictate all aspects of the series.

Playing the game in Auburn in 1989 (rather than in 1991) became a point of pride for Dye and Auburn and an absolute line in the sand that we would not give up. A compromise was worked out that allowed this to happen.

The game was played on December 2, 1989, in Jordan-Hare Stadium, for the First Time Ever. Auburn won the game. Auburn won in a place many Alabama people said was not capable of hosting the game. Auburn won in a place to which many Alabama people refused even to travel. Auburn won a game about which Alabama people had outright stated, "It won't happen"—the game will *never* be played there. And Auburn won it over an undefeated and second-ranked Alabama team loaded with weapons on offense and defense.

It happened.

Van Allen Plexico

The story of the Iron Bowl is the story of Auburn routinely having to deal with Alabama's (usually unreasonable) demands, and finding a way around them. The story of the 1989 Iron Bowl is the story of what happened when Auburn was finally in a position to push to get its way, and finally succeeded.

I believe Alabama really sort of lucked into the Birmingham situation, as part of the 1948 settlement to resume the series. But as playing the game there developed over the years into a serious edge for Alabama, I think they had no problem taking advantage of Auburn for as long as they could get away with it. By the 1980s, however, for various reasons, they could no longer really get away with it.

Auburn's biggest concern in the early Eighties was simply building a winning program. Once that was achieved, we could turn our attention to other issues. And when we started looking at where the Iron Bowl was being played every year, we got a little bit angry and resentful towards Alabama. And the attitude of the Alabama people at that point only made matters worse.

I have to add that I am struck by how little the SEC itself had to say or do with all of this. Never in our research did we find one mention that Southeastern Conference officials were ready to lay down the law and defend Auburn's right to host its own home game where it pleased. It's virtually impossible to imagine such a situation happening today, when the conference determines so much about how many games each team plays, and where, and when.

I think we as Auburn people were able to get a lot of motivation out of two areas of resentment toward Alabama here. One, we used our resentment over the game being played in Birmingham to fuel our efforts to move it to Auburn in the odd-numbered years, and to make it happen sooner rather than later—1989, not 1991 or later. Thanks to Bobby Lowder and David Housel and Pat Dye and the trustees and others, we got that done. Two, we used that same pent-up resentment and hostility toward Alabama to fuel the efforts of the players and coaches and fans, down on the field and in the stands around it, to win that First Time Ever game in 1989.

John Ringer

The football game played between the University of Alabama and Auburn University in Auburn on December 2, 1989 was the single most important game in Auburn history. I hope that this book has helped illustrate why I believe this to be true.

This game was a turning point in how Auburn fans saw themselves, their football team, and their rivals from across the state. And it was the final step in Auburn seizing control of its own destiny in football. Would everything be rosy every year afterward? Of course not. But no one else was going to take home games away from Auburn—and home games have often been Auburn's best weapon.

I have attended hundreds of college football games over the years at a variety of stadiums. Do the home fans cheer at every one of them, and try to support their team? Do the home fans try to cause problems for the opposing team? Yes. Does it work? Sometimes. LSU and Florida are tough places to play as a visitor. Auburn's Jordan-Hare Stadium is a tough place to play as a visiting team. But I truly believe that the will of the crowd and the energy that it generated helped to lift that Auburn team up that one December day. It helped them to play just a little bit better than they normally could; to go a little bit longer at maximum effort; to recover a little bit more quickly; to run just a bit faster.

Often I have seen the home crowd impact a visiting team with noise that disrupts communication and disorients players. And this crowd did try to impact the Alabama team's offense. But this one example stands up to me as a positive vibe and energy from a fan base that thought, "Come on—you have got this! We believe in you!" It was real and it mattered. Even when Alabama took the lead, it was not the nervous, "Oh, here we go again!" reaction that you see from some fan bases.

I was there that day and, watching the game again, I remember the feeling. For this one day, this one time, it really did matter, and it helped tip the scales. The spirit and will of that crowd was a real and tangible thing that impacted the outcome of the football game by lifting up the Auburn team. The collective will of Auburn—players, coaches, and fans— was far stronger than Alabama's that day.

There are football games that matter for bowl eligibility or a chance to play in a conference championship game or, soon, for the playoffs. But there are very, very, very few college football games that *matter*. This game *mattered* and I am very thankful that I got to be there that day with my family, my friends, and so many good Auburn people who made this day happen.

Van Allen Plexico

The last thing I want to touch on here is this: What if we had *lost*?

In the days leading up to the game, Coach Dye and David Housel, among others, tried to emphasize the historical nature of Alabama coming to Auburn at all. And that's totally fair. But what they were also doing, intentionally or not, was minimizing the game's *outcome* beforehand, in case Auburn lost.

Had Auburn lost the game, it would still have been a historic moment, absolutely. It would have been, as Dye and Housel said, a grand accomplishment. It would also have been a line item to check off on the list of milestones chronicling the rise of Auburn football.

"Moved the home game with Georgia Tech to Auburn: *check*. Moved the home game with Tennessee to Auburn:

check. Won the SEC a few times: *check*. Won the Heisman Trophy: *check*. Moved the home game with Alabama to Auburn: *check*."

Had Auburn *lost* the game, as time went by, we might still occasionally look back at that day and think, "Thank goodness we were able to move the game to Auburn. It was a big thing just to do that. And then of course later on we actually *won* a game there." We'd be happy about the overall accomplishment. But we wouldn't be celebrating that day. We wouldn't think of December 2, 1989, as something like a holy day, I don't think.

By winning the game, Auburn elevated the moment, the day, the occasion, the event to legendary status. It went from being a very important milestone for happening at all, to a *singular, triumphant* moment in Auburn history.

It would still have been the First Time Ever. But we wouldn't want to look back on it, aside from appreciating the pageantry of the day. We would have no interest in reliving the game itself, or all the moments afterward. The talk would be about how we had this amazing Tiger Walk, and had all that excitement and electricity in the air—and then we *lost*. We would probably justify it by talking about how Alabama was, after all, an undefeated team, on their way to playing Miami for the national championship, and they were just too much for us on that day. The excitement of the fans, we would tell each other, can only go so far and do so much. The players themselves had to win the game, and *gosh darn it*, we shouldn't have *expected* them to work miracles against a superior opponent out there on the field. We would remind one another that the historic nature of the event couldn't make our backs run better or our line block better or our receivers catch the ball better or our defense tackle better—not after the initial adrenaline wore off, anyway.

I found an interview with Alabama quarterback Gary Hollingsworth, conducted in 2020. They discussed his biggest games ever in his career. The 1989 Iron Bowl wasn't even *mentioned*. He was the starting quarterback for one side of one of the most important college football games ever played, anywhere, ever. And for them it's like it never happened.

Alabama fans have very little interest in talking about it. I don't think that's precisely how we'd look at that day, if we'd lost. But it's probably closer to it than we'd like to admit.

I was at the first Iron Bowl played in Auburn that *Alabama* won, in 1999. It was *horrible*.

It took them until their fifth try, with us having four wins there under our belt, before they pulled it off. We were used to beating them there. We had a padding of wins. Losing that one game only made it 4-1 our way. And even so, it was an absolutely horrible experience.

Losing the game on December 2, 1989, would have been fifty times worse than that. A *hundred* times worse.

But we *didn't* lose.

The running backs *did* run better. The line *did* block better. The receivers *did* catch the ball better. And the defense *did* tackle better.

Everyone in orange and blue had a hand in it, that day. Together, we all got it done. No explanations, no justifications, no excuses were necessary.

Playing the game at all was a historic event. *Winning* the game moved it from "an item to check off on a list" to an absolutely *legendary* day. A day, and a moment in time, we would cherish and remember and relive forever.

A day we would want to write a book about.

The day *Alabama came to Auburn*, and *Auburn won the day*.

War Eagle forever.

—Van Allen Plexico and John Ringer
Fall 2023

– NOTES –

In November 2022, the authors conducted new interviews with David Housel, former Athletic Director and Sports Information Director at Auburn University; Clyde Prather, former Public Safety Director, and Mark Murphy of *Inside the Auburn Tigers* and *Auburn Undercover*.

We would like to thank these gentlemen for giving so generously of their time.

In addition, Mr. Murphy provided several documents that were of great use in research for this book.

Several original and secondary sources were used throughout this book. Others were only used in specific locations.

Major sources *throughout* included:

The 1989 *Auburn Football Media Guide*

Auburn Football Illustrated program for the 1989 Iron Bowl

The Montgomery Advertiser

"'We'll play '89 in Auburn': How Pat Dye helped break Birmingham's 40-year Iron Bowl stranglehold," by Creg Stephenson, *AL dot com*, Nov. 25, 2019.

"'You sunk some deep roots here': 30 years later, Auburn still hasn't forgotten its 1st time," by Tom Green, Nov. 26, 2019.

"'Not nearly enough that day': 1989 Iron Bowl loss derailed Alabama's title hopes," by Creg Stephenson, AL dot com, Nov. 27, 2019.

Brief excerpts from the Foreword by David Housel to the book, *Tiger Walk to Victory*, by Liston Eddins, Barry Mask, and Mike Goodson, 1990.

"The most emotional day in Auburn history": Impact of 1989 Iron Bowl still being felt 30 years later - Josh Vitale, *Montgomery Advertiser*, 2019

"The real story: How Auburn dragged Alabama to Jordan-Hare Stadium" - Phillip Marshall, *Auburn Undercover*, Nov. 22, 2021

"Iron Bowl 1989: the first Iron Bowl at Jordan-Hare Stadium" - Jacob Waters, *Auburn Plainsman*, Nov. 27, 2021

"Mr. CFB: Pat Dye Changed the Dynamic of the Auburn-Alabama Game Forever" - Tony Barnhart, *TMG Sports*, June 3, 2020

"1989 Auburn Tigers gave 'whatever it took' to win 'First Time Ever' Iron Bowl" - Jeff Shearer, *AuburnTigers dot com*, April 13, 2020

"Iron Bowl 75: Alabama-Auburn disputes caused 41-year hiatus of the big game" by Jon Solomon - AL dot com, Nov. 24, 2010

"Iron Bowl History: The Missing Decades (1907-1949)" by John Cameron - *Mobile Press-Register*, Nov. 26, 2010

"Strange but true stories from the 40-year Iron Bowl hiatus" by Alex Scarborough- ESPN, Nov. 21, 2018

Additional Sources

Chapters 1-3
Sources for these chapters, as well as material about the earliest Iron Bowls in subsequent chapters, came primarily from accounts published the day after each game in the *Birmingham (Daily) News* and the *Montgomery Advertiser*. We discovered John Chandler Griffin's book, *Auburn Vs Alabama: Gridiron Grudge Since 1893* after our chapters were written. Griffin covers much of the same ground we covered here, and apparently using the same or similar sources, and therefore provided a good way to double-check some of the reporting for accuracy, as well as for the full names of players and coaches involved.

Chapter 4
Same sources as Chapters 1-3, plus the Alex Scarborough article on ESPN's website.

Supplemental material by Phillip Marshall, Michael Skotnicki and Will Collier.

Chapter 5
This chapter depended heavily on primary reporting from the earliest years of the rivalry in the *Montgomery Advertiser*, along with Zipp Newman in the *Birmingham News*. John Cameron's contemporary notes in the *Mobile Press-Register* proved valuable, as well as the ever-valuable writing in more recent years of Phillip Marshall in the *Montgomery Advertiser*, and our 2022 interview with David Housel.

Chapter 6
Reporting from the *Montgomery Advertiser* in 1972 contributed to this chapter, along with YouTube videos of the game. Mike McClendon of the AU-Sports Mailing List contributed contemporary analysis.

Chapter 7

Much information from this chapter came from reporting in the *Montgomery Advertiser*. The conversation between Pat Dye and Bear Bryant, over moving the Iron Bowl to Auburn, as recounted here, is an amalgamation of reporting and quotes by Creg Stephenson on AL dot com in 2019 and Ivan Maisel on the ESPN website in 2020. Mike McClendon of the AU-Sports Mailing List contributed contemporary analysis.

Chapter 8

A few quotes come from the "Decade of the Eighties" video tape Auburn produced circa 1990, and from the Auburn Football Review TV show. Other reporting came from the *Montgomery Advertiser* during that era.

Chapter 9

Mark Murphy and David Housel sat for interviews with the authors in November 2022. Mike McClendon of the AU-Sports Mailing List contributed material. Other reporting comes from the *Montgomery Advertiser*, as well as from *In the Arena* by Pat Dye (with John Logue) and *Touchdown Auburn* by Jim Fyffe (with Rich Donnell), and from writing by Creg Stephenson in 2019.

Chapter 10

The *Auburn Football Media Guide* contributed material about the Football Complex. The story of "the true, criminal origins of the Toomer's Corner tiger paw" was published on *The War Eagle Reader* web site on March 12, 2015, by Jeremy Henderson. More of the Mark Murphy and David Housel interviews were used here, as well as a 2022 interview with Auburn's former Public Safety Director, Clyde Prather. AP reporting was also used. Some player quotes are from "1989 Auburn Tigers gave 'whatever it took' to win 'First Time Ever' Iron Bowl" by Jeff Shearer, AuburnTigers dot com, April 13, 2020.

Chapter 11

The David Housel column appeared in *Auburn Football Illustrated*, the official game program, on December 2, 1989. The eagle statue information was provided to the authors by Everett

Duke, former AU Libraries development officer. Player quotes are from the *Montgomery Advertiser* and from Jeff Shearer's column (above). Quoting from Jim Nantz, Pat Haden and John Dockery are from the CBS television broadcast of the game, via authors' personal recordings collection and YouTube.

Chapters 12-15

Quoting from Jim Nantz, Pat Haden and John Dockery are from the CBS television broadcast of the game, via authors' personal recordings collection and YouTube. Player quotes come from the *Montgomery Advertiser* and other media sources, including columns by Creg Stephenson and Tom Green.

Chapter 16

Player quotes are from AL dot com, the *Montgomery Advertiser* and the Creg Stephenson and Tom Green columns noted above. Mark Murphy was interviewed by the authors in 2022.

Chapter 17

Some material here comes from the Creg Stephenson and Tom Green columns noted above. David Housel and Mark Murphy were interviewed by the authors in 2022.

– APPENDIX 1 –
1989 AUBURN TEAM ROSTER

The 1989 Pre-Season Depth Chart came from the 1989 *Auburn Football Media Guide*, provided by Mark Murphy of *Inside the Auburn Tigers* and *Auburn Undercover*.

1989 AUBURN TIGERS
Pre-Season Depth Chart

Offense:
Wide Receiver: 16 Greg Taylor, 18 Alexander Wright, 25 Andy Stidfole
Tight End: 87 Victor Hall, 86 Chris Gray, 82 Pat Autrey
Left Tackle: 70 Bob Meeks, 64 Anthony Brown
Left Guard: 67 Ed King, 73 Tim Tillman
Center: 66 John Hudson, 57 Travis Gallaway
Right Guard: 51 Mark Rose, 62 Brad Johnson, 71 Kevin Morgan
Right Tackle: 78 Rob Selby, 75 Jeff Catullo
Wide Receiver: 8 Shayne Wasden, 18 Alexander Wright, 4 Dale Overton

Quarterback: 17 Reggie Slack, 15 Frank McIntosh, 19 Matt Vogler

Fullback: 26 Teapot Brown, 33 John Stewart, 40 Alex Strong

Tailback: 32 Stacy Danley, 10 James Joseph, 40 Alex Strong

Defense:

Left Outside Linebacker: 94 Craig Ogletree, 99 Larry Young, 49 Hal Clemmer

Left Tackle: 72 Jon Wilson, 98 Mike Campbell, 77 Fernando Horn

Noseguard: 93 Richard Shea, 68 Mark Boring

Right Tackle: 95 David Rocker, 91 Lamar Rogers

Right Outside Linebacker: 47 Eltin Billingslea, 96 Clarence Morton, 49 Hal Clemmer

Sam Inside Linebacker: 41 Quentin Riggins, 59 Anthony Judge, 55 Wayne Bylsma

Mike Inside Linebacker: 43 Darrell Crawford, 38 Steve Brown, 46 Tim Garner

Left Cornerback: 27 Eric Ramsey, 9 John Wiley, 39 Charles Kelly

Strong Safety: 30 Dennis Wallace, 31 Roy Hunter, 22 Dennis Wright

Free Safety: 9 John Wiley, 29 Frank Stankunas, 24 Alex Thomas

Right Cornerback: 12 Corey Barlow, 13 Dominko Anderson, 23 Robert Zander

Specialists:

Punter: 5 Chris Dickinson, 1 Richie Nell

PlaceKicker: 6 Win Lyle, 2 Jim Von Wyl, 3 Clay Davis

Kickoffs: 2 Jim Von Wyl, 3 Clay Davis

Kickoff Returns: 8 Shayne Wasden, 18 Alexander Wright

Punt Returns: 8 Shayne Wasden, 4 Dale Overton

Snapper: 66 John Hudson, 57 Travis Galloway, 58 Ron Birchfield

– APPENDIX 2 –
1893 AUBURN TEAM ROSTER

The 1893 depth chart came from *Auburn vs Alabama: Gridiron Grudge Since 1893*, by John Chandler Griffin, as well as various original newspaper stories from that era.

1893 AUBURN TIGERS

Dr. George Petrie served as head coach of the first Auburn football team, which played its four games in the spring and fall of 1892.

D. M. "Pete" Balliet took over the job for one game, at the beginning of the Tigers' second season: the inaugural Iron Bowl, played in February, 1893. Auburn won it.

The Auburn roster for the first-ever Iron Bowl:

Quarterback: Dunham
Right halfback: Dorsey
Left halfback: Shackelford
Fullback: Daniels (captain)

Center: Shafer
Right guard: McKissick
Left guard: Brown
Right tackle: Buckalew
Left tackle: Redding
Right end: Foy
Left end: Riggs
Subs: Shafer, Stevens, Loveless, Powers

After Balliet departed, George Roy Harvey became head coach, prior to the fall portion of the 1893 season. He led the Tigers to victory in the second Iron Bowl ever played, in November of that same year.

– APPENDIX 3 –
MEMORIES

We asked the AU Wishbone's patrons, as well as Auburn fans on Twitter and Facebook, about their memories of the game. Their responses were instant and overwhelming. Space prohibits reprinting everything (and some have been edited slightly for clarity), but here is a nice, representative sample of what the Auburn Family said in response to these two questions:

What was the most memorable thing about the 1989 "First Time Ever" Iron Bowl?
How did it change Auburn and/or the Auburn Family?
Thanks & War Eagle!!

Bruce Pate
My most memorable thing was the stadium and the huge crowd. It was my first experience of the noise of a crowd that size, which was awesome. Although I spent my Freshman and Sophomore year at Alabama in Tuscaloosa, this Iron Bowl was the first college football game I had ever attended. I wasn't really

into football or any kind of sports during my life. I was a nerd and only went to high school football games because it was a band requirement. The only reason I went to this Iron Bowl was because my uncle had a group of alumni tickets and he offered me a seat. I was told to come early, I think so I could participate in tailgating activities, but I was not a social person, so I spent the early afternoon driving around town seeing the sights. I do recall driving on Shug-Jordan Parkway and Wire Road. I recall thinking, "If I were going to school here, I would feel safe riding my bike to class".

You see, where I was living in Tuscaloosa, I was not close to campus. There were maybe 10 traffic lights getting to class, and one place I lived had car break-ins on the regular. I could tell Auburn was like living on a farm. Chicken houses, horse pastures (vet school)... It seemed to be not a place I had to be, but rather a place I wanted to live.

After returning from the game, I started making plans to transfer to Auburn ASAP.

Patrick Williams
I was a senior in high school at the time of the 1989 Iron Bowl, and I had been attending a few games per season since the 1984 season. My most indelible memory of that game was how bizarre it was to see Alabama fans on Auburn's campus.

Also it is hilarious to me that Auburn had an extra player in formation on James Joseph's touchdown. Jim Fyffe's call of "full house backfield" was very true!

Mickey Howle
It was the biggest party in the state of Alabama.

Linda Kennedy Kilgore
Been an AU ticket holder since 1968! Go to all the games! There has never been another game to rival the 1989 Iron Bowl in Auburn! I stayed in Auburn from Thursday to Sunday (we rented a house)!

From the parade, pep rally and dance in Plainsman Park, and Tiger Walk, the atmosphere was electric! The stadium crowd roared the entire game!! It was intense!

One thing I loved the most and will never forget is how Pat Dye taught us, at the Pep Rally, how we as the crowd were going to help win the game! Coach Dye actually had the crowd practice how to yell when Alabama had the ball and how we were to be quiet when AU had the ball. We practiced several times. He and the players made us all believe there was no other way but to win, and win we did! Alabama fans were stunned! It was a rolling good time at Toomer's Corner!

James and Melissa Heron

Tiger Walk was phenomenal! There was a feeling early that morning (we got to our tailgate spot around 6:00 a.m.) that it was our day. No way we could lose. I have a friend who was on the Alabama team that year. He said the crowd made them uneasy going in. Their bus was being rocked by the fans. First time I think everyone (the nation) truly experienced what "the Auburn Family" is all about.

Beth Wages Johnson

1. The stadium was FULL two hours before kickoff, and many of us had already lost our voices from screaming by the time the paper shaker dust filled the air at kickoff.

2. It proved that what we'd said for years was true: "If we could only play them in Auburn...."

Jannie Whitt Smith

1. The thrill of being there for sports history in the making. We could feel like something special was about to take place, and it DID!!!

2. Auburn was no longer the step-child in the Alabama-Auburn rivalry!

Wendy Moore Jowers

Bama finally came to Auburn! They were undefeated. The atmosphere was unprecedented! The best thing was seeing the boxes of paper shakers by each entrance. EVERYBODY had a shaker and used it. It was an AUsome experience and one of my favorite memories!

Laura Kirkpatrick

I had been coming to every home Auburn game most of my life. I graduated from Auburn in 1987 and was then living in Birmingham which was mostly at that time a Bama town.

Traveling down 280 to Auburn that day was the most crowded I had ever seen that highway! I met up with all of my family from Dothan, we always parked at the old Amphitheater and had a tailgate prepared by my mama! The crowd that day was so electric, like none I had ever experienced! Tiger Walk was epic for sure! The game was amazing and the level of excitement carried on into the night!

I think it was a pivotal moment for the Auburn Athletic Dept. Bear Bryant said that game would never happen, and when it did, I believe it changed the country's view of Auburn Football. We were no longer just considered a stepbrother or a cow college. What a great experience for us all that were fortunate enough to be in attendance!

Roy Tona Hines

Having a bunch of Alabama fans as tailgating neighbors. Unlike bammers, they had some class (and actual connections to UA) and we really enjoyed being around them. It didn't change Auburn one iota; we already knew we were the best fans in America. Plus it got my road to Lake Martin (Highway 280) 4-laned, since most of Alabama state politicians were UA supporters (still are) and they didn't want to drive on that one-lane highway to Auburn every other year.

Lynne Stokley

1. Tiger Walk, easy—but the feeling I had after the pep rally at Plainsman Park on Friday was unbelievable. I knew, beyond any doubt, that we were going to win the next day. Listening to the players was awesome. I've never had that much confidence in a team or event—and it just carried over to Tiger Walk the next day!

2. Moving the game elevated Auburn in every way that matters and has been significant in the rivalry and series since. I'm thankful that Legion Field is a memory.

Iris Kerstan

The energy was amazing!

Mary Lee

I agree 100%, maybe once or twice in my life have I ever felt that pure energy and electricity in the air.

John Monroe

I was a sophomore at Auburn. I will never forget the blue & orange dust cloud from all of the paper shakers in the student section. Shakers for other home games were held back all year, and every student had a fist full of shakers for that game.

Kate Asbury Larkin

1. The atmosphere was like nothing I had ever experienced. I think my single most memorable thing was Tiger Walk; un-freakin-believeable crowd!

2. I think moving the game to Auburn made us more relevant.

Patsy Alford

1. The atmosphere was the most unbelievable ever.

2. Tiger walk had thousands; people were in the trees to see.

3. Stadium scene was exciting, moving and the best atmosphere anywhere.

4. This was Pat Dye's promise when he came.

Jamie Poland

1. The atmosphere was electric!!!!

2. Beating Bama on our home turf meant a lot that year to the Auburn Family and said a lot about the supposed neutral site of Legion Field.

Henry McMahan

I was there. Drove over from Starkville, MS. As I passed Loachapoka on 14, I was getting so excited that hairs were standing up on the back of my neck. I had seen a number of Auburn-Alabama games in Birmingham, but this one was different. I could feel it!!

Mike Henry

A man offered his car for a ticket at Tiger Walk (with) no takers.

I'm 75 years old, a lifelong sports fan. There has never been a sporting event that has ever come close. It's in a class by itself.

Judy Richeson

The atmosphere was absolutely ELECTRIC! But what I witnessed was Auburn fans being mostly courteous, although "War Eagle" was being yelled constantly. Several times we stopped some Bama fans and talked to them for a few minutes. We welcomed them, told them it was nice to meet them, hoped they had a good time in Auburn, seriously, may the better team win, and we all said it was time the games were being rotated between Auburn and Tuscaloosa.

This was SO financially important to Auburn University, the Auburn fan base, and the merchants to have the biggest rivalry in the Southeast played on home soil. And many who had never been to Auburn before, hopefully luring future students there. It was MEGA important for recruiting purposes too. I was so thankful and excited to be there that day! War Eagle!

Beth Jones

My son, Chris Jones played on the Special Teams in this game #43, defensive back! The atmosphere in Auburn was incredible all weekend! It was definitely "Great to be an Auburn Tiger" and always will be! Coach Dye had worked hard on getting this game moved to Auburn, it must have been a dream come true for this wonderful coach!

Peggy C. Vives-Austin

That it occurred, when Bear Bryant and all of the Alabama fanatics said it wouldn't. The crowd was so unbelievably happy. It made us feel we could do anything!

Shea Taylor Forman

As a member of the AU Marching Band down on the field, everything about that day seemed magical. The Auburn fans were there in force and were so incredibly loud. The team gave their all and the fans gave back. This time Bama was NOT going to win. This was OUR field, and OUR time. I still proudly wear the Tiger Rags game sweatshirt and it's an honor to tell my kids that I was there.

Sharon Griffin Fenn

It was amazing. The stadium was vibrating from the noise. I don't think anyone sat down for the entire game.

It gave Auburn a legitimate home game with Alabama.

Mary Baird
It was incredible! Best game ever! A victory on the field and a victory for Auburn against those who thought of us as the lesser team and university!

Tommy Snow
All the programs were sold out by 10 that morning and the campus was swarming like a bee hive.

David Reynolds
What I remember was the energy resonating throughout the entire stadium... Even though I was new to Auburn, I could feel all this energy from fans who had been told their whole lives Alabama would never play Auburn in Auburn, and now they were seeing it unfold in front of them. So much energy you just knew a win was a foregone conclusion. I think it changed the Auburn family because everyone knew there were no more "can't happens." We had arrived, forcing Alabama to treat us as a true equal, no more "little brother" for good.

Mr. NVRBRF on Twitter
I had withdrawn from school for the fall but already got my ticket. My childhood friend who was still enrolled, did NOT get a ticket through whatever lottery system they had.

He's still mad at me today.

AubieKong on Twitter
I was living in Texas at the time and watched it on TV. One of my close friends from high school is Win Lyle's uncle. Like other fans my age (70) it was a game I felt I had (waited) forever to see. A home Iron Bowl.

My friend told me later about his experience. He was allowed to hang around the athletic dorm all morning with Win and other players and coaches.

He said, "From the moment I walked through the door I KNEW we would win that game. The atmosphere of quiet confidence was incredible. The attitude of everyone in there was, "No way in hell are we gonna let them win this one!"

309

It was like the entire Auburn family collectively spent all of their energy directly on the team and the field that day to help win that game. NO ONE would even consider the possibility of not winning that day. We had waited too long to make them come to our house.

Win had 3 field goals and 3 extra points that day.

It was one of the most impressive wins I've ever seen.

Jen Hilton

I was there as a freshman. Woke up in Keller Hall on gameday to AU and Bama fans arguing in their RVs outside the window!

readandright on Twitter

I was there—living in Atlanta then. My dad had to work, and I came home and drove down to Auburn with my mom. The anticipation, the sense of redressing a grievous "thumb-on-the-scales" inequity in this series made the atmosphere electric. There was NO questioning Auburn victory.

Sandra Hutto

For me the most memorable thing about it was feeling the stands shaking in the student section and how loud it was! I think it helped show the Auburn Family that we belong and helped majorly boost confidence.

Aubiece on Twitter

Old school here—I grew up going to Legion Field for every Iron Bowl. "50/50 split," my butt. All the ushers there were decked out in Bama Gear, there were about 2500 gold stadium seats similar to TUFs for AU now that were all Bama. Have to remember Bama played all their big games in Bammerham, not Tuscaloosa. AU played UT and Bama in Bammerham. Bama played the rinky-dink teams in Tuscaloosa, big games AU, PSU, UT, LSU all in "Lesion Field."

Pat Dye standing up to them was Epic. They kicked and screamed and whined but had to come to Jordan-Hare. The stadium was electric that day. I remember the blue haze from the dust from the paper shakers.

As to changing the narrative, it gave AU a homefield which Lesion Field never was. Lesion Field was a dump in the early

Seventies when I played high school ball there, and nothing much has been done to it since. Jordan-Hare is a helluva home field advantage because of the AU Family and students. Coach Dye made that happen.

Marc Buffington on Twitter

I was there as a college student. We tried to rush the field, (but the police were) having none of that. Stayed so long we wandered into the press box and got play sheets and stuff. Crazy.

Beth Burgin Young

1. From a personal standpoint it was my first Iron Bowl and the last Auburn game I shared with my Daddy. The atmosphere before, during, and after was so electric.

2. The Auburn family finally got to host a true home game Iron Bowl!

Bob Clark

Tailgating for five days, watching the baseball team getting their SEC rings before the game, and then watching a great victory.

Horace Lee

It was on my birthday. I was 38. I took my Dad to experience it. We are both engineering graduates from Auburn. The most memorable thing I remember was that it was the first time I remember feeling electricity in the air. The crowd noise was awesome! It changed Auburn because more games were sold out after that game. Enthusiasm was alive and well after that game!

Howard Frontz

To be part of that Tiger Walk and the overall excitement of the whole day! We were equals to Alabama after that day, not just a "cow college"!

Kelli Donovan Hogue

I was a junior at Auburn. What I remember most was the cloud of shaker dust from all the paper shakers!!

Elisabeth Snell Wang

The Tiger Walk for that game was nothing short of sublime. It was other-worldly. We knew the day was special, but at that moment, we all knew we were a part of something that would never happen again.

Joy Givhan Bedsole

1. I was in the student section, and I remember the cloud of dust from the paper shakers. It was as far as I could see. And I still have my shakers!!

I also remember that there was absolutely no way that ANY Alabama team could have beaten Auburn that day. Auburn was unstoppable!!

2. In my Auburn eyes, Auburn was no longer overshadowed by big brother controlling us any longer — whether the other side agrees with us or not!

Kim Spencer

Most memorable was a toss-up between Tiger Walk (40,000 people and I was one!), the undeniable electricity in the air well before we even got to campus and the blue haze from the worn-out paper shakers by game's end!

It changed us because we knew we were finally on level ground with Alabama and Pat Dye had made good on his promise to make the Iron Bowl a home-and-home series like it always should have been. I will never forget that day.

Loring Muir

The Tiger Walk was incredible. I don't believe there has been another one quite like that one. That game validated that Auburn was no longer a little brother to UA.

Paul McCracken

I had to work so I watched the game on TV. Before the game, there was a shot of the Alabama team gathering in the portal from where I had seen opponents run out for years. I thought, "I guess they're just another football team now." Then it hit me: "I suppose that was the point."

Kathey McEachin

1. The excitement in the air all day. Tiger Walk was incredible. The haze in the stadium from the paper shakers. Orange and blue dust everywhere.

2. Gave us what was right—a home game.

Marla Brakefield Burch

1. The whole environment. I was a sophomore and the student section was crazy.

2. It literally put Auburn on the map and made Jordan-Hare a destination for people who've never been there for a game.

On a side note: My Dad bought season tickets to Auburn that year for that Alabama ticket. My dad was a die-hard Bama fan and their tickets were in the end zone next to the student section (this was before the student section was expanded through it). When we scored the last TD in that end zone, I could see my father, clear as day, in his red Bama sweatshirt scowling at everyone around him going crazy. He didn't speak to me for a week.

Donlyn Carpenter Sanders

1. The energy and 2. the orange and blue haze from the paper pom poms.

John Southerland

It was memorable for too many reasons, but one that stands out is the noise. I don't think I've ever heard a louder crowd anywhere for an entire game than what was experienced at JHS that day. Everyone seemed to be yelling full-throttle all the time.

2. It changed everything. For years we had complained about not getting to play Bama for a true home game, and finally, they were there. Playing that game on our terms for the first time ever was a crucial step in showing how far the football program had come, and how strong it could be going forward.

Joseph Scott Knight

1. Loudest I have ever heard the stadium. The paper shakers that everybody seemed to have, that created an orange and blue haze over the stadium.

2. Finally put us on even footing with Bama in the Iron Bowl. Legion Field was never an Auburn home game. We had to play

313

one more "home" game in Birmingham. The series is almost dead even since games have been played home and home.

Jan Boykin

The most memorable thing that I remember about the '89 game is the electric atmosphere. The Auburn family welcomed the UA fans to campus in true AU fashion. Moving this rivalry game on campus truly made it a "home" game for Auburn. The team and fans never felt like that while it was being played in Birmingham. WDE!

Jason Ross

1. My first Iron Bowl and the electrifying atmosphere. I knew there was no way we could lose!

2. It proved Auburn was here to stay and could go toe-to-toe with Bama and anyone. Jordan-Hare would be a factor from then on. War Eagle!

Melissa Montgomery

The most memorable thing to me is that I was in law school and had finals in five days but didn't think twice about going. I was there! I wouldn't have missed it. As a lifetime Auburn fan and former student, I was so excited they were playing in Auburn. I remember the feeling of all Auburn fans being so happy that day. The mood was great and it was a very friendly and welcoming experience for the Alabama fans. It changed Auburn because we felt the big game was finally home where it belonged.

Alison Watkins Walter

I was a student at the time and was there! It was an AUsome game and day! I remember the orange & blue fuzz from the paper shakers that permeated the sky.

Moving the game to Jordan-Hare meant a lot to the AU Family. Bama always claimed that Legion Field was a neutral site, but no way when at that time, they played about four or five of their games there each season (in addition to AU). I had a feeling it would be a good day and that we would "Cream Bama's Sugar" —and we did!!! My friends made a sign saying that—hoping to get on TV since the CBS Network carried the game.

Mark George

1) How electrical the environment was. The feeling was amazing and 70,000 orange shakers filled the air with orange dust.

2) By bringing the game home, we were finally recognized as being equal.

Robert Franklin

Watched on television. As a 2X Auburn graduate, former band member who grew up in Lee County, it brought tears to my eyes. You could feel the electricity in the air and the emotion and excitement of the day. Auburn had finally arrived. We were, begrudgingly, accepted as an equal to that school on the other side of the state! At least by their leadership!

Brian Hardin

1. I remember standing against the rail between Jordan-Hare and Plainsman Park to be able to see Tiger Walk. The feeling is one I've never had before or since—knowing we were going to win that day because of the moment. It was an emotional feeling that is unique to that day of all my Auburn memories.

2. I was a junior in high school but even at 16, I felt what it meant to have it finally in Auburn. The emotion of that day was something special - especially remembering how exciting it was for alumni like parents. It was a point of great pride to get to finally have the Iron Bowl in Auburn—to show why we love it so much—and to finally experience the atmosphere the AU Family knew we would have if we ever hosted Alabama in Jordan-Hare. We led the way because as we knew and deserved to have a true home Iron Bowl...and look who eventually followed.

Kevin Quinley

Finally got to see an Iron Bowl played in our stadium and the stands full of Blue & Orange!!!! Thank you, Coach Dye!!!

Sharon Lee

The game would NEVER be played in "Just Another Neutral Site." Who bought into that one anyway?

Jenny Wooddall Hunt

I was there and pregnant with our first child and morning sickness was an all day, all the time thing, but I made it. We stood the entire game. No one ever sat down and the noise meter that Jordan-Hare had then was almost always as high as it would go!

The pride that escalated in our home field and our fans and our school just went to an all-time high that day and kept soaring!

Mary Hendrix Knight

I was a senior at Auburn and it was the best game ever. The week leading up to the game was so electric around campus, and the atmosphere at the game was unlike any other! I remember seeing so much orange and blue dust from all the shakers, and was exhausted from standing and cheering so much during the game!!

Kelley MP

My husband and I were students there, dating at the time. We both agreed it was the most "alive" the fans had been about the game. You could feel the electricity in the air. To finally have a level playing field for this game was so exciting and to win just pushed the experience over the top. We had both been to the game in Birmingham, which always felt like an Alabama home game, so to finally feel validated was awesome.

Heather Witten

It was my first Iron Bowl my freshman year. It was such an electric atmosphere and solidified my love for Auburn and football.

I think the game being held at home was so special because the rivalry felt bigger and more personal.

Kathy Kimbrough Compton

Susan Bailey and I had a blast!!! It is a wonderful memory! There was a quietness before the game like none other and then a celebration of an AUsome win!!!! A game we will always treasure. War Eagle!!!

Laura Frances Griner

I remember the student section being full and loud an hour and a half before the game. We were packed in and never sat down.

It was a day that changed the dynamic of the rivalry. The Iron Bowl was no longer just another Bama home game every year.

Janet K Greer

It was one memorable event. Went with my Alabama fan husband and the win was so sweet.

Melissa Mount

1. The sea of fans at Tiger Walk set the tone for the rest of the day. There had never before been one where the team, coaches and cheerleaders had to walk single file because the streets were so packed.

2. The environment that day was a true testament for the Auburn spirit and our fan loyalty. I believe it set the tone for every "big" game since, because home field advantage just means more here!

Karen Marie Anderson Kulas

1. Auburn won!

2. I always felt like Birmingham was a home field advantage for Alabama. I love it when Bama fans have to come to Auburn.

Don Joe Mikell

For the first time Auburn finally had home field advantage. Legion Field was never a neutral field; Bama played half their games on it before they expanded the stadium in Tuscaloosa

Jimmy Harris

Remember crying when it was over. Was so happy. Was proud for coaches Jordan, Dye, Meagher, Petrie, and all our players who wore navy blue and burnt orange.

Stephen Livingston

1. The amount of fans was massive, the noise unbelievable.

2. The last great thing Pat Dye did for Auburn was force Alabama to rotate the rivalry between Auburn and Tuscaloosa, because the Iron Bowl was never fair to Auburn when it was

played in Birmingham, due to the fact that Alabama played half their home games there.

Rick Palmedo
1. The most memorable thing was being in the stands, shoulder-to-shoulder with my brother, and screaming in his ear, but still couldn't be heard because it was so loud the entire game.

I think "The Miracle at Jordan-Hare" (in 2013) might have the single loudest moment of any game I've ever been to, but 1989 was the loudest continuous noise level ever.

2. It felt like, for once, we were on an even playing field with that school across the state. Having them set foot in Auburn forever changed the Iron Bowl.

Ben Vanoy
I got there really early that morning. Parked in a spot that I could get out of really quick after the game. I knew we had a deadline to meet and could get caught up in traffic. I knew that I couldn't go through downtown. So I had to be strategic in my spot. Also couldn't get blocked in.

Parked between the Business building and the stadium. That way I could make a right turn onto Donahue.

On my way to the stadium I saw a fan wearing a red BAMA jacket. That is when it sunk in that we were about to play Alabama AT home in Jordan Hare.

The game from the sidelines was deafening. We were screaming at each other, but could not hear a word. I was blowing shaker dust out of my nose for days.

Biggest disappointment: We shot film in those days. We shot ten-plus rolls. Didn't know until we developed the film that I had broken the shutter on my camera very early during the game. Somehow a piece got stuck, so I had a silhouette of what looked like an eagle's head in the middle of every frame. I had nothing to print for the paper

It put us on an even playing field. No more "neutral" field crap. Come play us at on our field or stay home.

Jerome on Twitter
Thinking back, the most memorable thing about it was the feeling around town the entire week leading up to that Saturday. I was a first-quarter freshman, but was also a local. The

electricity in town was like no other game week I had experienced. You could see the "change" in the Auburn Family. The way they talked and carried themselves.... like we have arrived. We aren't second-fiddle to anyone.

Walking through Beard-Eaves parking lot on game day at about 6 am, I saw a pair of tickets change hands for $2000.

That day meant so much to Auburn people and you could feel it. Tiger Walk was like a sold-out Prince concert...you couldn't move. But I will never forget the moment the team took the field. I have never heard Jordan-Hare louder than that. And the paper shakers that were given out, as the crowd went nuts, created a haze over the field that hung over for a while as the game started. I shook mine so hard on Alexander Wright's catch on the first drive that the stick broke and the shaker head flew about ten rows down.

Too many unforgettable moments to tell them all. I will say this to wrap up: Losing that game was never an option. The electricity that the Auburn Family had all week was going through that stadium and through all the players. To me, it is still the greatest day in Auburn Football history. It showed the nation that day, who had the most beautiful stadium in this state, and there were two premier football programs that were now on even footing.

Harris A Pippen III

At the time, I was in graduate school and teaching at the University of Alabama. I can remember my wife and I leaving T-Town to meet up with friends on Friday night, and then we all sat together at the game. I have been to any number of incredible Auburn games in Jordan-Hare, but none will ever compare to the atmosphere of the stadium on that evening. It was electric. It was loud. But the most memorable thing about it was watching those jackasses run out of the tunnel onto OUR field.

Yes, it changed Auburn and the Auburn Family. Somehow by having the game played in our house on our ground, it legitimized us in the state. And it epitomized what it means to have home field advantage.

And...somehow...I knew we would win.

WAR DAMN EAGLE!

Robin Hinds Martin

I was ten and my parents left the house planning to sell their tickets. They turned down some offers thinking they'd get more money closer to the stadium and closer to game time. I remember getting the call from them, I think from a pay phone close to the stadium: "It's just too exciting! We're going in!"

Patrick Campbell

Just the electricity surrounding the game the whole week. RVs arrived very early in the week; cars parked two-wide on both sides of Magnolia Ave.; the orange and blue fog created by those shakers; that first drive of the game sent the crowd into a frenzy.

One thing I witnessed as we were walking to the stadium…all the game programs sold out. We saw a lady without a ticket to the game offer a guy $100 for his game program. They later made extra copies and sold them at the 'Bama basketball game in January or February.

How did it change Auburn? We finally met Alabama on our turf and our terms.

Durb on Twitter

I have never been to a game that was as loud as that day and I have been a season ticket holder since 1998. Sustained energy from the time we set foot in that stadium. There was no way Alabama was winning that day and the fans meant it. The haze from the shakers is still my favorite memory from Jordan-Hare - it's above the Kick Six for me. Just an unreal environment.

Rusty Owens

The most memorable thing to me was the atmosphere the week leading up to it. Friends of mine who weren't even sports fans were excited. I think it was single-handedly the best thing Coach Dye ever did. He made us believe that we didn't have to think of ourselves as second-class citizens to Alabama.

GME2 on Twitter

Seeing and hearing bama fans on campus was both sweet and bitter. I had walked the gauntlet through bama fans at Legion Field. Watching them trying to navigate the sea of Tiger fans at Tiger Walk and seeing the shock on their faces was a proud moment. They came in not respecting Auburn people and they thought they would take over our stadium. I think most of them only then realized that the Auburn Family was much larger than they gave credit. Every Auburn person there felt this energy driven by a desire to win and we were also terrified of losing. I think the adrenaline started flowing at the baseball field on Friday and didn't stop until Sunday.

Tiger Walk morphed into something new that day. And soon after every school in the country started trying to copy it. But playing at home in Jordan-Hare was such a relief after years of abuse playing at Legion Field. If someone asks when did Auburn fans become a family, my answer is 2 December 1989.

Craig from Zion on Twitter

My parents attended. For context, we are from a tiny town between Tuscaloosa and Mississippi. While en route to Auburn, they decided to fall in with the Bama caravan leaving Tuscaloosa whilst flying their Auburn flags from their vehicle. Resulted in quite the reaction from the Tuscaloosa crowd. Got hooked up with some of the fraternity guys in Auburn (the full-body painted ones) and my uncle and dad found their way into the parade. I am told some kindly State Troopers escorted them out after a while. They were there rocking the team bus when Bama arrived at the stadium. It was quite the trip.

Walt Mussell

There are many things I remember. I'll mention four off the top of my head.

I remember the pep rally where Pat Dye said about one of the players, "When (player) was being recruited, Alabama told him he would never win an Iron Bowl if he went to Auburn. This weekend he's going to make it four in a row."

I remember being afraid of losing, as Alabama was undefeated and we had two losses, and I knew we'd never live it down if we lost the first one at home.

I remember starting to relax when it was 27-10, but finally feeling relief when we made it 30-20.

I remember being a little ticked off that Alabama was still invited to the Sugar Bowl anyway after it was over.

As for how it changed Auburn, I felt like we finally had a bit of control. One thing I remember about the Iron Bowl from my years at Auburn (I graduated Spring of '88) was the time in '87 when I noticed that Alabama was the "visitor" in the Iron Bowl. In '87, they played their entire home schedule that season at Legion Field, due to stadium renovations, and had been playing three games a season there for a few years. And yet the Alabama fans and the Birmingham-based media BS continued to talk about how this was a "neutral site." Even playing at home in '89, I realized we would have to put up with that fiction for '91, but by getting the game there in '89, we at last had the ability to control our own destiny.

I honestly believed at that time that, had we waited until '91 to play our first home game at Auburn, that some legal maneuvering would have been successful enough to force us to continue playing at Legion Field for a few more years.

Zac Richardson

What sticks out is Auburn running onto the field. I still have goosebumps thinking of that moment. What changed was it brought Auburn out of the little brother stage. Auburn definitely had a coming-out party in the 1980s, and having that game in Auburn put an exclamation point on the end of that decade.

Dad of Leopold Bloom on Twitter

First of all, when we received our tickets, we were pumped for the season to get started. Just the sight of the ticket made your heart pump faster, eyes widen, and shoot, I might have even spoken faster from the excitement just by seeing the ticket with bama coming to Auburn finally. People arrived early for game day activities. The excitement level was out of this world.

Going into the stadium, the student section was full and loud an hour before kickoff. The game had typical Auburn ebbs and flows, but we all knew there was no way we were going to lose this game. We were better and the stadium was rocking to create that extra adrenaline to keep us focused.

Being to many Iron Bowls in Birmingham before, having this game in Auburn at least gave Auburn a true home field advantage and it showed in this game. That's how it changed Auburn. The most important game was affected by the home crowd and Auburn showed how the fans can make a difference, which has led to other amazing wins in big games!

You could physically feel the sound rolling over you. I checked my heart rate several times during the game and it was over 140 beats per minute. That's like running a marathon for 3 and 1/2 hours. The other 48 games I have been to with my brother have all been memorable but none have measured up for the entire drama.

It's cool thinking back to this game. This year will be the 50th Iron Bowl my brother and I have attended; many satisfying wins, but this was my favorite. It was college football at its best, the Iron Bowl at its best, and that Iron Bowl made Auburn THE best!

AU80 on Twitter

I was there, but not in the stadium. I didn't have tickets, but I legitimately needed to be there. My wife, a Bama fan, was given a ticket and went with friends. I was literally on the outside looking in. I graduated in 1980 and had been an Auburn fan since the mid-1960s. I grew up loving Connie Fredrick, Mickey Zofko, Tucker Fredrickson and Buddy McClinton and, of course, Pat and Terry. So, obviously, I endured the futility of the 70s. You asked last week about the 1972 game. After that one, I was crazy with joy. Walking around that stadium in 1989, knowing Alabama was finally in town, I was just proud- of Auburn, of Pat Dye, and of my connection with a place and a people like Auburn. I'll never forget the electricity, the anticipation and the knowledge that something unique was happening. There are fewer and fewer of us older Auburn fans around. We remember Coach Jordan's dignity, Bear Bryant's dismissive arrogance and Cliff Hare Stadium without an upper deck. We remember when Haley Center was new and Petrie Hall was already old. We remember Scott Hunter throwing the ball out of bounds to stop the clock on fourth down. We remember the Sani-Flush and a good man named Barfield. I wish Coach Jordan had lived to see it because there was nothing like 1989.

Marc Tillis on Twitter

Walking through the corridor in section 1 with my grandfather... I had never seen Bama in person before. They were warming up right in front of us. My granddad looked at me and said "I never believed this would ever happen. Bama coming to our house."

Auburn men and women, admit it or not, had an inferiority complex when it came to our cross-state rival. Bama's superiority complex and their refusal to come play at Auburn was that last psychological play they had.

Pat Dye and his answer of "60 minutes" to the question of "how long will it take you to beat Bama" changed all of that. Getting the crimson uniforms on our field, in front of our fans— that was the final nail in the coffin. We were on equal footing for the first time.

George Gaston
The excitement on campus was palpable, and I was blown away at the sights and sounds of Tiger Walk. I was nervous knowing Alabama had an undefeated team and was fully capable of spoiling the day, but Auburn had a good team and had won its fair share of games during the first decade of my lifetime. It was a fun game, and Auburn came out strong and held on for a convincing victory. My mom cross stitched a "Night Before Christmas" poem that ended in "Ho! Ho! Ho! and four in a row!" to commemorate the occasion.

Only later would I appreciate the battles the Auburn family had fought and won merely to see the Iron Bowl played on home soil. Auburn was capable of anything, and it has accomplished almost everything in the decades that have followed. War Eagle!

David Knight
Most memorable: The unmatched atmosphere, particularly the orange and blue "dust" from the paper shakers.

Change: It put Auburn on an equal footing with that other school at last.

Greg Lathem
I have lots of memories of that game, and they started the week before. I was a junior that fall. As a lifelong Auburn fan, I was super-stoked to have Bama come to our house. There was a parade on Friday, and my fraternity built a float for it. It was a Tiger head with its mouth open and tongue out. We had the fangs and all. On his tongue, we made a couple of Bama football players and Big Al. Our theme was "Roll out the red carpet for Bama."

Friday comes and we line up for the parade. I just remember the streets were packed with people. I had never seen a parade route more crowded in Auburn. When I talk about it, I tell everyone that there probably isn't a person on that parade route who was holding a camcorder that doesn't have me running right up to the lens screaming and yelling.

The parade ended at Plainsman Park for a pep rally. All the participants gathered on the outfield as they came off the route. The stands were packed. As we were waiting for the parade to finish, one of my fraternity brothers and I ran over to the seats and started leading the fans in cheers before the cheerleaders arrived. It was awesome.

The day of the game comes and I am still stoked. We tailgated across from the coliseum in the lot that is now the Arena. Back then, the opposing team buses came in on that road. I went and stood on the sidewalk with my arms folded and a mean stare on my face as the buses went by. I am sure the Bama players were super intimidated by me! (Laughs.)

The next thing I remember is the Tiger Walk. I fought my way to the front row on the ropes and yelled as loud as I could as the team walked in. For years after that, I never went back to Tiger Walk, because in my mind, I had been to the ultimate Tiger Walk. There would never be one greater.

Finally, the game comes, and of course we win. I remember Ace Wright's over-the-shoulder catch and James Joseph diving in for a score. I remember the kick that sealed the victory, getting us to 30 points (Win Lyle). And of course the haze from the paper shakers is legendary.

As for change, I believe David Housel put it best. It was the final brick in the wall. Having always been the "little brother" in this rivalry, we made them come to us, and we won the game. There was no fluke. No blocked punts. We were the better team. I can't imagine any other outcome. If we had let them win, it would have been such a letdown. Looking back, it was Coach Dye's final legacy. I think we lost to Bama the next two seasons that I was in school. (I stuck around for one last football season in '91.) WDE!

JD Willyerd on Twitter

It was 33 years ago so some of this may have moved from actual memory into lore. First a little backstory on me for context. Summer before my Junior year in high school we moved to Atlanta from Oregon. I knew no better, so there are a ton of pictures in my high school yearbook of me wearing Georgia garb. I went to a couple of UGA games in high school and it was fun, but it never really felt like it was where I should be.

Came down to Auburn with a girl I was dating, to stay with her brother for 1984 A-Day. Never made it to the game, but had a blast and knew I had found a home. I started out with much more disdain for Georgia than Bammer, but six seasons on the Plains will change you.

That whole week it just kept building. Even the football-hating professors had to admit this was a big deal. Friends of friends that were at Bama started showing up on Thursday. It made the campus seem dingier. By Saturday, everyone was in a frenzy. My now-wife had graduated, but was back down for the game. We were waiting in line in the SE Corner to get into the stadium with two and a half hours to game time. Back then, the visitors pulled down to what is now Tiger Walk court or whatever. The street was packed and the buses had to cut through the crowd slooowly. A group of guys started pounding on the lead bus and then started rocking it back and forth. We thought it was going over!

The game was loud—and I mean constantly loud. When Auburn had the ball, during commercial breaks, and especially when Bama had the ball. I have heard it louder since, but not as consistently loud the entire game. There was kind of a purple haze covering the student section from the old paper shakers. After the game Toomer's Corner was EPIC! I have never seen that much toilet paper used up. It was waist-deep in places. Some poor soul decided to come through in his Triumph and it was like he was in a snow drift. Folks started piling TP in his car which he dragged halfway down N. College.

Coming to AU from Atlanta, I did not understand that the deck was stacked against Auburn with all of the lawyers and judges and politicians having come from Bammer. Getting the game moved and then beating them on a field where it was not 65% Bama fans put us on a more equal footing. We did not have to kowtow to the mighty Capstone, and we did not have to pay $2 to pee in someone's house while tailgating near the Old Gray Lady. They might continue to beat us after that, but they would have to do it looking us in the eye.

Rob Chaney

Even growing up cheering for the other side, I had attended a handful of games in Auburn. None of those games came close to the environment of 1989, and I immediately believed there was no way Auburn would lose on that given day.

Two things have continued to resonate thirty-four years later: Like so many others, I vividly remember the blue cloud (from the shakers) hovering above the student section, which was easy to see from the West Upper Deck. Secondly, the roar from the crowd when Slack hit Wright on Auburn's first drive was unbelievable.

Beyond the feeling of being on a level playing field with UA, I think the '89 game may have demonstrated just how magical Jordan-Hare can be and how much of a lift the crowd can give the team.

Laura Alldredge

Iron Bowl '89 was memorable because of the absolute electric atmosphere that day, and even the days leading up to it. I was in the flag corps with the AU Marching Band, and marching out of the tunnel and onto the field was always a thrill, but that Saturday was exceptional. I've never forgotten the blue and orange haze created by the paper shakers that we used back then. It was magical! The haze, the cheering, the music—all of it!

I was born and raised in Montgomery and had lived with being taunted by both friends and family for being an Auburn fan. That Saturday things changed. We finally got to host that rivalry game in our town, on our campus. I never bought into the idea that Legion Field was a neutral site. There was a statue of Bear Bryant outside, for crying out loud! I remember a friend's grandmother even slammed my sweet school when they announced that the game would be held in Auburn, claiming that a "little town like that couldn't handle an Iron Bowl and all the fans." Well, we showed her!!!

It was a proud moment and I believe it changed the way the rest of the state looked at our "cow college" and the Loveliest Village. We could hang with the big boys and host the game as well as, if not better than, those folks in Tuscaloosa. I think the playing field was finally evened, just like Pat Dye wanted.

Thanks for taking the time to read my thoughts. My husband and I are both third generation Auburn folks and our kids are fourth generation. War Eagle!

Bill Brown (an Alabama fan on Twitter)

I think the most memorable thing (from an Alabama perspective) was the absolutely insane noise for the "First Time Ever," largely peaking with that bomb to Wright on the first drive. Back in 1989, as you know, teams generally did not come out throwing the ball to start the game, but Auburn ran several pass plays and got the crowd right into the game, which in all honesty was a key component to them keeping momentum.

I realize I'm committing heresy as an Alabama fan, but despite us entering that game undefeated, I really never thought we were going to win because I'd watched both teams play. Alabama historical revisionism convinces itself that, "If only that game had been in Birmingham, we'd have been undefeated and playing for the national championship." Okay, I guess it's conceivable they're saying "Auburn's home field was worth 10 or more points that day," which I'd take as a huge compliment.

As far as how it changed Auburn, my perception is that Auburn people felt (for lack of a better word) more "on even ground" with Alabama. A lot of Tide fans forget that Alabama WAS actually pretty successful in the Eighties—by all standards except the ones Bryant had set. Alabama won (or shared) two SEC titles, which was topped only by (wait for it) Auburn and Georgia. It appeared to some Tide fans that Auburn's belief "the only difference between us and them is Bryant is there" was largely vindicated by the Eighties, and the move of the Iron Bowl was simply the last step (I believe Dye called it the final brick).

Let me add a personal note: I never personally had a problem with Auburn insisting they had autonomy to determine where games were played as some Alabama folks did, but I'm Gen X, too. I would rank it similar, for its time, to when Georgia Tech stunned their state by winning a share of the 1990 national title, which gave UGA fans their own case of "what's going on."

Rob Sherrill, Alabama fan

Honestly, (playing the Iron Bowl in Auburn) wasn't that big of a deal. My brother is an Auburn grad. He was going on and on about how now Bama wasn't going to have a home field advantage and that sort of thing. But this was also around the time that Alabama was going to start playing exclusively in Tuscaloosa. I had some fun times in Birmingham but I was fine with the game starting to alternate and I was more than fine with moving all of our home games to Tuscaloosa.

I think a lot of the rank-and-file Auburn fans wanted the move. I think a lot of the rank-and-file Alabama fans were somewhat indifferent. I get the feeling that the "fat cats" were the ones that it mattered to.

Joseph A. Miller

Memory: The orange and blue dust from the paper shakers, and the roar of the crowd. It was a roar the entire game, and on big plays you could not hear a word.

(Moving the game to Auburn) changed AU by bringing the game away from the "Neutral Site" (my butt) Lesion Field. It let Jordan-Hare become one of the great homefields in the country. It showed what the AU Family was capable of doing with a competitive team. A decent AU squad has a puncher's chance against anyone, no matter how high they are ranked. Not sure the homefield advantage would be as great if there was not a 1989. War Damn Coach Pat Dye!

Joe Swart

My favorite memory: I was a sophomore at Auburn at the time. I was standing in the student section with about 5-6 friends and our respective girlfriends before the game watching the Bama players warm up.

Bama players. On *our* field. It was surreal.

About that time, one of my friend's girlfriends said, "I think the world is going to come to an end before kick-off." A 30-year-old Auburn fan hearing that today would think it was absolutely crazy, or at least extreme hyperbole. But at that moment in 1989, it sounded like a perfectly rational statement.

My FIRST memory of that game was from at least 10 years prior. Sometime in the late Seventies (probably 78 or 79, as I was about 8 or 9), I was sitting at my grandparent's kitchen table listening to my mother talk to my grandfather (AU class of '42 and Board of Trustees member from 1948-60) about how we had to "get Bama down in Auburn." It wasn't going to be fair until

329

the day that we finally "get them down in Auburn." Honestly, I barely understood what they were talking about at the time. But from that moment forward I knew it was important that we "get Bama down in Auburn."

Like everyone, I remember the orange and blue haze from the paper shakers that were distributed.

Gumby was in the student section that day. He and I must have gone to Auburn at the same time, because Gumby was in the student section for a lot of games in the late Eighties.

Ace's over the shoulder catch on the first drive was right in front of me. I can't say "I knew we were going to win," but it sure felt good.

The last 5 minutes felt like it lasted 5 hours.

After Rolling Toomer's, we all went to The Heart of Auburn Motel because a girlfriend's parents were staying there and she wanted to see them. She went to their room while the rest of us waited in the lobby. On the tv there, we saw a replay of Dye's post-game interview from the field. He was asked, "Who deserves to go to the Sugar Bowl?" And said, "Tennessee has a great team. Alabama has a great team. We ain't too bad."

I had yelled so much during the game that I was still hoarse was when I got home for Christmas break. I was taking to a high school friend (a big Bama fan) about something unrelated and he said, "Damn, listen to your voice! You must have yelled your ass off at the game!" I said, "I wanted to give all I could and do my part." He smiled and said, "Bastard!"

– APPENDIX 4 –
OTHER MASSIVE EVENTS
THAT TOOK PLACE IN 1989

It's somehow fitting that perhaps the most significant year in Auburn football history also turned out to be one of the most significant years in *world* history overall.

The First Time Ever Iron Bowl slotted itself in alongside these monumental events of 1989:

January 7: Emperor Hirohito of Japan, who presided over that country during World War II, passes away.

January 11: The Lexus and Infiniti car brands are launched.

January 20: Ronald Reagan's second term as President of the United States ends, and George H. W. Bush is sworn in as the 41st president.

February 2: The last Soviet armored column leaves Kabul, ending the nine-year occupation of Afghanistan by the USSR.

February 14: Ayatollah Khomeini of Iran issues a death order on Salman Rushdie over his novel, the *Satanic Verses*. (Rushdie would remain in hiding for years; partly in Atlanta.)

March 4: Time, Inc. and Warner Communications merge to form Time-Warner.

March 12: Tim Berners-Lee produces the proposal document that will become the blueprint for the World Wide Web.

March 24: The Exxon Valdez spills 240,000 barrels of oil in Alaska's Prince William Sound.

March 26: The Soviet Union holds its only contested elections for the Soviet parliament, resulting in Communist Party losses.

April 5: Poland restores legal status to the Solidarity trade union, touching off the Revolutions of 1989, against communist dictatorships in Eastern Europe.

April 14: The Savings and Loan Crisis in the US begins.

April 15: The Hillsborough Disaster in Sheffield, England: 94 Liverpool soccer fans are crushed to death due to poor crowd control by police.

April 19: The Central Park Jogger rape and assault takes place in New York City, leading to convictions of five men. The convictions will all be vacated in 2002.

April 21: The massive Tiananmen Square pro-democracy protests begin in Beijing, China.

May 3: Construction begins on the first McDonald's restaurant in the Soviet Union.

May 4: Oliver North is convicted on charges stemming from the Iran-Contra Affair.

June 3: Ayatollah Khomeini of Iran, who had presided over the American hostage crisis of 1979-1981, dies.

June 4: The Chinese military begins a violent crackdown on pro-democracy protesters in Tiananmen Square.

June 4: Solidarity defeats the Communist Party in the national legislative election in Poland.

June 23: The "Batman" movie, starring Michael Keaton and Jack Nicholson, is released.

July 14: France celebrates the 200th anniversary of the French Revolution.

July 31: Nintendo releases the Game Boy.

September 22: Hurricane Hugo hits the southeastern US.

October 17: An earthquake strikes the San Francisco Bay Area just prior to the start of the World Series between Oakland and San Francisco, resulting in the deaths of 63 people and a 10-day postponement of the Series.

November 9: Amid weeks of anti-government protests in East Germany, the Berlin Wall is accidentally opened, allowing East Germans to travel to the West.

November 17: The Velvet Revolution against communism begins in Czechoslovakia. A week later, the leaders of the Communist Party resign.

December 1: The East German parliament votes to end the Communist Party's monopoly on power. The Politburo and Central Committee members resign two days later.

December 2: The "First Time Ever" Iron Bowl is played in Auburn, Alabama.

December 3: President Bush meets with Mikhail Gorbachev of the USSR at Malta and they announce moves toward ending the Cold War.

December 16: The Romanian Revolution against their country's communist regime begins.

December 20: President Bush orders the invasion of Panama, "Operation Just Cause," to overthrow dictator Manuel Noriega.

December 22: The communist government of Romania is overthrown after a week of street battles between the Romanian army and the secret police.

December 29: Czechoslovakia elects playwright Vaclav Havel as its first post-communist president.

December 31: Poland ends communism in favor of a capitalist system. The Warsaw Pact (Soviet military alliance) is abandoned.

ABOUT THE AUTHORS

Van and **John** have been recording episodes of the **AU Wishbone Podcast** almost every Monday since fall 2012.

Van Allen Plexico is an award-winning author who managed to attend Auburn (and score student football tickets) for some portion of every year between 1986 and 1996. He teaches college near St Louis, and also hosts a number of different podcasts, appears at pop culture conventions, and writes and edits novels, stories, nonfiction works and articles for a variety of publishers. Find links to his various projects at *www.plexico.net*.

John Ringer graduated from Auburn in 1991 (which may be the greatest time ever to be an Auburn student — SEC titles in 1987, 88 and 89 and the 1989 Iron Bowl). His family has had season tickets every year since well before he was born and he grew up wandering around Jordan-Hare on game days. He currently lives in Richmond, Virginia where he spends way too much time reading about college football and basketball on the internet.

You can hear Van and John discuss the latest in Auburn Football— with lots of humor and fun thrown in—every single week:
Just search "AU Wishbone" on your favorite podcast app, or go to
www.AUWishbone.com

ALSO FROM THE AU WISHBONE CREW:

HOSTS OF THE AU WISHBONE PODCAST
AND BEST-SELLING AUTHORS OF *DECADES OF DOMINANCE*

WE BELIEVED

A LIFETIME OF AUBURN FOOTBALL

VOLUME 1: 1975-1998

VAN ALLEN PLEXICO
AND
JOHN RINGER

WE BELIEVED
A LIFETIME OF AUBURN FOOTBALL
Vol 1: 1975-1998

Meticulously researched and created using the same style as
AUBURN BASKETBALL: FROM BARKLEY TO BRUCE,
WE BELIEVED Vol 1 dives deep into the Pat Dye era of Auburn
Football. Filled with memories, full game descriptions, player stats
and much more, it's the indispensable work on Auburn in the 1980s
& 1990s. At nearly 500 pages, it's $19.95 wherever books are sold!
ISBN: 979-8536996751
www.whiterocketbooks.com

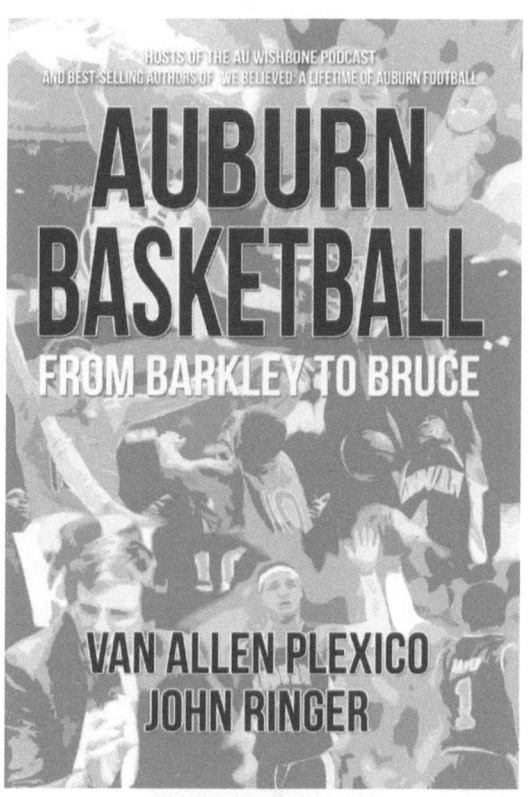

AUBURN BASKETBALL:
From Barkley to Bruce

"The best and most comprehensive book ever written on Auburn Basketball." —David Housel, Auburn Athletic Director Emeritus
Covering every basketball season from 1978 — 2022 and featuring a new interview with Auburn's legendary Coach Sonny Smith, this book takes you from Charles Barkley in the Olympics and NBA (and Waffle House!) to the hiring of Bruce Pearl and his magical Final Four run, and everything in between.
It's $16.95 wherever books are sold!
ISBN-13: 9798353194996
www.whiterocketbooks.com